Opening Up By Cracking Down

How did democratic developing countries open their economies during the late twentieth century? Since labor unions opposed free trade, democratic governments often used labor repression to ease the process of trade liberalization. Some democracies brazenly jailed union leaders and used police brutality to break the strikes that unions launched against such reforms. Others weakened labor union opposition through subtler tactics, such as banning strikes and retaliating against striking workers. Either way, this book argues that democratic developing countries were more likely to open their economies if they violated labor rights. *Opening Up By Cracking Down* draws on fieldwork interviews and archival research on Argentina, Mexico, Bolivia, Turkey, and India, as well as quantitative analysis of data from over one hundred developing countries to places labor unions and labor repression at the heart of the debate over democracy and trade liberalization in developing countries.

ADAM DEAN is an assistant professor of political science at George Washington University. His first book, *From Conflict to Coalition* (Cambridge University Press, 2016), was a finalist for the J. David Greenstone Book Prize.

POLITICAL ECONOMY OF INSTITUTIONS AND DECISIONS

Other books in the series

Alberto Alesina and Howard Rosenthal,
Partisan Politics, Divided Government and the Economy
Lee J. Alston, Thrainn Eggertsson and Douglass C. North, eds.,
Empirical Studies in Institutional Change
Lee J. Alston and Joseph P. Ferrie,
Southern Paternalism and the Rise of the American Welfare State: Economics, Politics, and Institutions, 1865–1965
James E. Alt and Kenneth Shepsle, eds.,
Perspectives on Positive Political Economy
Josephine T. Andrews,
When Majorities Fail: The Russian Parliament, 1990–1993
Jeffrey S. Banks and Eric A. Hanushek, eds.,
Modern Political Economy: Old Topics, New Directions
Yoram Barzel,
Economic Analysis of Property Rights, 2nd edition
Yoram Barzel,
A Theory of the State: Economic Rights, Legal Rights, and the Scope of the State
Robert Bates,
Beyond the Miracle of the Market: The Political Economy of Agrarian Development in Kenya
Jenna Bednar,
The Robust Federation: Principles of Design
Charles M. Cameron,
Veto Bargaining: Presidents and the Politics of Negative Power

(*continued after the Index*)

Opening Up By Cracking Down

Labor Repression and Trade Liberalization in Democratic Developing Countries

ADAM DEAN
George Washington University

Shaftesbury Road, Cambridge CB2 8EA, United Kingdom

One Liberty Plaza, 20th Floor, New York, NY 10006, USA

477 Williamstown Road, Port Melbourne, VIC 3207, Australia

314–321, 3rd Floor, Plot 3, Splendor Forum, Jasola District Centre, New Delhi – 110025, India

103 Penang Road, #05–06/07, Visioncrest Commercial, Singapore 238467

Cambridge University Press is part of Cambridge University Press & Assessment, a department of the University of Cambridge.

We share the University's mission to contribute to society through the pursuit of education, learning and research at the highest international levels of excellence.

www.cambridge.org
Information on this title: www.cambridge.org/9781108745895

DOI: 10.1017/9781108777964

First published 2022
First paperback edition 2023

A catalogue record for this publication is available from the British Library

ISBN 978-1-108-47851-9 Hardback
ISBN 978-1-108-74589-5 Paperback

Dedicated to Naomi and Talia
&
In Memory of Marilyn Simonson

Contents

Figures

Tables

Acknowledgments

Writing a book during the COVID-19 pandemic required an unprecedented amount of support. My family helped in ways I never imagined I would need. When schools closed in March 2020, my family and I left Washington, D.C. and moved closer to my parents. My wife and I split childcare (60–40, at my best), and my parents watched our kids in the afternoons. George Washington University granted me a year and half of leave, from Spring 2020 through Spring 2021. I had the privilege to write while almost all other professors learned how to teach on Zoom. There is no way I could have finished this book without all of these advantages.

The relative isolation of the pandemic also made it clear how much I have always relied on intellectual guidance and support from my colleagues and friends. Take away the chat over coffee and the quick question in the hallway, and my work started to suffer. Like a lost driver who doesn't stop to ask for directions, I took some long detours. This became clear during a (virtual) book conference I organized at the height of the 2020–2021 winter COVID-19 surge. It would be hard to exaggerate how much Jeff Frieden, Ernesto Calvo, Henry Farrell, Margaret Levi, Paul Poast, and Manny Teitelbaum improved this manuscript – revising the argument, developing an analytical framework for the case studies, and carefully choosing which battles to fight. They saved me from myself.

After the book conference, my family and I moved to Vermont, where I rewrote the entire book. During that final push, I was lucky to have almost daily discussions with Jonathan Obert and Jamie McCallum, my best friends from graduate school and my first academic job, respectively. They both read each chapter and helped me figure out how to revise the manuscript while still writing the book that I wanted to write. During this time, I also got crucial advice from Jeff Colgan and Eric Grynaviski, who helped me to turn labor history into political science. David Miranda Hardy and Carmine

Grimaldi – filmmakers and friends – generously read parts of the manuscript and encouraged me to embrace the dramatic details of the stories I had to tell.

Of course, I am lucky to have started this project long before the pandemic, giving me many years to collect feedback from colleagues and friends. At GW, I benefitted from discussions and advice from Celeste Arrington, Michael Barnett, Bruce Dickson, Henry Farrell, Harvey Feigenbaum, Marty Finnemore, Charlie Glaser, Eric Grynaviski, Stephen Kaplan, Eric Kramon, Janet Lewis, Yon Lupu, Cynthia McClintock, Mike Miller, Kimberly Morgan, Harris Mylonas, David Szakonyi, Manny Teitelbaum, and Chris Warshaw.

I thank all those who attended talks I gave at McGill; University of Wisconsin; Georgetown; Oxford; LSE; University of Sussex; Stanford; Texas A&M; University of Gothenburg; University of Chicago; and the D.C. Area Labor and Working-Class History Seminar, as well as conference participants at APSA, MPSA, and REPAL. During these and other trips I had the opportunity to get friendly feedback from Faisal Ahmed, Eric Arnesen, Andy Baker, David Burk, Bill Clark, Jeff Colgan, Gregory Distelhorst, Sebastián Etchemendy, Leon Fink, Nikhar Gaikwad, John Gaventa, Kemi Fuentes-George, Judy Goldstein, Sebnem Gumuscu, Will Howell, In Song Kim, Atul Kohli, Walter Mattli, Kate McNamara, James Morrison, Layna Mosley, Abe Newman, Erica Owen, Didem Özkiziltan, Stefano Pagliari, Héctor Palomino, Krzysztof Pelc, Jon Pevehouse, Stephanie Rickard, Ron Rogowski, David Rueda, Ken Shadlen, Alberto Simpser, Dan Slater, Duncan Snidal, David Steinberg, Sarah Stroup, Todd Tucker, Steve Weymouth, Kevin Young, Amy Yuen, and many others. I am especially grateful for the opportunities I have had to work with Robert Dreesen, my editor at Cambridge University Press. I am lucky to have his trust.

I am also grateful for excellent support from research assistants at GW and Middlebury College, including Samer Anabtawi, Sebastian Kern, Alex Kirss, Jiya Pandya, Aparna Ravi, Navodhya Samarakoon, and Karlo Skarica. I owe a special thanks to Rocío López Karababikian, a research assistant in Argentina who gathered old newspapers and union documents and helped to schedule, conduct, and transcribe the interviews I conducted in Buenos Aires in December 2019. During that trip, I also had unique assistance from Saulito Ubaldini, the son of the deceased Argentine labor union leader, Saúl Ubaldini. I thank Saulito for his help arranging interviews and granting me access to his family's collection of union documents. I also thank the staff at the Library of Congress in Washington, D.C., whose collection of newspapers from around the world allowed me to conduct archival research just a short bike ride away.

I thank my family, especially my parents and in-laws, for their support and enthusiasm. In my first book, I wrote that my wife, Elana, has kept me happy, motivated, and intellectually honest. Six years later, it's still true. I think of her when I'm writing, hoping that when she reads the next draft she'll give me an A+. Together, we've now added two books and two children to the world.

Our daughters, Naomi and Talia, are constant sources of fun and daily reminders that life begins where work ends. This book is dedicated to them. Last, this book is written in memory of my grandmother, Marilyn Simonson, who had the rare ability to make you feel like you were the center of the world whenever you were with her.

Introduction

Saúl Ubaldini's Ford Falcon exploded a few minutes before 2 A.M. on the morning of August 17, 1989. The bomb threw the car several feet into the air and shattered the windows on the first floor of the *Confederación General de los Trabajadores* (CGT), Argentina's main labor union federation.[1] "For us," asserted a longtime CGT organizer, "it was the government."[2] Thirty years later, Ubaldini's assistant – the man who parked the car the night it blew up – explained that "Saúl knew, and I saw it in his eyes. He knew he was going up against something big, something that wanted to shut him up."[3]

What Ubaldini, the Secretary General of the CGT, was going up against was a set of neoliberal economic reforms proposed by Argentina's newly inaugurated President, Carlos Menem.[4] From 1983 through 1988, Ubaldini's CGT launched thirteen general strikes against similar reforms proposed by Raúl Alfonsín, the country's previous President. Those strikes paralyzed the economy, stopped the reform process, and destabilized Alfonsín's rule, all while establishing the CGT as one of the most important social forces in Argentina. When Menem announced his intentions to open and deregulate the Argentine economy, Ubaldini's CGT was the indisputable symbol of resistance.

The battle lines were clear; as one Argentine periodical summarized, the Menem administration "will have to destroy the CGT as a major factor of power if it is to succeed in its aims of setting out new rules for the economic

1 "La Noche Bomba de Ubaldini," *Página/12*, August 18, 1989.

2 Author interview with Julio Mirogui, December 6, 2019.

3 Author interview with Darío Nazar, December 2, 2019.

4 As discussed in Chapter 4, the bombing of Ubaldini's car was neither investigated nor solved by the police. At the time of the attack, journalists, politicians, and union members speculated that the bomb may have been planted by rival union leaders that were collaborating with President Menem to remove Ubaldini from his leadership of the CGT. For example, see "Debajo de la Alfombra," *Página/12*, August 18, 1989 and "Los fantasmas del pasado," *Página/12*, August 18, 1989.

game."[5] Menem quickly ousted opposition union leaders, broke strikes with the military, and ultimately banned strikes in the public sector before slashing Argentine tariffs by more than 40 percent.[6]

Half way around the world, a similar dynamic was playing out in India. In the mid-1980s, Prime Minister Rajiv Gandhi announced privatization and trade policy reforms that triggered widespread general strikes from India's labor unions.[7] Gandhi, like Argentina's Alfonsin, gave in to such labor opposition and gave up on his economic reforms.[8] In the early-1990s, India's newly-elected Prime Minister, Narasimha Rao, would propose a similar package of reforms with his New Economic Policy.[9] Rao, like Argentina's Menem, unleashed a campaign of labor repression aimed at squashing labor union protests against his reforms. As India's *The Hindu* newspapers explained, "Once labour becomes seriously aroused, it becomes necessary to resort to repression if the reforms are not to be abandoned."[10]

Instead of car bombs, India's labor unions faced the explosive use of what the Indian government calls "preventive arrests." On June 16, 1992, over ten million Indians joined a nationwide general strike in opposition to Rao's reforms.[11] But before the first strikers could even enter the streets of New Delhi and Calcutta, 25,000 union members had already been arrested and imprisoned throughout the country.[12] The government's basic strategy – coordinated between the central government and state-level Chief Ministers aligned with Rao's Congress Party – was to prevent union members from picketing, disrupting public transportation, and spreading the general strike.[13] In the southern state of Tamil Nadu, 4,000 union members were held in a crowded prison and beaten my guards with batons.[14] At least one union member died while in police lockup.[15] Union leaders immediately denounced "the unprecedented repression by the state government."[16]

Four days after the general strike, with the immediate threat of labor opposition overcome, all imprisoned union members were released without any charges being pressed.[17] When unions launched another general strike ten months later, the Indian government again preventively arrested more

[5] "One Foot in the Stirrup," *The Review of the River Plate*, June 30, 1989.

[6] "On the Labour Front: Divided Loyalties," *The Review of the River Plate*, August 25, 1989; "La Marche del Adjuste," *Clarín*, September 10, 1990; "The Right to Strike: the Decree and the Possible Bargains," *The Review of the River Plate*, November 14, 1990. pg. 294. Tariff decrease based on author's calculation using data from the World Bank.

[7] Varshney 1998. [8] Kohli 1989. [9] Jenkins 1999; Teitelbaum 2011; Kohli 2012.

[10] "Squeeze on Labour Already on," *The Hindu*, June 21, 1992.

[11] "Forward to June 16 Countrywide Strike," *The Working Class*, June 1992.

[12] "1000s Held Over Strike Call," *Times of India*, June 14, 1992.

[13] "Centre Gears up for Bandh," *Hindustan Times*, September 9, 1993.

[14] "Lathicharge in Jail," *The Hindu*, June 15, 1992.

[15] "Strike Hits Banks, Airlines," *Times of India*, June 17, 1992.

[16] "Unprecedented Repression in TN: Union Leaders," *Indian Express*, June 17, 1992.

[17] "CM orders Release of Agitators," *The Hindu*, June 21, 1992.

than 10,000 union members in an attempt to make sure that turnout for this general strike was lower than the previous one – a downward trend they would highlight as evidence that there was growing consensus in favor of their economic reforms.[18] Unlike Gandhi, whose reforms were stalled by union opposition, Rao used preventive arrests to limit the scale of general strikes before lowering India's tariffs by more than 50 percent.[19]

These stories illustrate broader themes about the politics of free trade not just in Argentina and India, but in developing countries around the world at the end of the twentieth century. In short, developing countries with democratic governments repeatedly opened their economies while cracking down on labor unions. *Opening Up By Cracking Down* explains how democratic developing countries used labor repression – the violation of workers' basic rights to act collectively – to overcome labor union opposition to trade liberalization. Some democratic governments brazenly jailed union leaders and used police and military violence to break the strikes that unions launched against whole packages of neoliberal economic reforms. Others weakened labor union opposition through subtler tactics, such as restricting workers' rights to organize, banning strikes, or threatening to retaliate against striking workers. Either way, the reality is that democracy and trade liberalization were more likely to go together when governments were willing to violate labor rights. Far from guaranteeing workers' basic freedoms, democratically-elected governments routinely violated their rights to act collectively. What follows in this book is a revisionist account – both theoretical and empirical – of the process through which many developing countries embraced free trade.

In brief, this book argues that democratic developing countries were more likely to open their economies during the late twentieth century if they violated workers' basic rights to organize and strike. The more democracies adopted such labor repression, the more likely they were to embrace free trade. The more democracies respected workers' rights, in contrast, the more likely they were to maintain high tariffs.

To understand why, consider that most developing countries entered the late twentieth century with autocratic governments in which trade policy was dominated by a small group of protectionist, import-competing businesses. The stable trade policy outcome was a closed economy walled off by high tariffs. When many of these autocracies transitioned toward democracy, they opened their political arenas to general publics that were more supportive of trade liberalization. Whether individuals were driven by the promise of lower consumer prices, higher rates of economic growth, and new employment opportunities, or by the growing ideological consensus that economic crises had discredited protectionist policies, the reality was that the majority of the public

18 "Partial Response," *Times of India*, September 10, 1993.
19 Author's calculation using tariff data from the World Bank.

in developing countries often held favorable views of international trade.[20] Democracy also often empowered the pro-trade demands of export-oriented businesses, which organized lobby groups and funded political parties that supported their economic policy agenda.[21] These new domestic demands for trade liberalization, from the general public as well as organized businesses, had the *potential* to push trade policy toward greater openness.

However, greater levels of democracy also increased the political influence of labor unions, which vehemently opposed free trade during this period.[22] The more a democratic government respected labor rights, the more likely workers were to organize powerful labor unions and to launch protests and strikes against trade liberalization. Such strikes informed governments about the salience of economic reforms, demonstrated the extent of public opposition, hinted at the political costs to which trade liberalization might lead, and made governments more likely to maintain high tariffs.[23] In contrast, the less a democratic government respected labor rights, the less likely labor unions were to counterbalance demands for trade liberalization. Limits on the right to organize reduced the size of labor unions and restrictions on the right to strike reduced their ability to launch influential strikes against free trade.[24] In other words, democracy empowered new domestic demands for free trade and labor repression helped to overcome a major barrier to such reforms.

Among the many developing countries that combined democracy with labor repression there were two different paths toward free trade. The first path started with labor repression and then added democracy. This path was followed by countries that transitioned to democracy while maintaining the high level of labor repression that was practiced by the previous autocratic regime. Turkey, for example, transitioned to democracy in 1983 but maintained the military dictatorship's strike bans and limits on union activities.[25] The new democratic government quickly liberalized trade policy while the country's union leaders were still imprisoned and on trial facing the death penalty.[26]

The second path toward free trade, however, started with democracy and then added labor repression. This path was followed by countries that transitioned to democracy and respected labor rights, only to later increase labor repression. Argentina and India, as discussed above, were both established democracies when their governments increased labor repression in order to weaken union opposition to trade liberalization in the 1990s. In both of these

[20] Przeworski 1991; Rodrik 1992; Grinspun and Kreklewich 1994; Garrett 2000; Stokes 2001; Blyth et al. 2002; Fourcade-Gourinchas and Babb 2002; Weyland 2002; Harvey 2005; Milner and Kubota 2005; Sheppard 2005; Eichengreen and Leblang 2008; Baker 2009; Babb 2013.

[21] Olson 1965; Grossman and Helpman 1994; Ziblatt 2006; Acemoglu and Robinson 2008; Albertus and Menaldo 2014.

[22] Geddes 1995; Kohli 2004; Spalding 2014.

[23] Tarrow 1994; Burstein and Linton 2002; Uba 2005; Giugni 2008.

[24] Freeman and Pelletier 1990; Godard 2003; Lindvall 2013; Gourevitch 2018.

[25] Özkiziltan 2020. [26] Nichols et al. 2002.

pathways, labor repression played a pivotal and previously overlooked role in the process of trade liberalization in democratic developing countries.

This book's focus on the interaction between democracy and labor repression sheds new and critical light on when and how a large swath of humanity joined the global economy. There were roughly sixty-five developing countries with democratic governments in 1992, and at the turn of the century there were as many as 100. By 2000, more than 2.5 billion people lived in developing countries with democratic governments.[27] *When* did developing countries open their economies? Trade liberalization was frequently triggered either by (1) an increase in democracy when the level of labor repression was high or (2) an increase in labor repression when the level of democracy was high. *How* did democratic developing countries implement trade liberalization? Often, by repressing labor unions that demanded continued trade protection.

While such labor repression was nearly ubiquitous in democratic developing countries that opened their economies, it is important to clarify that neither democracy nor labor repression were strictly necessary for trade liberalization. Many developing countries, such as Chile, South Korea, and China opened their economies without democratizing first.[28] Moreover, many democratic developing countries faced so many different pressures to lower their tariffs that they may have done so, albeit more slowly, even if they had not repressed labor unions. For example, many countries faced external pressure from international institutions and the United States, while others were heavily influenced by pro-trade government technocrats, multinational corporations, transnational networks, and the broader battle of ideas about economic policy.[29] With these numerous explanations in mind, it is important to state clearly that this book's goal is not to develop an all-encompassing explanation for why developing countries opened their economies, but rather to highlight the important and often-overlooked ways in which democratic developing countries frequently used labor repression to facilitate trade liberalization.

The many instances of labor repression documented throughout this book clearly demonstrate that democracy is by no means a guarantee of respect for labor rights. Throughout the late twentieth century, there were many developing countries that were commonly viewed as democracies – countries with competitive elections, broad suffrage, and basic constraints on executive authority – and yet regularly violated workers' rights to act collectively.[30]

[27] https://ourworldindata.org/democracy.

[28] Deyo 1989; Ianchovichina and Martin 2001; Fischer 2009.

[29] Centeno 1993; Blyth et al. 2002; Chorev 2005; Harvey 2005; Gallagher 2007; Margheritis and Pereira 2007; Chwieroth 2009; Kay 2011; Babb 2013; Fairbrother 2014; Manger and Shadlen 2014; Kentikelenis et al. 2016.

[30] This basic definition of democracy builds on the Polity IV Project, the most widely used measure of political regime type in the social science, see Marshall et al. 2002. Chapter 2 demonstrates that despite definitional difference between Polity IV, the Unified Democracy Score, and Varieties of Democracy, all three of these common measures of democracy are weakly associated with respect for labor rights.

In other words, democracies vary widely in their level of respect for labor rights and therefore differ in the political influence that they grant to organized labor.[31] In theory, it may sound strange, but in practice, democratic governments regularly reduced labor union opposition to trade liberalization by resorting to labor repression.

THE CONSEQUENCES IN THEORY AND PRACTICE

Trade liberalization in developing countries contributed to increases in international trade that transformed the global political economy and continue to shape the contemporary world. On the one hand, trade stimulates innovation and economic growth that helps to reduce income inequality between rich and poor countries.[32] At the same time, trade increases wages for each country's relatively-skilled individuals and therefore fuels growing income inequality within countries.[33] These distributional consequences are driving a growing backlash against globalization and the rise of authoritarian populism around the globe.[34] With the global economy once again moving toward closure, it has never been more important to understand the political process through which developing countries joined an open international trade system in the late twentieth century.

At the core of this puzzle is a longstanding debate about the relationship between democracy and international trade. Early research on this topic argued that democracies were unlikely to open their economies because they faced powerful opposition from labor unions and other groups that would be harmed by trade liberalization.[35] But when many democratic developing countries lowered their tariffs in the 1980s and 1990s, scholars began to develop new explanations for how democratic governments could implement trade liberalization.[36] One influential approach argued that democracy led to trade liberalization simply because it empowered domestic groups that favored free trade. According to some, international trade benefits society overall and political leaders that are democratically accountable to the public therefore maintain lower trade barriers.[37]

During this period, many countries faced economic crises that helped to discredit protectionist policies and contributed to a growing public consensus that "there is no alternative" to trade liberalization and other neoliberal

[31] Western 1997; Korpi 2006; Davenport 2007, 2017; Albertus and Menaldo 2018.

[32] Held et al. 1999; Reuveny and Li 2003; Bhagwati 2007; Lockwood 2020.

[33] Acemoglu 2003; Hanson 2003; Goldberg and Pavcnik 2007; Meschi and Vivarelli 2009; Pavcnik 2017; Menendez et al. 2018.

[34] Rodrik 2018; Broz et al. 2019.

[35] Haggard 1990; Przeworski 1991; Bates et al. 1993; Haggard and Kaufman 1995.

[36] Geddes 1995. [37] Garrett 2000; Stokes 2001; Weyland 2002; Eichengreen and Leblang 2008.

economic reforms.[38] Others argue that the link between democracy and trade is especially strong in developing countries, where export-led growth may increase employment opportunities and wages for the majority of workers.[39] As Milner and Kubota explain, "in developing countries, workers and the poor tend to gain from trade liberalization–Democratization will thus enfranchise a new group of voters with preferences for lower levels of protectionism."[40] And it is true that many developing countries – from Bangladesh to Turkey, Nicaragua to the Philippines – transitioned to democracy and then rapidly moved toward free trade during the late twentieth century.

Yet many other democratic developing countries maintained high tariffs or only gradually liberalized their trade policies. In the mid-twentieth century, India, Nigeria, and Malaysia, for example, all transitioned to democracy and then pursued the high tariffs and import-substitution industrialization supported by their countries' labor unions and nascent industrial manufacturers.[41] Argentina and Bolivia both transitioned to democracy in the early 1980s, but maintained high tariffs after their government's efforts at economic liberalization triggered massive labor-led general strikes.[42] According to one estimate, 42 percent of developing countries that transitioned to democracy between 1978 and 2000 subsequently maintained high levels of trade protection.[43]

Understanding how some democratic developing countries liberalized their economies more than others requires examining not only the ways in which democracies empowered pro-trade groups, but also how they overcame opposition from protectionist groups such as labor unions. Some asserted that economic crises simply weakened labor unions and reduced their ability to mobilize workers against neoliberal economic reforms.[44] Others pointed to welfare benefits, such as unemployment insurance and job retraining programs, that democratic governments provided to compensate workers dislocated by globalization.[45] Still others argued that partisan ties between labor unions and political parties led to union restraint and acquiescence to trade liberalization.[46] Some even argued that democratic leaders implemented a "reform by stealth" strategy that confused labor union leaders and limited their mobilization.[47]

38 Rodrik 1992; Grinspun and Kreklewich 1994; Blyth et al. 2002; Fourcade-Gourinchas and Babb 2002; Harvey 2005; Sheppard 2005; Babb 2013.

39 O'Rourke and Taylor 2006; Milner and Mukherjee 2009; Mukherjee 2016; Zucker 2020.

40 Milner and Kubota 2005, 116.

41 For India and ISI following independence and democracy in 1947, see Kohli 1989. For Nigeria and ISI following Independence and democracy in 1960, see Oyejide 1973. For Malaysia and ISI following Independence and democracy in 1957, see Kuruvilla 1995.

42 Dunkerley 1990; Murillo 2001.

43 Mukherjee 2016.

44 Nelson and Waterbury 1989; Geddes 1995.

45 Cameron 1978; Schamis 1999; Adsera et al. 2002; Etchemendy 2011.

46 Murillo 2001; Levitsky 2003; Teitelbaum 2011.

47 Jenkins 1999.

At the heart of these approaches, however, is the mistaken assumption that democracies cannot and do not use labor repression to reduce labor unions' influence on trade policy. For example, Adsera and Boix explain that democracies compensate "trade losers" because the only alternative would be "excluding in a systematic manner – that is, through authoritarian rule – those sectors that may lose from increasing economic integration."[48] Similarly, Haggard and Kaufman's work on democracy and economic reform starts from the assumption that "the freedom of association that allows interest groups to organize and press their claims on the state" is one of the "constitutive features of democratic rule itself."[49] Starting from these premises, scholars repeatedly overlook how democratic developing countries around the world often used a mix of strike bans, mass arrests, physical violence, and legislative restrictions to weaken labor union opposition and thereby facilitate the process of trade liberalization. While I share the normative belief that democracies ought to respect workers' rights, the descriptive reality is that many countries that are widely seen as democratic regularly violated workers' basic rights.

Did trade liberalization deliver sufficient benefits to justify the labor repression that democratic governments often used to achieve it? According to some, trade liberalization increased wages for low-skilled workers and spurred economic growth in developing countries.[50] These claims support a worldview without tradeoffs, a vision in which democracy led to free trade, and free trade led to the alleviation of poverty. But we also know that labor repression has direct and negative consequences that include lowering workers' wages, increasing income inequality,[51] and weakening demands for welfare spending.[52] By weakening the power of labor unions, labor repression may even undermine the very sustainability of democracy itself.[53] Is free trade beneficial if it comes at the cost of labor repression? What if free trade comes at the longterm cost of democracy itself? As Atul Kohli once warned, "the normative implication then is to treat with suspicion claims that trade-offs are not necessary and that all good things can readily go together."[54]

RESEARCH METHODS

The field's main theoretical approaches to international trade tend to obscure the actual role that labor repression played when democratic developing countries opened their economies in the late twentieth century. Research in these traditions regularly tells the story of trade policy reform without reference to or serious consideration of the labor repression that often helped to pave

48 Adsera et al. 2002, 254. 49 Haggard and Kaufman 2008, 13.

50 Held et al. 1999; Reuveny and Li 2003; Milner and Kubota 2005; Bhagwati 2007; Eichengreen and Leblang 2008; Chaudoin et al. 2015.

51 Kerrissey 2015. 52 Rudra 2002; Yang and Kwon 2019.

53 Schmitter 1993; Budd et al. 2018; Baccaro et al. 2019. 54 Kohli 2004, 422.

the way toward free trade. Despite thirty years of scholarship on economic reform in Argentina and India, for example, neither the story of Ubaldini's car bomb nor that of Rao's preventive arrests has ever been told.[55] In general, the existing literature overlooks major instances of labor repression on its way to concluding that other factors explain how democratic developing countries implemented trade liberalization.

This book carefully revisits the empirical evidence that supports the field's dominant theories in order to demonstrate that democratic developing countries frequently used labor repression to overcome labor union opposition to trade liberalization. Such revisionist research is most compelling when based on well-known cases that the extant literature explains without reference to the factors highlighted by a new theory.[56] This book therefore presents in-depth case studies of trade liberalization in India and Argentina in the 1990s, two cases with enormous literatures that are nearly silent on the role of labor repression. In both cases, I document that labor unions opposed trade liberalization and that governments' non-repressive tactics failed to stop unions from launching strikes and protests against such reforms. I then demonstrate how previously overlooked instances of labor repression weakened labor union opposition and thereby facilitated the implementation of trade liberalization. Similarly, I revisit the cross-national quantitative evidence that suggests that democracy is associated with trade liberalization in developing countries and demonstrate how these results are actually driven by the subset of democratic developing countries that aggressively repressed labor unions.

Studying the history of free trade and labor repression therefore requires a multi-method approach that combines archival research, fieldwork interviews, and statistical analysis. Archival documents, such as local newspapers and labor union pamphlets, help identify episodes of labor repression that were well-documented scandals when they occurred but were overlooked in later scholarly accounts. Interviews with labor union leaders and government officials from these periods help to add new details on the lived experience and strategic logic of labor union members resisting economic reforms. Cross-national statistical analysis demonstrates that the basic dynamics identified using qualitative methods are generalizable beyond the small number of cases studied. In over one hundred developing countries, the association between democracy and trade liberalization was strongest when governments heavily repressed labor unions; when governments maintained high levels of respect for labor rights, democracy was associated with the maintenance of high tariffs.

55 Ranis 1992; Levitsky and Way 1998; Jenkins 1999; Murillo 2001; Levitsky 2003; Etchemendy 2011; Candland 2007; Teitelbaum 2011; Kohli 2012; Sinha 2016.

56 George and Bennett 2005, 253.

PLAN FOR THIS BOOK

The remainder of this book is organized into five chapters. Chapter 1 presents my theory of trade politics in developing countries. It presents a deductive theory of domestic actors' policy preferences as well as a theory of how these societal preferences are aggregated by a set of two domestic institutions – political regime type (democracy vs autocracy) and labor rights regime (respect for labor rights vs labor repression). While this focus on preferences and institutions is rooted in the open economy politics (OEP) approach, my argument uses these building blocks to construct a less rosy story about globalization than is usually found in this tradition.[57]

Chapter 2 tests my argument using quantitative data on average tariff levels in over one hundred developing countries from 1985 through 2010. The regression analysis focuses on the interaction between the level of democracy and the level of respect for labor rights.[58] The results demonstrate that an increase in democracy was associated with trade liberalization when respect for labor rights was low, but continued trade protection when respect for labor rights was high. The results also suggest that at high levels of democracy, an increase in labor repression was associated with a decrease in tariff levels. In short, the analysis supports my argument that democratic governments in developing countries were more likely to open their economies if they cracked down on labor unions.

Chapter 3 presents case studies of trade politics in Argentina, Mexico, Bolivia, Turkey, and India during the late twentieth century. I use this diverse set of countries and a series of cross-case and within-case comparisons to illustrate the mechanisms that link democracy and labor repression to trade liberalization.[59] These include cross-case comparisons of Argentina (1983–1989), Mexico (1982–1994), and India (1985–1989), a within-case comparison of Bolivia (1982–1984 vs 1985–1989), and a within-case comparison of Turkey (1961–1980 vs 1983–1989). I present each case study in three sections, each of which illustrates a different causal mechanism of my theory. First, I examine whether democracy increased demands for trade liberalization. Second, I explore whether labor repression decreased union mobilization. In cases where governments respected labor rights, I describe how such protections enabled unions to mobilize against trade liberalization. Third, I discuss whether union opposition influenced trade policy outcomes. Overall these cases provide examples of how (1) increases in democracy led to the maintenance of high tariffs if governments respected labor right, (2) increases in democracy led to

57 Lake 2009.

58 For the level of democracy, the analysis uses Polity as well as the Unified Democracy Score. For labor rights, the analysis uses Mosley and Marx's data on collective labor rights as well as labor union density from Martin Rama.

59 Goertz 2017, 56.

trade liberalization if governments repressed labor unions and (3) increases in labor repression by an established democracy led to trade liberalization. The case studies of India and Argentina in the 1980s also set the stage for the next two chapters, which explore trade liberalization by both countries during the 1990s.

Chapter 4 returns to the story of India's path from the blocked trade policy reforms of the 1980s to the successfully implemented reforms of the 1990s. India's liberalization in the 1990s represents an especially hard case for my theory due to its reputation for strong respect for labor rights. Influential work in comparative political economy argues that the Indian government followed a strategy of "reform by stealth" that confused and demobilized opposition groups and reduced "the possibility that more strident versions of trade union resistance would spread."[60] Others suggest that partisan ties between the ruling Congress party and the country's largest labor union, INTUC, contributed to labor restraint and acquiescence to Rao's reforms.[61] In contrast, this chapter describes general strikes that mobilized tens of millions of Indian workers and uncovers shocking episodes of labor repression – such as the preventive arrests mentioned above – that sheds new light on the process through which India implemented trade liberalization in 1990s.

Chapter 5 returns to the story of Argentina's path from democratization, respect for labor rights, and high tariffs in the 1980s, to the increased labor repression that facilitated trade liberalization in the 1990s. Argentina has a large economy that is intrinsically important and its pursuit of import-substitution industrialization is broadly representative of Latin American developmental history. The literature on Argentine economic reforms argues that Menem overcame potential labor opposition because of close partisan ties between his political party and the country's labor movement, as well as the government's use of welfare compensation for reform losers.[62] In contrast, I draw on archival documents and interviews to show how Menem used labor repression to split the Argentine labor movement in half and then to isolate and squash those unions that continued to resist his reforms. As Carlos Tomada, Argentina's Minister of Labor from 2003 to 2015, explained, "Menem destroyed the labor movement as if we were in a dictatorship, of that there can be no doubt."[63] When paired with the previous chapter's analysis of Argentina in the 1980s, this case study of Argentina in the 1990s allows for a within-case comparison that illustrates how democracies can increase labor repression in order to reduce labor union opposition and thereby facilitate trade liberalization.

[60] Jenkins 1999, 149. [61] Teitelbaum 2011.
[62] Levitsky and Way 1998; Murillo 2001; Levitsky 2003; Etchemendy 2011.
[63] Author interview with Carlos Tomada, December 19, 2019.

The book concludes with a final chapter that summarizes my theory and evidence and reflects on the broader implications for political economy research, our understanding of the history of international trade, and the future prospects for an open global economy. Overall, this book demands that we think differently about the politics of free trade in democratic developing countries, the relationship between democracy and respect for labor rights, and the overall process through which the international trade system opened in the late twentieth century.

1

Open Democracies

How Labor Repression Facilitates Trade Liberalization

How did developing countries with democratic governments open their economies during the late twentieth century? More specifically, how did they overcome opposition from protectionist labor unions that demanded the continuation of high tariffs? In short, this book argues that democratic developing countries often used labor repression – the violation of workers' basic rights to organize and strike – to weaken labor union opposition and ease the transition toward free trade. This book therefore places labor unions and labor repression at the heart of the debate over democracy and trade liberalization in developing countries.

There were two different "ideal-typical" paths through which democratic developing countries used labor repression to facilitate trade liberalization. The first path started with labor repression, and then added democracy. This path was followed by developing countries that transitioned to democracy while maintaining the high level of labor repression that was practiced by the previous autocratic regime. The second path started with democracy, and then added labor repression. This path was followed by developing countries that transitioned to democracy and respected labor rights, only to later increase labor repression. On both paths, labor repression played a crucial role in reducing labor union strikes and protests against trade liberalization.

This chapter presents my theory of trade policy in developing countries in four steps. First, it explains why labor unions in developing countries opposed trade liberalization during the late twentieth century. This prediction is derived from my previous research on profit-sharing institutions, which explains the trade policy preferences of capital and labor based on their sector of employment and whether or not workers' wages rise along with profits. This section explains how import-substitution industrialization led to powerful labor unions, profit sharing, and protectionist workers in capital-intensive, import-competing industries. In contrast, export-oriented industries faced global competition that led to weak unions, wages that lagged behind profits, and workers that lacked the interest and ability to demand trade liberalization. In import-competing industries, capital and labor formed cross-class coalitions in favor of trade protection; in export-oriented industries, capital supported free trade on their own, while labor sat on the political sidelines.

Second, this chapter explains how the process of trade policymaking differs across two different domestic institutions: political regime type and the level of respect for labor rights. Political regime type determined which domestic groups were able to influence trade policy. In autocracies, trade policy was often dominated by just one group: protectionist, import-competing capital. In democracies, however, trade policy was open to numerous domestic groups including the general public, import-competing capital, export-oriented capital, and, potentially, labor unions. The degree to which labor unions were able to organize and act collectively to influence trade policy was heavily shaped by the government's level of respect for labor rights. The more labor rights were protected, the more likely labor unions were to launch influential protests and strikes against trade liberalization. The less labor rights were protected, in contrast, the less likely labor unions were to mobilize powerful protests and strikes that could impede trade liberalization.

Third, this chapter explains how these theoretical micro-foundations lead to parsimonious predictions about the implementation of trade liberalization, including the two ideal-typical paths discussed above. In short, the more democratic developing countries repressed labor unions, the more likely they were to open their economies. Finally, this chapter discusses the origins of the two paths mentioned above and explores why some democratic developing countries may respect labor rights more than others as well as why some democratic developing countries that respect labor rights may later decide to increase labor repression.

POLICY PREFERENCES, INSTITUTIONS, AND TRADE POLICY

My overall theory of international trade policy in developing countries has two main building blocks. The first building block is a theory of trade policy preferences, which explains which groups supported trade liberalization and which preferred continued trade protection. The second building block is a theory of domestic institutions, which explains how some countries privilege the trade policy preferences of some groups over others. By combining my theory of trade policy preferences with my theory of domestic institutions I am able to explain who wants what, and when and why they are able to get it.[1] Countries with

[1] My theoretical framework is therefore consistent with the Open Economy Politics paradigm, which "begins with individuals, sectors, or factors of production as the units of analysis and derives their interests over economic policy from each unit's position within the international economy. It conceives of domestic political institutions as mechanisms that aggregate interests (with more or less bias) and structure the bargaining of competing societal groups" (Lake 2009, 225).

different sets of institutions, in other words, took the same sets of trade policy preferences and turned them into different types of trade policy outcomes.[2] This section presents these building blocks, starting with my theory of trade policy preferences and then moving on to my theory of domestic institutions.

Trade Policy Preferences

In developing countries during the late twentieth century, who supported free trade and who opposed it? Previous research suggests that a majority of the general public in developing countries often supported trade liberalization.[3] Starting in the 1970s, many developing countries faced low rates of economic growth, hyperinflation, and mounting debt crises that helped to discredit the high tariffs and protectionist policies associated with import-substitution industrialization.[4] According to some scholars, members of the public rationally anticipated that lower tariffs would reduce consumer prices, increase aggregate economic growth, and create new employment opportunities.[5] For others, public support for trade liberalization was driven less by individuals' material interest and more by partisan rhetoric or ideological trends; a growing consensus spread across both developed and developing countries that famously concluded that "there is no alternative" to trade liberalization and other neoliberal economic reforms.[6]

Yet international trade policy is not determined by public opinion alone; as Grossman and Helpman explain, "in representative democracies, governments shape trade policy in response not only to the concerns of the general electorate, but also to the pressures applied by special interests" such as business lobbies and labor unions.[7] How can we understand the trade policy preferences of these different interest groups? Drawing on my previous research, I argue that the trade policy preferences of these groups depend on two key factors: industry of employment and profit sharing between capital and labor. I use a simple model with two industries – export-oriented and import-competing – and a binary distinction between industries with and without profit sharing. For capital, my theory makes the same predictions as the well-known Ricardo–Viner model of international trade; capital in export-oriented industries benefits from, and therefore supports, trade liberalization, while capital in import-competing industries benefits from, and therefore supports, trade protection.[8] To predict labor's trade policy preferences, however, we need to know more than just workers' industry of employment; we also need to know whether or not an increase in industry profits will lead to an increase in workers' wages.

2 Rogowski 1987; Bailey et al. 1997. 3 Baker 2009. 4 Rodrik 1992; Blyth et al. 2002.

5 Stokes 2001; Baker 2005; Milner and Kubota 2005; Chaudoin et al. 2015; Zucker 2020.

6 Grinspun and Kreklewich 1994; Harvey 2005; Medrano and Braun 2012; Hicks et al. 2013.

7 Grossman and Helpman 1994, 833. For a recent study that finds that consumer interests do not drive trade policy outcomes, see Betz and Pond 2019.

8 Frieden 1991.

The key insight is that workers do not automatically benefit from trade policy reforms that benefit their industry of employment. When workers have little bargaining power, trade policy reforms tend to increase the profitability of an industry without leading to an increase in wages.[9] Trade liberalization can increase profits for export-oriented industries without increasing wages for workers in those industries, just as trade protection can increase profits for import-competing industries without increasing wages for those industries' workers.[10] In contrast, when workers organize labor unions, bargain collectively, and threaten to strike, their wages are more likely to rise along with their industry's profits.[11] My model therefore predicts that workers are more likely to share the same trade policy preferences as their employers when the profits generated by trade policy are shared with workers.[12]

In developing countries during the late twentieth century, such profit sharing was common in import-competing industries but very rare in export-oriented industries. These sectoral differences in profit sharing had both political and economic origins. Profit sharing in import-competing industries was rooted in the policies of import-substitution industrialization, a set of economic policies that included protectionist trade barriers and labor market regulations that fostered union organizing in protected industries.[13] Workers in these capital-intensive, import-competing industries – such as steel and automobiles – organized powerful labor unions that were able to bargain with their employers for a share of their industry's profits.[14] In contrast, workers in labor-intensive, export-oriented industries found it very difficult to organize labor unions and bargain for a share of their industry's profits.[15] These industries faced low profit margins and global competition that put downward pressure on wages and often led employers to resist recognizing and bargaining with labor unions.[16]

The result was that labor unions in import-competing industries were powerful and regularly opposed trade liberalization, while workers in export-oriented industries were less likely to be unionized and rarely provided organized support for trade liberalization. When labor union confederations – peak organizations that represent unionized workers throughout the economy – debated international trade, they therefore faced much stronger demands for trade protection than for trade liberalization. In addition, import-competing unions were frequently joined by unions representing workers in state-owned enterprises, which were threatened by the privatization proposals that governments often bundled together with trade liberalization.[17] The end result was that

[9] Levy and Temin 2009; Kerrissey 2015. [10] Wallerstein 1987; Kuruvilla 1996; Dean 2015b.
[11] Blanchflower et al. 1996; Dean 2015a. [12] Frieden 1991; Hiscox 2002; Dean 2016.
[13] Kohli 2004. [14] Weyland 2002; Dean 2016. [15] Kuruvilla 1996. [16] Silver 2003.
[17] Boix 1997; Uba 2005; Simmons 2016.

labor union confederations, the best-organized and most politically relevant representatives of the working class, regularly opposed trade liberalization.[18]

Domestic Institutions

Now that we know which groups supported and opposed trade liberalization, we now turn to see how different domestic institutions shaped the ability of these different groups to influence trade policy.[19] This section explains how two domestic institutions – political regime type and labor rights – determine which groups shape international trade policy. In short, the transition from autocracy toward democracy empowered groups that favored trade liberalization, while the level of respect for labor rights shaped the degree to which protectionist labor unions were able to defend trade protection.

Political Regime Type: Democracy vs. Autocracy

Many developing countries entered the 1980s with autocratic regimes and relatively closed economies, along with a domestic coalition of import-competing industrialists that supported both.[20] For example, Weyland explains that "business associations, which were once dominated by protectionist sectors," played a particularly influential role in supporting authoritarian governments and trade protection in Latin America.[21] During this period of trade protectionism, the general public and export-oriented businesses favored trade liberalization but were unable to influence trade policy. As long as domestic groups that supported trade liberalization were excluded from policymaking, protectionism survived without political assistance from labor unions, which were usually politically weak under authoritarian regimes.[22]

This previously stable equilibrium of trade protectionism was often upset if and when developing countries moved toward greater democracy. Whether it was incremental reforms that broadened the franchise or increased competition between political parties, or sudden transitions from autocracy to democracy, such political regime changes opened the policymaking arena to new groups. Higher levels of democracy increased the political influence of the general electorate, which often believe that trade liberalization would lower consumer prices, increase economic growth, and create new employment opportunities.[23] Although members of the general public rarely organize around trade policy issues, democratically elected politicians may still face incentives to lower tariffs

18 For an alternative explanation for limited labor support for trade liberalization in developing countries, see Menendez et al. 2018, which uses the Melitz model and "new new trade theory" to explain trade politics in developing countries.

19 Rogowski 1987; Frieden 1999; Milner and Kubota 2005; Lake 2009.

20 Edwards 1996; Bates 2014. 21 Weyland 2002, 60. 22 Collier and Cardoso 1979.

23 Weyland 2002; Milner and Kubota 2005; Baker 2009; Chaudoin et al. 2015; Mukherjee 2016. The trade policy preferences of voters with little knowledge about international trade may also be influenced by political parties, see Medrano and Braun 2012; Hicks et al. 2013; Guisinger 2017.

if they anticipate that it will lead to economic growth and future electoral benefits.[24] Beyond empowering average citizens, democracy also increased the political influence of export-oriented businesses, which had often been excluded from policymaking under autocracy. Compared to the general public, the relatively small number of such export-oriented businesses made it easier for them to overcome collective action problems and to organize lobby groups and fund political parties that supported their economic policy agenda.[25]

But protectionist and pro-trade capital are not the only interest groups looking to shape trade policy in democratic developing countries. Democracy can also empower labor unions – especially the protectionist labor union confederations discussed above – to pressure elected officials.[26] Labor unions educate their rank-and-file members about trade policy,[27] mobilize their members to vote based on salient economic policies,[28] influence public opinion on economic reforms,[29] regularly lobby the government over economic policy,[30] have significant influence on legislative voting,[31] and can paralyze the economy with protests and strikes.[32] In these ways, protectionist labor unions have the potential to pressure democratic developing countries to maintain high tariffs, thus counterbalancing pro-trade demands for trade liberalization. While the shift from autocracy to democracy therefore increased the political influence of pro-trade groups, it did not necessarily lead to trade liberalization.[33]

Labor Rights: Respect vs. Repression

Why does democracy lead to trade liberalization in some developing countries but continued trade protection in others? Among democratic developing countries that open their economies, why do some open quickly and others more slowly? One key factor is the degree to which democratic developing countries respect labor rights – that is, the degree to which they protect workers' basic rights to organize, collectively bargain, and strike. The more democratic developing countries respect labor rights, the more labor unions are empowered to organize and act collectively to defend high levels of trade protection.[34] In developing countries during the late twentieth century,

[24] Garrett 2000; Stokes 2001.

[25] Olson 1965; Thacker 2000; Osgood et al. 2017. This book neither theorizes nor empirically tests the degree to which the link between democracy and trade liberalization is driven by the pro-trade preferences of the general public or organized business. For an important contribution to this debate, see Betz and Pond 2019.

[26] Geddes 1995; Kuruvilla 1996.

[27] Ahlquist et al. 2013; Kim and Margalit 2017. [28] Rosenfeld 2010.

[29] Ahlquist and Levi 2014. [30] Freeman and Medoff 1984. [31] Wilhite 1988.

[32] Tarrow 1994. [33] Bearce and Velasco-Guachalla 2020.

[34] Labor rights and labor union power are co-constitutive. On the one hand, labor unions often pressure governments to protect workers' basic rights to act collectively (Tilly 1995). On the other hand, labor rights fundamentally influence labor union power by shaping their ability to organize and strike (Kerrissey 2015). In new democracies, low levels of respect for labor rights are associated with unions that lack political influence due to low union density and

one of the most important labor union tactics was the launching of general strikes. General strikes often mobilized hundreds of thousands or even millions of union members and clearly demonstrated the breadth of working-class opposition.[35] Such large and public demonstrations can build solidarity and shift public opinion, thus increasing the size of the coalition opposed to government reforms.[36] In turn, growing public criticism of government reforms can lead opposition parties to champion the cause of the protests; at times, union opposition can even attract support from dissenting members of the political party implementing unpopular reforms.[37] General strikes that paralyze the economy for any length of time can also inflict enormous economic costs, which democratic leaders must be especially sensitive to during periods of economic crisis.[38] Short of general strikes, labor unions also launched industry-level strikes, protests, marches, and demonstrations that influenced government policy through similar mechanisms.

The less democratic developing countries respect labor rights, however, the more they can use labor repression to weaken labor unions, limit general strikes and other protest tactics, and thereby reduce the influence of union opposition. As Lukes and Gaventa explain, governments have two very different ways in which they can use their power to reduce the political influence of labor unions.[39] What these scholars call the "first face" of power is on display when the government uses violence in open conflict with workers. In this vein, democratic governments often responded to general strikes and protests by arresting union leaders and rank-and-file members and by unleashing police brutality on strikers. In many instances, democratic governments used their own police or militaries to break strikes launched against government reforms.[40]

The "second face" of power, in contrast, is on display when the government changes the "rules of the game" to deter groups from organizing, mobilizing, and openly and effectively expressing their demands. In this vein, democratic

restrictions on their ability to act collectively. In established democracies, a decrease in respect for labor rights decreases unions' political influence by limiting their ability to translate their organizational power (union density) into collective action. It is beyond the scope of this book to settle whether labor rights or labor power determines labor union influence on trade policy.

35 Lindvall 2013. 36 Tarrow 1994. 37 Hamann et al. 2013. 38 Wisniewski et al. 2020.

39 Gaventa 1982; Lukes 2004. This book does not explore Lukes' "third face" of power, which explains how dominant groups can use power over oppressed communities to convince them to support policies that are materially harmful to themselves. While power may have played such a role in many cases, this book focuses on the concrete and empirically observable ways in which governments used the first two faces of power to weaken labor union opposition to trade liberalization.

40 For examples from Bolivia, see Nazmi 1995; for Argentina, see "Alsogaray Defends Actions," *Buenos Aires Herald*, September 9, 1990; for India, see "1000s Held Over Strike Call," *Times of India*, June 14, 1992.

governments often restrict workers' rights to organize unions, declare strikes to be illegal, threaten to fire workers that join strikes, interfere with union elections, or co-opt union leaders through the manipulation of union finances.[41] In many instances, democratic governments threatened to de-certify labor unions that launched "political" strikes aimed at blocking government reforms. While democratic governments may hesitate to exclude labor unions from politics with the first face of power, they frequently weakened and politically excluded unions with the more subtle second face of power.[42]

To be clear, democracy is not a guarantee of respect for labor rights, and democratic governments regularly weakened labor union opposition to trade liberalization through labor repression. In theory, a government can restrict workers' rights to organize, collectively bargain, and strike (labor repression that limits their political power) without limiting the franchise, competitive elections, or constraints on the executive (democracy). In practice, common indices of democracy and respect for labor rights are almost completely statistically independent; the correlation between the Polity score and the measure of labor rights used in this book was only 0.08 in developing countries from 1985 through 2010. This book analyzes shocking instances of labor repression in Argentina, Bolivia, India, and Turkey during periods when all four countries were widely seen as democracies.

The fundamental difference between democracy and respect for labor rights is on clear display in developed countries as well. The members of the OECD are all considered full democracies, yet these countries vary tremendously in their level of respect for labor rights. Similarly, American history demonstrates that consistently high levels of democracy were associated with widely varying levels of respect for labor rights, including the violent labor repression of the Gilded Age, the increased respect for workers' rights during the New Deal, and the steady decline of labor rights and the political power of labor unions since the 1980s. Labor unions and activists often argue that workers' rights are human rights and that democratic governments therefore should not violate labor rights.[43] The reality, however, is that democratic governments regularly violate labor rights and weaken labor unions without ceasing to be viewed as democracies.

41 Valenzuela 1989.

42 Valenzuela 1989; Davenport 2007. This book argues that labor repression, on average, reduces labor unions' ability to mobilize workers and therefore decreases their influence on government policy. In specific instances, labor repression may attract additional media coverage and public attention and therefore amplify unions' policy demands. More research is needed to understand the unique conditions under which a government's use of labor repression may "backfire" in this way.

43 Kolben 2009.

TWO PATHS TOWARD FREE TRADE: DEMOCRACY OR LABOR REPRESSION FIRST?

Among the many developing countries that combined democracy with labor repression there were two different "ideal-typical" paths toward free trade.[44] The first path started with labor repression, and then added democracy. This path was followed by countries that transitioned to democracy while maintaining the high level of labor repression that was practiced by the previous autocratic regime. New democratic governments then faced increased demands for trade liberalization from the general public and export-oriented capital without countervailing pressures from protectionist labor unions.[45] For developing countries that followed this first path, trade liberalization was triggered by an increase in democracy when respect for labor rights was low.

The second path started with democracy, and then added labor repression. This path was followed by developing countries that transitioned to democracy and provided strong protections for labor rights that fostered powerful labor unions. This type of democratic transition enabled protectionist labor unions to help import-competing capital counterbalance the pro-trade demands of the general public and export-oriented capital. On this second path, democratic developing countries maintained high tariffs until an increase in labor repression weakened union opposition to trade liberalization. Some democratic developing countries respected labor rights and maintained high tariffs for decades. Others increased labor repression and lowered their tariffs within just a few years. The crucial point is that for developing countries that followed this second path, trade liberalization was triggered by an increase in labor repression by an established democratic government.

The basic predictions of my theory, along with these two ideal-typical paths toward free trade, are displayed below in Figure 1.1. As explained above, my theory starts with developing autocracies with closed economies. The first step in the argument is an increase in democracy. Whether or not this increase in democracy leads to trade liberalization or continued trade protection depends on the level of respect for labor rights. If respect for labor rights is low (representing continued labor repression from the prior regime), then an increase in democracy leads to trade liberalization. This is the first path that many democratic developing countries took toward free trade; they started with labor repression and added democracy.

44 As discussed in the Introduction, these were not the only two paths toward free trade for developing countries. Many developing countries lowered their tariffs without democratizing, and many democracies faced external pressures that may have led to trade liberalization independent of their level of respect for labor rights.

45 After the transition from autocracy to democracy, import-competing capital continued to favor trade protection. But in democracies that did not respect labor rights, protectionist capital was left to lobby for high tariffs without political assistance from labor unions.

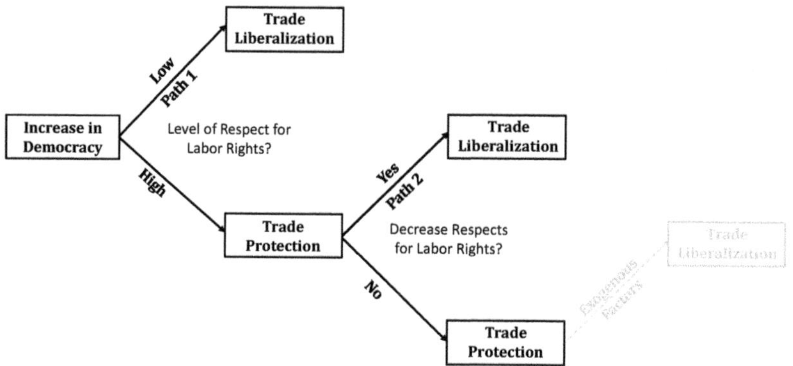

FIGURE 1.1. Two paths toward free trade for democratic developing countries

If respect for labor rights is high, however, then an increase in democracy leads to continued trade protection. For these new democracies that respected labor rights and maintained high tariffs for a period of time, trade liberalization came later on after a decision to decrease respect for labor rights. This is the second path that many democratic developing countries took toward free trade; they started with democracy and added labor repression. Beyond these two paths, Figure 1.1 also displays that additional exogenous factors may cause democratic developing countries to implement trade liberalization (in gray). This book focuses on how democratic developing countries used labor repression to facilitate trade liberalization and acknowledges that additional factors – such as external pressure, government technocrats, and the influence of ideas – also play independent roles in the political economy of international trade.

On both of these ideal-typical paths toward free trade, the extent of trade liberalization depended upon the degree of labor repression. On the first path, the level of labor repression determined the extent to which an increase in democracy led to lower tariffs. When respect for labor rights was low, an increase in democracy led to a large decrease in tariff levels; at incrementally higher levels of labor rights, an increase in democracy led to smaller tariff reductions; when respect for labor rights was high, an increase in democracy led to the maintenance of high tariffs. On the second path, the degree to which a democratic developing country increased labor repression determined the extent of the subsequent trade liberalization. Large increases in labor repression were associated with large tariff reductions, while small increases in labor repression were associated with small tariff reductions. While labor unions were rarely able to block trade liberalization completely, their efforts slowed down the process of reform and granted workers more time to adjust to economic changes. As Polanyi reminds us, "the rate of change is often of no less importance than the direction of the change itself"; therefore "why should the ultimate victory of a trend be taken as proof of the ineffectiveness of the efforts to slow down its progress?"[46] In these ways, labor unions were often influential on the margins; the more respect for labor rights enabled unions to influence trade policy, the less democratic developing countries lowered their tariffs.

DEMOCRACY AND LABOR RIGHTS

This book's primary goal is to demonstrate that democratic developing countries often used labor repression to overcome union opposition to trade liberalization. But this focus on labor repression raises important questions about variation in labor rights across democratic developing countries as well as the longer historical processes behind the politics of trade liberalization. With regard to the first path, why did some new democracies respect labor rights while others repressed labor unions? With regard to the second path, why did established democracies sometimes increase labor repression? While there are many factors that may influence respect for labor rights across democratic developing countries, this section highlights three important dynamics: (1) who led a country's struggle for democracy, (2) realignment of political parties, and (3) learning from failed economic reforms. While more research is needed on this topic, these dynamics shed light on how many developing countries eventually adopted democracy, labor repression, and trade liberalization.

Top-Down and Bottom-Up Democratization

While there are many reasons why new democracies may or may not respect labor rights, prior scholarship suggests that differences in each country's struggle for democracy may play an important role. As Collier explains, countries have historically followed two different trajectories from autocracy to democracy; bottom-up democratization led by labor unions and top-down democratization led by political and economic elites.[47] When labor unions led a bottom-up democratization struggle, new democracies were more likely to respect labor rights and empower labor unions to influence economic policy.[48] In some cases, new democratic governments drafted constitutions that guaranteed workers' rights to organize, collectively bargain, and strike. In other cases, labor union leaders and union-affiliated political parties won elections and governed the country with a commitment to fostering powerful labor unions. In short, the more labor unions led the struggle for democracy, the more new democracies respected labor rights, and the more labor unions were subsequently able to defend high tariffs.

This dynamic played out clearly in India in the 1940s. Labor unions led the fight for independence and democracy and were rewarded with a constitution that protected workers' rights to unionize and to strike. Unions then used

[46] Polanyi 1944, 36–37. [47] Collier 1999. [48] Rueschemeyer et al. 1992.

their political influence to successfully demand high tariffs for the next forty years. The link between independence, democracy, and trade policy were clear to Polanyi, who argued that the "revolt against imperialism" was mainly an attempt by colonized people to protect themselves from a flood of European imports; without political independence, colonies lacked the ability to use tariffs and other trade barriers to "shelter themselves from the social dislocations" caused by international trade.[49] Similar stories unfolded in Argentina and Bolivia in the early 1980s, where labor unions led struggles against their countries' military dictatorships and were then rewarded with improved labor rights and political influence after the transition to democracy.

In contrast, when political and economic elites led a top-down democratization struggle, new democracies often maintained low levels of respect for labor rights and thereby limited the ability of labor unions to influence economic policymaking.[50] In some cases, new democratic governments simply maintained the labor repression practiced by the previous authoritarian regime. In other cases, economic elites pushed for new labor rights restrictions that further weakened labor unions and undermined their political influence. As Collier explains, elites are often "willing to come to some understanding with the authoritarians and engineer a transition to democracy on mutually acceptable terms – an understanding that, analysts often assert, involves compromising the interests of labor."[51] In short, the more elites led the struggle for democracy, the less new democracies respected labor rights, and the less labor unions were subsequently able to defend high tariffs.

The potential effect of top-down democratization on labor rights and trade policy can be seen in Mexico during the late twentieth century. Internationally-oriented businesses, unhappy with the government's protectionist economic policies, sponsored a new political party that increased political competition.[52] In response, Mexico's dominant political party, the PRI, underwent "a fundamental transformation in the structure of power...which, among other things, reduced labor's say in national policy making."[53] As the country gradually moved toward greater democracy in the 1980s, the same internationally-oriented businesses used their new political influence to push for lower tariffs, membership in the WTO, and the negotiation of NAFTA.[54]

While the struggle for democracy may influence respect for labor rights, trade policy in developing countries cannot be reduced to the idea that bottom-up democratization led to high tariffs and top-down democratization led to trade liberalization. Some developing countries transitioned to democracy without labor-led struggles and then went on to respect labor rights and

49 Polanyi 1944, 192. 50 Thacker 2000; Ziblatt 2006; Albertus and Menaldo 2014.
51 Collier 1999, 8–9. 52 Thacker 2000. 53 Davis 1992, 16.
54 Thacker 2000; Shadlen 2002. For an argument that public support for trade played an important role in Mexico's trade liberalization, see Stokes 2001.

maintain high tariffs. For example, labor unions did not lead the struggle that culminated in Turkey's transition to democracy in 1961. Nonetheless, Turkey's new democratic government wrote a new constitution that protected workers' rights to organize and strike, and labor unions subsequently used their political influence to help maintain high tariffs.[55]

Other developing countries transitioned to democracy after labor-led struggles but then continued to repress labor unions. For example, Bangladesh transitioned to democracy in 1991 after a campaign led by industrial workers. Nonetheless, Bangladesh's new democratic government continued the labor repression practiced by the prior authoritarian regime; throughout the 1990s, Bangladeshi workers were regularly arrested for union activities, fired for strikings, harassed, attacked, and even murdered.[56] The case studies presented in this book explore how bottom-up and top-down democratization contributed to labor rights and trade policy outcomes in Argentina, Mexico, Bolivia, India, and Turkey, but more research is needed to understand variation in respect for labor rights across new democracies.[57]

Increased Repression by Democracies

In democratic developing countries that maintained high levels of respect for labor rights, why did governments sometimes increase labor repression? Although there are many reasons why democracies may decide to restrict basic labor rights, this book highlights two related political processes. The first process was that democracies restricted labor rights when left parties abandoned labor unions in search of new political constituents. In developing countries that pursued import-substitution industrialization, such party realignments were common when economic growth rates began to slow in the 1970s and 1980s. Although left parties had long supported labor unions – in exchange for labor union campaign assistance and votes – economic stagnation left labor unions deeply weakened on the economic front. While unions successfully bargained with employers for higher wages and benefits when ISI was profitable in the 1960s, unions found it increasingly difficult to negotiate with less-profitable employers after the oil crises of the 1970s. With labor unions in relative economic decline, left parties began to worry about where they would find the resources and votes to win future elections. The answer, for many new left parties in the 1980s and 1990s, was a shift away from labor unions and toward the middle class and business. Through this dynamic, the economic decline of labor unions triggered a political decline that culminated in anti-labor reforms that further weakened labor unions on both the economic and political fronts.

55 Ahmad 1993. 56 International Confederation of Free Trade Unions 1993; Mosley 2011.
57 Greenhill et al. 2009; Mosley 2010.

Without strong support from a political party, labor unions found their rights to organize, collectively bargain, and strike increasingly under threat.

The second process was that democracies learned from previous experiences of failed economic reforms. Some of the learning came from the experience of previous administrations that proposed reforms only to back down in the face of widespread opposition from labor unions. Other learning was done on the job, when non-repressive efforts to curtail labor opposition failed to stop general strikes and widespread worker protests. In Argentina, for example, thirteen CGT general strikes during the 1980s paralyzed the economy and blocked Raúl Alfonsín's economic reforms. When Menem assumed the presidency in 1989, the Argentine press stated the obvious: the new administration "will have to destroy the CGT as a major factor of power if it is to succeed in its aims of setting out new rules for the economic game."[58] When Narasimha Rao was elected Prime Minister of India in 1991, he had a similar past example to study: Rajiv Gandhi's package of reforms launched in the mid-1980s was similarly sidelined by a series of labor-led general strikes. Similar stories unfolded in Turkey and Bolivia in the 1980s, where democratic governments were keenly aware that labor-led general strikes had blocked the economic reforms proposed by prior administrations; in both countries, democratic governments then implemented trade liberalization with the help of increased labor repression.

Of course, there were many ways that developing countries may have arrived at the combination of democracy, labor repression, and trade liberalization. Top-down democratization, left parties searching for new electoral allies, and democratic governments learning from previous reform failures were just three of many possible different trajectories. While the case studies explore these historical causes of labor repression by democracies, the main point of this book is to demonstrate that democratic governments in developing countries often used labor repression to overcome union opposition to trade liberalization.

SCOPE CONDITIONS

The theory developed in this chapter has important scope conditions about what, where, and when it seeks to explain: international trade policy in developing countries at the end of the twentieth century. My focus on international trade means that I do not examine how labor repression by democratic developing countries may have influenced other neoliberal economic policy reforms that were often proposed alongside trade liberalization, such as privatization and labor law reform. This means that my theory is not able to explain within-country variation in the implementation of different economic policies opposed by labor unions.[59] While more research is needed to explore the generalizability

58 "One Foot in the Stirrup," *The Review of the River Plate*, June 30, 1989.

59 For examples of studies that explore such variation, see Murillo 2001; Madrid 2003.

of my theory to other policy areas, the logic of my argument suggests that democracies could use labor repression to facilitate the implementation of any policy opposed by labor unions.

My theory is also specific to developing countries in the late twentieth century. This means that developed countries did not face the same constraints and trade-offs when they opened their economies in the decades after World War II. One key difference between developing countries in the late twentieth century and developed countries in the mid-twentieth century was the type and profitability of the goods they exported.[60] This helped to determine whether workers' wages rose with export-led profits, whether or not labor unions joined their employers in support of trade liberalization, and whether or not the political influence of protectionist labor unions could be counterbalanced with the pro-trade demands of other labor unions.

In the mid-twentieth century, developed countries exported differentiated, capital-intensive goods such as steel and automobiles. The high profit margins in these industries enabled – though did not guarantee – workers' wages to rise along with profits.[61] If governments supported unionization in these export-oriented industries, labor unions captured a share of the profits and supported trade liberalization. Although labor unions in import-competing industries demanded continued protection, the pro-trade demands of labor unions in export-oriented industries provided a crucial political counterweight. In other words, the presence of pro-trade labor unions enabled democratic governments in developed countries to implement trade liberalization without labor repression. Previous research shows how such pro-trade labor unions enabled trade liberalization in the United States in the 1940s and throughout the "small states" of Europe in the mid-twentieth century.[62]

As explained above, the situation in developing countries during the late twentieth century was very different. These countries exported standardized, labor-intensive goods such as textiles and clothing.[63] The low profit margins in these industries put downward pressure on wages and working conditions, making it all but impossible for workers' wages to rise along with profits.[64] Without such profit sharing, workers in export-oriented industries were unlikely to provide influential political support for trade liberalization.[65] Democratic developing countries were therefore unable to counterbalance the protectionist demands of some labor unions with the pro-trade demands of other labor unions. When faced with labor-led general strikes and protests against trade liberalization, democratic governments in developing countries either backed down and maintained higher tariffs or used labor repression to weaken union opposition and facilitate trade liberalization. In these ways, developing countries faced constraints and trade-offs that developed countries avoided by empowering labor unions in export-oriented industries.

60 Schumpeter 1928. 61 Silver 2003. 62 Katzenstein 1985; Dean 2016.
63 Razmi and Blecker 2008. 64 Arrighi et al. 2003. 65 Dean 2016.

CONCLUSION

Most developing countries entered the 1980s with autocratic governments and inward-looking economies protected by high tariffs. Thirty years later, the majority of developing countries had democratic governments and relatively open economies. Ever since, scholars have asked whether or not democracy led to trade liberalization in developing countries. If so, how did democratic developing countries overcome opposition from labor unions that demanded continued trade protection? This book argues that democracy had the potential to lead to trade liberalization, as it opened the political arena to domestic groups that were more supportive of international trade. However, democracy also increased the political influence of labor unions, which vehemently opposed trade liberalization during this period.

The more democratic developing countries respected labor rights, the more workers were able to organize powerful labor unions and to launch protests and strikes against trade liberalization. Therefore, democratic developing countries were more likely to open their economies if they used labor repression – the violation of workers' basic rights to organize and strike – to weaken union opposition. In short, democracy empowered new domestic demands for trade liberalization and labor repression helped to overcome a major barrier to such reforms.

This book now begins to test my argument with a multi-method approach that includes quantitative data analysis and qualitative case studies supported by archival research and fieldwork interviews. The next chapter uses statistics from over 126 developing countries to demonstrate that trade liberalization is associated with democratic governments that repress labor unions. As predicted, an increase in democracy is associated with more trade liberalization in countries that have lower levels of respect for labor rights. At high levels of respect for labor rights, an increase in democracy is associated with the maintenance of high tariffs. Similarly, the results suggests that in established democracies, an increase in labor repression is associated with a lowering of tariffs. While neither democracy nor labor repression were strictly necessary for trade liberalization, democratic developing countries frequently used labor repression to weaken union opposition on their way to opening their economies.

2

Trade Liberalization Around the World

Cross-National Quantitative Tests

Most developing countries entered the late twentieth century with autocratic governments and high tariffs. When many of these countries transitioned toward democracy, their subsequent international trade policies depended crucially on the degree to which they protected labor rights. While democracy empowered new domestic demands for lower tariffs, respect for labor rights enabled protectionist labor unions to launch protests and strikes that impeded trade liberalization. The more democracies used labor repression to weaken union opposition, the more they moved toward free trade. This chapter tests this argument concerning the political economy of international trade using quantitative data from 126 developing countries from 1985 to 2010.

The results support my argument that there were two ideal-typical paths through which democratic governments in developing countries used labor repression to facilitate trade liberalization. The first path was followed by developing countries that increased democracy while maintaining the low level of respect for labor rights practiced by the prior regime. Consistent with this prediction, I find that the degree to which an increase in democracy was associated with trade liberalization depended upon the level of respect for labor rights. When respect for labor rights was low, an increase in democracy was associated with a relatively large decrease in tariffs. In contrast, when respect for labor rights was high, an increase in democracy was associated with the maintenance of high tariffs. The second path was followed by developing countries that transitioned to democracy and initially maintained high levels of respect for labor rights and high tariffs. For these countries, trade liberalization was associated with an established democratic government increasing labor repression. Consistent with this prediction, I find that at high levels of democracy a decrease in respect for labor rights is associated with a decrease in tariffs.

This chapter first introduces cross-national data on tariffs, democracy, and labor rights and describes how theses measures varied over time. In general, developing countries lowered their tariffs, became more democratic, and decreased their respect for labor rights around the turn of the twenty-first century. Second, it presents a descriptive analysis of how democracy, labor rights, and tariffs varied overtime within specific countries. A plot of the data suggests that democratic transitions were followed by greater trade liberalization in developing countries that had a low level of respect for labor rights than in those that had high levels of respect for labor rights. Third, it discusses the additional data and regression methods used to conduct a more systematic analysis that controls for alternative explanations and potential confounders. Fourth, it presents the results from the main regression model and a series of robustness checks. Last, it discusses the strengths of the the regression analysis, as well as the limitations that motivate the qualitative case studies presented in the remainder of this book.

DATA TO TEST THE ARGUMENT

This book explores the relationships between three main concepts – trade policy, democracy, and labor rights – all of which pose important conceptual and measurement challenges. In order to test my argument, I gathered data on these, and other related variables, for 126 developing countries from 1985 through 2010.[1] Figure 2.1 displays the broad spread of these countries across Latin America, Africa, the Middle East, Asia, and Eastern Europe.[2]

Tariff Levels

A country's openness to international trade can be measured in various ways, including actual trade flows and various policies that generate import barriers. Following prominent studies of trade policy in developing countries, the dependent variable in this chapter is the average tariff rate measured at the country-year level.[3] More specifically, I use the Most-Favored Nation applied tariff rate that countries annually supply to the WTO.[4] In 1985, the mean tariff

1 My analysis includes all countries for which data was available in Latin America, Africa, the Middle East (excluding Israel), Asia (excluding Japan), and Eastern Europe. The regression results reported below are substantively similar when limiting the analysis to countries that were not members of the OECD.

2 For a list of the 126 developing countries included in the analysis, see the Appendix.

3 Milner and Kubota 2005; Oatley 2011; Chaudoin et al. 2015.

4 As discussed below, I also use eight additional measures that include bound and applied tariffs, weighted and unweighted tariffs, and tariffs for all products and manufactured products only. All trade policy measures used are available from the World Bank.

FIGURE 2.1. Developing countries included in analysis

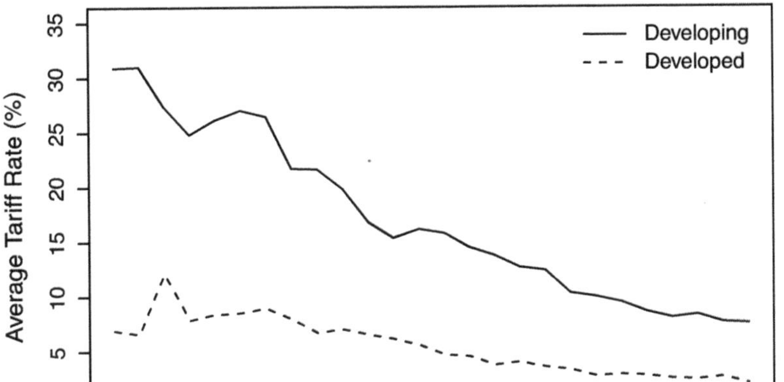

FIGURE 2.2. Trade liberalization in developing and developed countries

rate across developing countries was 31 percent; by 2010, following twenty-five years of trade liberalization, the mean tariff rate stood at less than 8 percent (Figure 2.2). In comparison, tariff rates in developed countries began this period at roughly 7 percent and were gradually lowered to 2 percent. During the period covered in this book most developing countries implemented major trade policy reforms that opened their economies to an increasingly interconnected global economy.

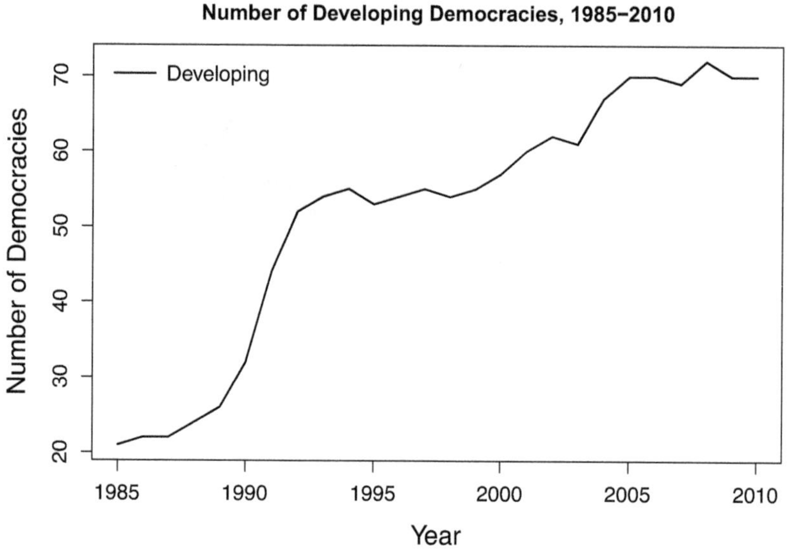

FIGURE 2.3. Number of democracies in developing countries

Democracy

The late twentieth century also witnessed what is often called the "third wave" of democratization and a rapid increase in the number of developing countries with democratic governments.[5] In 1985, there were only twenty-one developing countries with democratic governments; the number of democracies in developing countries rapidly grew after the collapse of the Soviet Union and then gradually increased to roughly 70 by 2010 (Figure 2.3).[6] Given these nearly simultaneous trends in economic and politic reform in developing countries, scholars have long debated whether democracy and international trade policy are related.

Early research on this topic used the well-known Polity index to measure the degree of democracy in developing countries.[7] The Polity index focuses on five factors that measure the institutional differences between democracies and autocracies, each of which focuses on political competition and the breadth of a country's political franchise. The continuous Polity index ranges from −10 (autocracy) to 10 (full democracy); countries receiving scores of 6 or above considered democracies.[8] In order to keep my analysis comparable to previous studies, the baseline model uses *Polity* as a continuous measure of political regime type.[9]

5 Huntington 1993. 6 Estimates based on the Polity index (>5) for 148 developing countries.

7 Milner and Kubota 2005. 8 Marshall et al. 2002.

9 To ease the interpretation of the interaction term in the regression model, I transform the Polity index by adding 10 so that the final measure ranges from 0 to 20.

While Polity remains the most widely used measure of political regime type, there is still no scholarly consensus on exactly how to conceptualize and measure democracy.[10] Researchers associated with the Varieties of Democracy (V-Dem) project recently developed an alternative measure of democracy that takes into account a broader range of characteristics evaluated by teams of country experts.[11] V-Dem's electoral democracy index (called "polyarchy"), for example, measures the extent to which a country's rulers are held accountable by citizens through fair elections, extensive suffrage, freedom of association, and freedom of expression supported by an independent media. This polyarchy measure ranges from 0 to 1, with countries receiving scores of 0.5 or above considered democracies.[12] As an alternative to these Polity and V-Dem indices, some scholars use the Unified Democracy Score (UDS), a composite of 13 different measures of democracy constructed using a Bayesian statistical measurement model.[13] This UDS index ranges from −2 to 2; countries receiving scores of 0 or above are considered democracies.[14]

The conceptual and methodological differences across these three measures of democracy mean that there is occasionally disagreement about whether a given country in a specific year was a democracy.[15] While all three measures agree that India was a democracy throughout the 1980s and 1990s, there are often disagreements about the exact year that developing countries transitioned to democracy. For example, consider Bolivia. According to Polity and UDS, Bolivia transitioned to democracy in 1982, the year that military rule ended and democratically-elected President Siles Zuazo entered office. V-Dem, in contrast, codes Bolivia's democratic transition as occurring in 1985, the year that Siles lost an election to President Paz Estenssoro.[16]

How widespread are such disagreements, and how might using different measures of democracy affect the results of cross-national statistical analysis? Using the thresholds mentioned above, Table 2.1 presents the Pearson correlation between the three binary measures of democracy based on Polity, V-Dem, and UDS.[17] Although the correlations between these measures are relatively high, I perform robustness checks using each of these three binary measures of

[10] Marshall et al. 2002. [11] Coppedge et al. 2017. [12] Teorell et al. 2019. [13] Pemstein et al. 2010.

[14] Polity and V-Dem's polyarchy index are both included in the composite UDS.

[15] I thank Paul Poast for his advice regarding different measures of democracy. For his discussion of Polity's recent decision to code the United States as a non-democracy in 2020, see https://twitter.com/ProfPaulPoast/status/1347566184749789188.

[16] The difference is likely driven by a disagreement about how to interpret Siles' election, which took place in 1980 but was not ratified by the Bolivian Congress until 1982 due to an intervening military coup. Whereas Polity and UDS focus on the return of democratic rule in 1982, V-Dem asserts that we cannot call a regime democratic in any sense unless it holds elections – a criteria that Bolivia did not meet again until 1985, see Collier 1999; Coppedge et al. 2017.

[17] Out of the 1,422 country-year observations used in the baseline regression analysis, the binary measures from V-Dem and UDS disagree in 320 (22.5%) cases. The binary measures from Polity and V-Dem disagree in 133 (9.4%) cases.

TABLE 2.1. *Correlations between binary measures of polity, V-Dem, and UDS*

	Polity	V-Dem	UDS
Polity	1		
V-Dem	0.81	1	
UDS	0.86	0.80	1

democracy to make sure that my main results using the continuous measure of Polity are not driven by idiosyncratic disagreements about specific cases. Using these different binary measures of democracy also helps to address concerns that a one point increase from a very low Polity score might represent something qualitatively different than a one point increase from a middle or high Polity score.

Labor Rights

As discussed in the previous chapter, democracy and respect for labor rights are distinct theoretical concepts. Whereas democracy is usually defined to include electoral competition and the right to vote, labor rights are about workers' rights to organize, collectively bargain, and strike. While some democratic governments in developing countries, such as Uruguay, maintain high levels of respect for labor rights, others, such as Colombia, are notorious for the frequent assassination of labor union leaders. In short, a country can have a democratic government as well as low levels of respect for labor rights. These conceptual and empirical differences between democracy and labor rights are especially important for the regression analyses discussed in this chapter, which revolve around the interaction between a country's level of democracy and level of respect for labor rights.

To measure respect for labor rights, this chapter draws on the *Collective Labor Rights Dataset* collected by Mosley and updated by Marx, Soares, and Aker.[18] Whereas earlier measures of labor rights often focused narrowly on laws but not actual practices, this data considers the legal rights of workers to organize, associate freely, bargain collectively and strike, as well as the observation of these rights in practice.[19] The *LaborRights* index is based on recorded violations of 37 specific labor rights in six broad categories; freedom of association and collective bargaining-related liberties; the right to establish and join worker and union organizations; other union activities; the right to bargain collectively; the right to strike; and rights in Export Processing Zones. These 37 violations are based on "core" labor rights as promulgated by the

[18] Mosley 2011; Marx et al. 2015. [19] Mosley 2010.

International Labour Organization and encompass the *absence* of legal rights, the *limitation* of legal rights, and the *violation* of legal rights by the government or employers.[20]

After documenting labor rights violations, the scale is reversed so that higher values represent countries with fewer violations of labor rights. A decrease in the scale therefore represents an increase in the violation of labor rights, or labor repression.[21] The dual focus on labor rights in law, as well as practice, assures that a country cannot receive a high *LaborRights* score by simply withholding legal protections for workers, and then not having any domestic labor laws to violate.[22] In these ways, *LaborRights* measures the degree to which domestic institutions provide the antecedent conditions for worker collective action and political influence. Importantly, *LaborRights* varies across time within countries, thus allowing us to estimate its association with trade policy while also including country fixed-effects that control for omitted, time-invariant variables.[23]

Not only is labor repression by democratic governments a conceptual possibility, this measure of respect for labor rights suggests that it was increasingly common in developing countries in the late twentieth century. Figure 2.4 displays the average level of respect for labor rights across 185 developed and developing countries from 1985 to 2012. The mean level of respect for labor rights in developed countries – all of which Polity, V-Dem, and UDS code as democracies – gradually decreased from 35 to 32 during this period, while labor rights in developing countries dropped from 28 to 23 (0.64 standard deviations).

The raw data also suggests that labor rights were no better protected in developing countries with democratic governments than in those with non-democratic governments; from 1985 to 2012 the mean level of respect for labor rights in developing countries with democratic governments was 23.3, compared to 23.9 for non-democracies – a difference that is not statistically significant ($p = 0.18$). In developing countries, the Pearson correlation between *Polity* and *LaborRights* is only 0.08. Similarly, the correlation between

20 Mosley's methodology assigns a weighting to each violation, with more serious violations, such as general prohibitions on unions, weighted more heavily than others. However, due to a high correlation between respect for different types of labor rights, the correlation between the weighted and unweighted indices is 0.89. The regression results reported below are based on the weighted index.

21 In order to reduce bias, violations of these thirty-seven labor rights were drawn from three sources: the U.S. State Department annual Country Reports on Human Rights Practices; reports from the International Labor Organization's Committee of Experts on the Applications of Conventions and Recommendations and the Committee on Freedom of Association; and the International Confederation of Free Trade Unions' Annual Survey of Violations of Trade Union Rights.

22 This framework also allows *LaborRights* to be disaggregated into respect for labor rights in law, on the one hand, and respect for labor rights in practice, on the other.

23 Beck 2011.

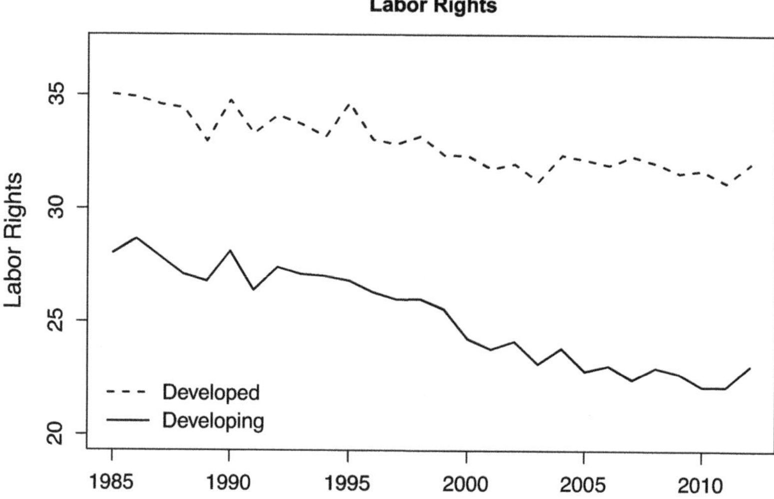

FIGURE 2.4. Labor rights in developed and developing countries, 1985–2012

LaborRights and V-Dem's polyarchy index, which explicitly claims to take into account freedom of association for political and civil society organizations, is only 0.15.

However, the low correlation between *LaborRights* and different measures of democracy should not reduce our confidence in the ability of the *Collective Labor Rights Dataset* to capture important differences in respect for labor rights across time and space. Previous research finds that respect for labor rights is associated with the types of economic outcomes that we would expect when labor unions are more powerful, such as workers' wages rising along with productivity gains and lower levels of income inequality.[24] Moreover, the secular decrease in *LaborRights* over time is also consistent with the downward trend in labor union density across developing countries during this period. Although data on union density is only available for twenty-eight developing countries from 1985 to 1999, this alternative measure of labor union power gradually decreased from 21.4 to 14.9 during this time period.[25] Similar to *LaborRights*, the correlation between labor union density and *Polity* in developing countries is only 0.13, further demonstrating the important differences between democracy and labor union power.

[24] Dean 2015a; Kerrissey 2015.

[25] Labor union density in developing countries is available from Martin Rama and the World Bank.

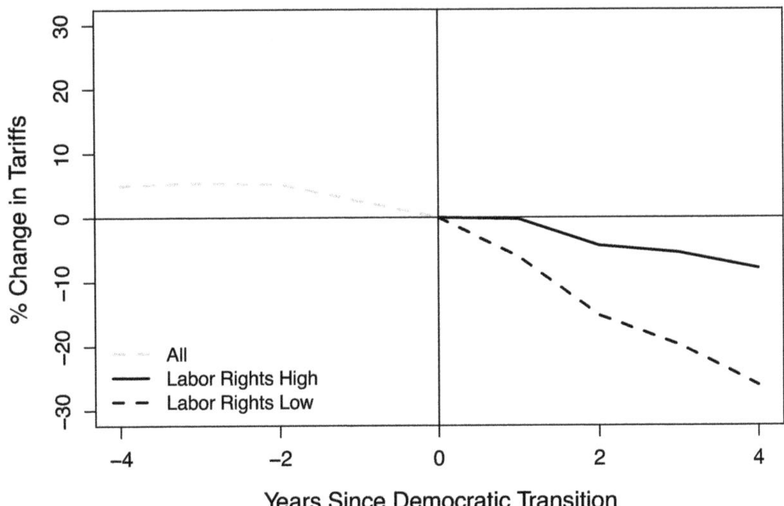

FIGURE 2.5. Labor rights, democratic transitions, and tariffs

Tariffs, Democracy, and Labor Rights

Over the course of the late twentieth century, developing countries became more democratic, lowered their tariffs, and decreased respect for labor rights. These general trends are broadly consistent with my argument that trade liberalization in developing countries was associated with the combination of democracy and labor repression, but how were these trends related to one another within specific countries? Did countries that became more democratic implement more trade liberalization than those that remained autocracies? When countries transitioned to democracy, did their level of respect for labor rights shape the degree to which they lowered their tariffs? Preliminary answers to these questions can be found in Figure 2.5, which shows how tariffs changed in thirty-nine developing countries that transitioned to democracy during the period of study.

The dashed gray line represents the mean tariff rate in all thirty-nine countries during the years before their transitions to democracy. On average, tariff rates were relatively stable during this period, dropping just a few percentage points in the years before a democratic transition. After a democratic transition, however, tariff rates dropped dramatically in developing countries that maintained low levels of respect for labor rights (dashed black line). In contrast, developing countries that maintained high levels of respect for labor rights (solid black line) gradually lowered their tariffs.[26] Within four years of a democratic transition, developing countries with high levels of respect for labor rights had lowered their tariffs by roughly 8 percent while those with low levels of respect for labor rights had lowered their tariffs by roughly 26 percent. In other words, developing countries that had low levels of respect for labor rights went on to lower their tariffs more than three times as much as developing countries that had high levels of respect for labor rights.

This plot tells a simple story that is consistent with my theory's first path toward free trade; developing countries were more likely to liberalize trade policy following an increase in democracy when respect for labor rights was low. However, this descriptive plot should only be seen as suggestive evidence in favor of my argument; the plotted tariff rates do not account for potential confounders and are based on a relatively small number of countries. In order to conduct a more systematic analysis, I therefore also gathered data on a series of domestic and international variables that may influence international trade policy.

Controls

Previous research has identified numerous factors that may be associated with trade liberalization. I gathered data on GDP per capita (*GDPpc*), total population (*Population*), and WTO membership (*WTO*) to control for the possibility that countries that are wealthier, smaller, and members of the WTO are more likely to liberalize trade policy.[27] To address the possibility that unions restrain their opposition to economic reform when a labor-aligned leader is in power, I control for whether a country has an executive from a left-wing party.[28] Since governments may use welfare spending to compensate trade losers and facilitate trade liberalization, I also control for government social spending and welfare and insurance spending.[29]

Beyond these alternative explanations, I also gathered data on two important sources of endogeneity between tariff levels and respect for labor rights: import-substitution industrialization (ISI) and pressure from the IMF. Previous research finds that ISI often led to high tariffs as well as strong protection of labor rights[30] The model therefore controls for manufacturing output as a percentage of GDP (*Manufacturing*), a proxy measure for the development of an industrial economy. Past studies also find that the IMF may influence trade policy and labor market regulations in developing countries through the conditionality

[26] In order to define low and high levels of respect for labor rights for this plot, I first calculated each country's mean level of *LaborRights* during the four years after a democratic transition. The 20 countries below the median value of 24.9 were coded as "low" and the 19 countries above the median were coded as "high."

[27] Katzenstein 1985; Wade 2010. [28] Beck et al. 2001; Murillo 2001.

[29] Cameron 1978; Albertus and Menaldo 2014. [30] Gereffi and Wyman 1990; Kuruvilla 1996.

attached to their loans.[31] The model therefore controls for the level of trade (*IMF-Trade*) and labor policy (*IMF-Labor*) conditionality that each country negotiated with the IMF.[32] Descriptive statistics for all variables included in the regression analyses are presented in the Appendix.

REGRESSION ANALYSIS: MODEL AND METHOD

My main arguments about domestic trade politics in developing countries is captured by an interaction term between *Polity* and *LaborRights*. The baseline model can be specified in the following way:

$$\begin{aligned} Tariff_{jt} = {} & \beta_1 Polity_{jt} + \beta_2 LaborRights_{jt} + \beta_3 (Polity_{jt} * LaborRights_{jt}) \\ & + \beta_4 Year_t + \sum_k \beta_k Controls_{jt} + \gamma_j + \epsilon_{jt} \end{aligned} \tag{2.1}$$

Where j identifies country and t identifies year. The γ_j represent fixed-effects at the country level.[33] These fixed-effects, along with a time trend, help to address the problem of omitted variable bias.[34] The time trend also helps to address concerns that the relationship between trade policy, democracy, and labor rights is driven by all three variables trending in one direction over time. The main model uses an AR(1) correction to address problems related to serial correlation. Importantly, the results are robust to alternative approaches to serial correlation, such as including a lagged dependent variable on the right hand side of the equation instead of an AR(1) correction, and calculating Newey-West standard errors.

Trade policy, democracy, and labor rights all potentially vary from year to year within each country and therefore the country–year is the basic unit of analysis. The data set in this analysis has 126 units (countries) and a maximum of twenty-six time periods (years). Due to missing observations for some country-years, the data set is an unbalanced panel. In order to control for the panel heteroskedasticity and contemporaneously correlated errors associated with panel data, the main model is estimated using OLS with country-level fixed-effects and panel corrected standard errors.[35] Even with these modeling techniques and the numerous controls discussed above, more research is needed to determine if the correlations identified below represent causal relationships.

One potential limitation of this analysis is reverse causality; some previous studies argue that a decrease in tariffs leads to democracy, rather than

31 Stone 2008. 32 Kentikelenis et al. 2016.

33 A Breusch and Pagan Lagrangian multiplier test rejects the null hypothesis of no country-specific variance and a Hausman test confirms that estimating the model with fixed effects is preferable to random effects.

34 Green et al. 2001.

35 Panel corrected standard errors are estimated in accordance with Beck and Katz 1995, 1996.

democracy leading to decreased tariffs.[36] This reverse causal argument suggests that trade liberalization increases wages for workers, who then use their new economic resources to collectively struggle for democracy.[37] While this general dynamic is possible, it does not pose a direct threat to my argument that labor rights moderate the relationship between democracy and tariff levels. A reverse causal interpretation of my argument, and the evidence presented below, would be that a decrease in tariffs is more likely to lead to democracy when respect for labor rights is low. This reverse argument is not logically compelling, as previous scholarship argues that tariff reductions lead to democracy via the collective action of workers.[38] In other words, there is little reason to believe that trade liberalization is more likely to lead to democracy when governments have little respect for workers' rights to act collectively.

It is also possible that trade liberalization may lead to an increase in labor repression. This might occur if governments in countries with open economies seek to improve economic competitiveness by weakening unions and suppressing workers' wages.[39] While this dynamic is plausible, it does not pose a direct threat to my interactive argument about democracy and labor rights. A reverse causal interpretation of the interaction term in my regression model would not just suggest that trade liberalization leads to labor repression; rather, it would imply that democracies are more likely than autocracies to repress labor unions after lowering their tariffs. While this book shows that democracy is not a guarantee of respect for labor rights, I am unaware of any theoretical reason to expect that democracies with open economies repress labor unions more than autocracies with open economies. The case studies in Chapters 3 through 5 further support my interpretation of the regression results; these cases illustrate how democratic developing countries often increased labor repression in order to implement trade liberalization, rather than trade liberalization later leading to labor repression.

Hypotheses

My theory suggests four hypotheses concerning the relationship between labor rights, democracy, and trade policy. First, when respect for labor rights is low an increase in democracy is associated with a decrease in tariffs. This type of increase in democracy empowers the pro-trade demands of the general public and export-oriented capital at the same time that high levels of labor repression weaken the protectionist demands of labor unions. The result is a move toward free trade following the first path predicted by my theory.

> **Hypothesis 1** Democracy is negatively associated with tariffs when respect for labor rights is low. This suggests that the coefficient on *Polity* will be negative at low levels of *LaborRights*.

[36] Rudra 2005; Eichengreen and Leblang 2008.
[37] Acemoglu and Robinson 2006. [38] Tilly 1995; Collier 1999. [39] Kuruvilla 1996.

Second, when respect for labor rights is high an increase in democracy is associated with the maintenance of tariff levels. When a country respects labor rights, an increase in democracy empowers new domestic groups that favor trade liberalization, as well as the countervailing protectionist demands of labor unions. The result is continued trade protection.

> **Hypothesis 2** Democracy is associated with no change in tariffs when respect for labor rights is high. This suggests that the coefficient on *Polity* will be zero at high levels of *LaborRights*.

The first two hypotheses explore the ideal-types of democracy with labor repression and democracy with respect for labor rights. In reality, the level of respect for labor rights varies on a continuous spectrum between these two extremes. The more that labor rights are respected, the more influence that protectionist labor unions are able to have on trade policy. Therefore, the degree to which an increase in democracy is associated with a decrease in tariffs depends upon the level of respect for labor rights. More specifically, as the level of respect for labor rights decreases, an increase in democracy is associated with larger decreases in tariff levels as protectionist labor unions have less influence on trade policy.

> **Hypothesis 3** Respect for labor rights moderates the relationship between democracy and tariffs. This suggests that the coefficient on the interaction between *LaborRights* and *Polity* will be positive.

Some developing countries became more democratic while also maintaining high levels of respect for labor rights. For various reasons, many established democracies subsequently turned their back on labor unions and increased labor repression. Such increased repression – the banning of strikes, the arrest of union leaders – reduced the political influence of protectionist labor unions and shifted trade policy toward free trade. Therefore, in developing countries with high levels of democracy, a decrease in respect for labor rights is associated with a decrease in tariff levels. As my theory's second path predicts, in established democracies an increase in labor repression is associated with trade liberalization.

> **Hypothesis 4** Respect for labor rights is positively associated with tariffs when democracy is at a high level. This suggests that the coefficient on *LaborRights* will be positive when *Polity* is at high levels.

MAIN RESULTS

The regression results presented below provide strong evidence in favor of my theory. As Path 1 predicts, an increase in democracy is associated with a decrease in tariffs when respect for labor rights is low. As respect for labor rights increases incrementally, the negative association between democracy and tariffs decreases in magnitude. When respect for labor rights is high, an increase in democracy is associated with no reduction in tariff levels. As Path 2 predicts, at high levels of democracy, a decrease in respect for labor rights is associated with a decrease in tariffs. In short, in developing countries with democratic governments labor repression was associated with trade liberalization.

Table 2.2 presents the results of five regression models that test my predictions. Model 1 starts by including the Polity index, population, GDP per capita, membership in the WTO, country-level fixed effects, a time trend, an AR(1) correction, and panel-corrected standard errors. This model demonstrates the familiar negative correlation between democracy and trade policy. The coefficient on *Polity* is negative and statistically significant, which means that an incremental increase in democracy is associated with a decrease in tariffs. This finding forms the basis of the popular claim that democratization in developing countries leads to trade liberalization through the free trade demands of newly enfranchised workers.[40]

Model 2 and Model 3 begin to test my argument by introducing respect for labor rights (*LaborRights*) and then an interaction between *Polity* and *LaborRights* to the regression model. The decrease in observations after Model 1 is due to a drop in the number of countries for which *LaborRights* data is available after 2002. As discussed above, this interaction term allows us to explore whether or not the association between trade policy and democracy varies based on a country's level of respect for labor rights.

There are four important findings from Model 3. First, as predicted by Path 1, an increase in democracy is associated with a decrease in tariffs when respect for labor rights is low (0). This can be seen in the coefficient on *Polity*, which is negative and statistically significant. Second, respect for labor rights moderates the relationship between democracy and trade policy. This can be seen in the coefficient on the interaction between *Polity* and *LaborRights*, which is positive and statistically significant. In other words, as respect for labor rights increase, an increase in democracy is associated with less and less trade liberalization.

Third, when respect for labor rights is high, an increase in democracy is associated with no change in tariff rates. This can be seen clearly in Figure 2.6, which displays how the marginal effect of democracy on tariff levels changes with the level of respect for labor rights. Once *LaborRights* is equal to or greater than twenty, democracy no longer has a significant negative association with tariffs.[41] Fourth, as predicted by Path 2, an increase in labor repression is asso-

40 Milner and Kubota 2005; Oatley 2011; Chaudoin et al. 2015.

41 A large portion of my sample (33 percent) falls within the region of significance (*LaborRights* < 20), see Brambor et al. 2006. Using a binning estimator for three equal sized bins, I found that the marginal effect of *Polity* on *Tariffs* is negative and statistically significant for the bottom tercile but not for the second and third terciles; the marginal effects increase between the three binned groups in a roughly linear fashion, as assumed by the linear interaction model, see Hainmueller et al. 2019. Last, the visual overlap in the confidence intervals for the marginal effects across the range of *LaborRights* does not imply that the interaction between *Polity* and *LaborRights* is statistically insignificant; the coefficient on the interaction term is the formal test of whether the effect of *Polity* on *Tariffs* depends on the value of *LaborRights*, see Pepinsky 2018 and Franzese and Kam 2007, 50.

TABLE 2.2. *Trade policy and labor rights in developing countries*

OLS Regression Results. DV = Tariff Level					
	(1)	(2)	(3)	(4)	(5)
Polity	−0.174**	−0.096	−0.380**	−0.343*	−0.357*
	(0.061)	(0.076)	(0.146)	(0.167)	(0.151)
Population	2.021	4.041	3.316	8.913	−0.862
	(2.018)	(3.338)	(3.397)	(4.917)	(4.225)
GDPpc	−3.092**	−1.820	−1.652	−0.289	−3.861*
	(1.125)	(1.364)	(1.343)	(2.502)	(1.691)
WTO	−2.160**	−2.213*	−2.328**	−1.892*	−1.846*
	(0.700)	(0.884)	(0.888)	(0.802)	(0.875)
Year	−0.649***	−0.730***	−0.713***	−0.879***	−0.702***
	(0.069)	(0.099)	(0.100)	(0.148)	(0.116)
LaborRights		0.056	−0.073	−0.090	−0.051
		(0.033)	(0.063)	(0.069)	(0.068)
Polity × LaborRights			0.012*	0.011*	0.011*
			(0.005)	(0.005)	(0.005)
Welfare Spending				−0.021	
				(0.099)	
Left Exec					1.135
					(0.663)
Manufacturing					0.129
					(0.074)
IMF-Trade					−0.072
					(0.045)
IMF-Labor					−0.066
					(0.061)
Debt Crisis					−0.006
					(0.898)
Banking Crisis					−0.597
					(0.522)
Currency Crisis					0.630
					(0.541)
Country Fixed-Effects	yes	yes	yes	yes	yes
Observations	2030	1422	1422	709	1243
R^2	0.696	0.719	0.723	0.774	0.738

AR(1) Correction, and PSCE in parentheses.
$^{*}\ p < 0.05$, $^{**}\ p < 0.01$, $^{***}\ p < 0.001$.

ciated with trade liberalization in established democracies. This relationship is displayed in Figure 2.7, which plots the marginal effect of democracy on the relationship between labor rights and tariff levels. When *Polity* is at relatively high levels, respect for labor rights is positively associated with tariff levels.

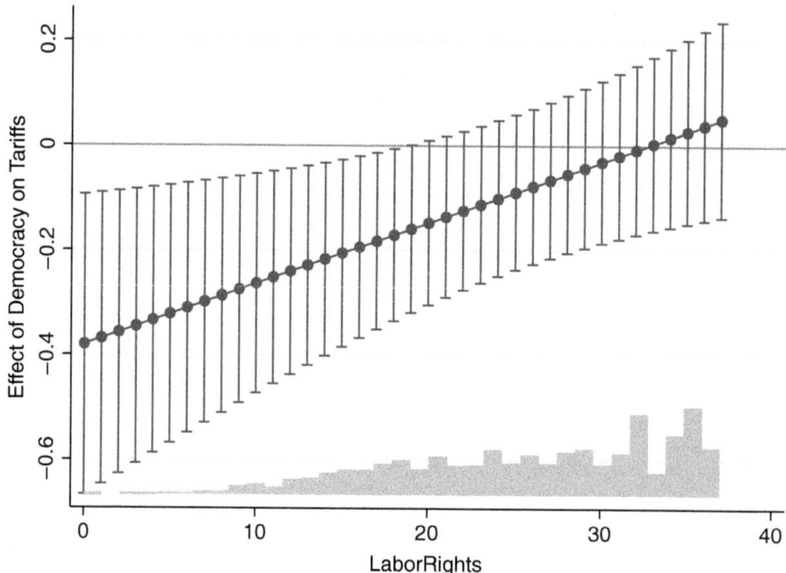

FIGURE 2.6. The marginal effect of democracy on tariff rates

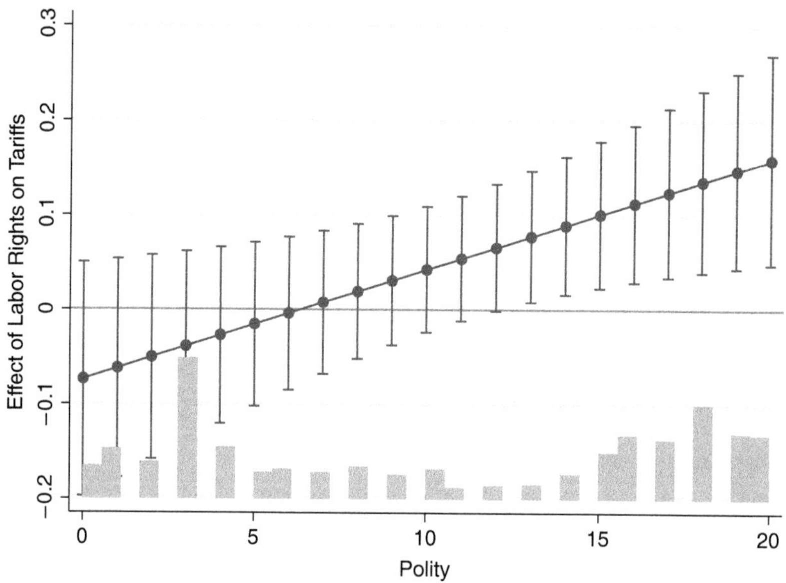

FIGURE 2.7. The marginal effect of labor rights on tariff rates

This means that in established democracies an increase in labor repression is associated with a decrease in tariffs.

Models 4 and 5 further demonstrate the robustness of these results by introducing additional controls. Model 4 controls for government spending on social insurance; due to a lack of data for forty-two of the developing countries in my dataset, including this control decreases the number of observation from 1,422 to 709. Model 5 drops this measure of social insurance and adds controls for left party executive, manufacturing as a percentage of GDP, IMF conditionality for trade and labor policy, and debt, banking, and currency crises. Although some of these controls limit the number of countries and observations in the regression analysis, the coefficient on the interaction between *Polity* and *LaborRights* remains positive, of a similar magnitude, and statistically significant in all models.

The regression results in Table 2.3 use binary measures of democracy, rather than the continuous Polity index, to explore the association between democracy and tariffs. Model 1 uses a binary measure of democracy ($Polity_{binary}$) based on the Polity index. Model 2 uses a similar binary measure of democracy ($V\text{-}Dem_{binary}$) based on the polyarchy index from the Varieties of Democracy dataset. Model 3 uses a binary measure of democracy (UDS_{binary}) based on the Unified Democracy Score dataset. The coefficient on these binary measures of democracy represent the association between democratic transitions and tariff levels when respect for labor rights is low. In all three models, the association between democracy and tariffs is negative, of a similar magnitude ($\sim$5.0), and statistically significant when respect for labor rights is equal to zero. The interaction between democracy and labor rights is also positive, of a similar magnitude ($\sim$0.15), and statistically significant for all three measures; the negative relationship between democracy and tariff levels gets smaller and smaller as respect for labor rights increases.

Not only are the regression results statistically significant, they also suggest that labor repression played a substantively important role in international trade policy in developing countries. Consider the association between democratic transitions and tariff levels presented in Table 2.3. When labor rights are one standard deviation below the mean, a democratic transition is associated with a 2.7 percentage point decrease in average tariff levels. Given that the mean tariff rate in developing countries during the period of study was roughly 17 percent, this suggests that a democratic transition with low levels of respect for labor rights is associated with a 16 percent reduction in tariff levels. When labor rights are one standard deviation above the mean, in contrast, a democratic transition is associated with zero change in average tariff levels. In other words, the results suggest that the degree to which an increase in democracy leads to trade liberalization depends crucially on the level of respect for labor rights; at high levels of labor, an increase in democracy is associated with the maintenance of high tariffs. Another way of thinking about these regression results is to revisit Figure 2.5, which showed how tariff rates changed after democratic transitions in two groups of developing countries – those that had low levels of respect for labor rights and those that had high levels of respect for labor rights. In short, the regression results suggest that the key insight displayed in that figure – democratic transitions lead to more trade liberalization when respect for labor rights is low – is statistically significant even after controlling for potential confounders.

TABLE 2.3. *OLS regression results. DV = Tariff level*

	Polity	UDS	V-Dem
Polity_{binary}	-5.499^{**}		
	(1.801)		
LaborRights	−0.018	−0.019	0.007
	(0.042)	(0.042)	(0.038)
Polity_{binary} × LaborRights	0.176^{*}		
	(0.070)		
UDS_{binary}		-4.982^{*}	
		(1.841)	
UDS_{binary} × LaborRights		0.155^{*}	
		(0.066)	
V-Dem_{binary}			-5.001^{**}
			(1.768)
V-Dem_{binary} × LaborRights			0.140^{*}
			(0.062)
Population	2.833	0.997	2.819
	(3.439)	(3.898)	(3.428)
GDPpc	−1.541	−1.875	−1.685
	(1.320)	(1.430)	(1.314)
WTO	-2.295^{**}	-1.812^{*}	-2.194^{*}
	(0.883)	(0.872)	(0.890)
Year	-0.716^{***}	-0.755^{***}	-0.708^{***}
	(0.102)	(0.107)	(0.101)
Country FEs	yes	yes	yes
Observations	1422	1258	1421
R^2	0.724	0.725	0.724

AR(1) Correction, and PSCE in parentheses.
$^{*}\ p < 0.05$, $^{**}\ p < 0.01$, $^{***}\ p < 0.001$.

ROBUSTNESS TESTS

To assess the robustness of these main results I estimated a series of alternative regression models. First, I modeled serial correlation in tariff rates using a lagged dependent variable instead of the AR(1) correction commonly used in previous studies.[42] Second, I estimated a Tobit model to address censoring of the dependent variable due to the fact that average tariffs cannot be set below zero. Third, I modeled the secular changes in tariff rates, democracy, and labor rights with year-level fixed effects instead of a time trend. Fourth,

[42] Milner and Kubota 2005; Oatley 2011; Chaudoin et al. 2015.

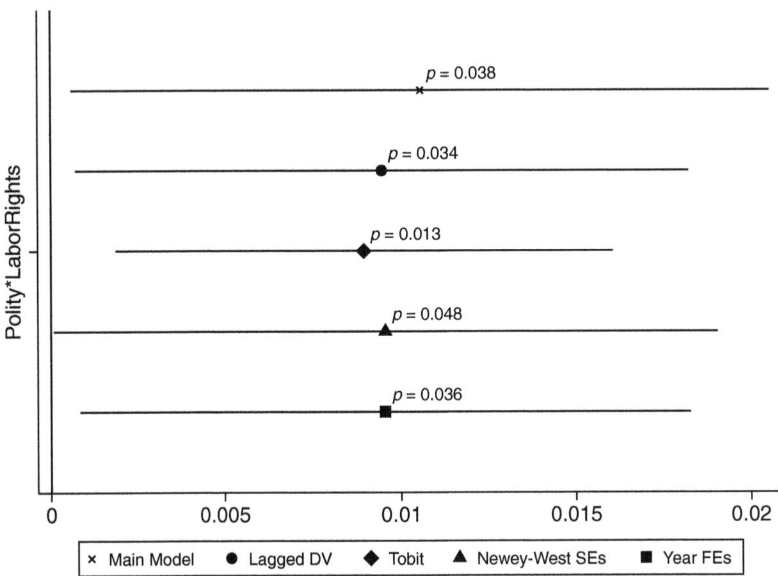

FIGURE 2.8. Interaction of democracy and labor rights in alternative models

I estimated Newey–White standard errors to address concerns that serial correlation among the residuals may extend for a longer period of time than assumed by the panel-corrected standard errors used in the main model.[43] As Figure 2.8 shows, the coefficient for the interaction between democracy and respect for labor rights remains positive and statistically significant in all four of these robustness tests.

The main regression results are also robust to using alternative measures of the dependent and main independent variables. As shown above, the main results using the continuous Polity index are robust to using binary measures of democracy from Polity, V-Dem, and UDS. In addition, the results are robust to using alternative measures of tariff rates and labor union political influence. For alternative dependent variables, I used eight different tariff measures to explore the potential differences between bound and applied tariffs, weighted and unweighted tariff averages, and tariffs for all goods and tariffs for manufactured goods. Figure 2.9 plots the coefficient for the interaction between democracy and labor rights when using these alternative measures, along with 90% confidence intervals and *p*-values. These coefficients are statistically significant at the 0.05 level for four of the models, statistically significant at the 0.10 level for three of the models, and just miss this cut off in one the models (the highest *p*-value is 0.119). In general, the results are more robust when using

43 This model drops *Population* and *GDPpc*, both of which are relatively time-invariant within countries and are therefore highly collinear with the country fixed effects. When these variables are included, multicollinearity increases the standard errors and the *p*-value to 0.067.

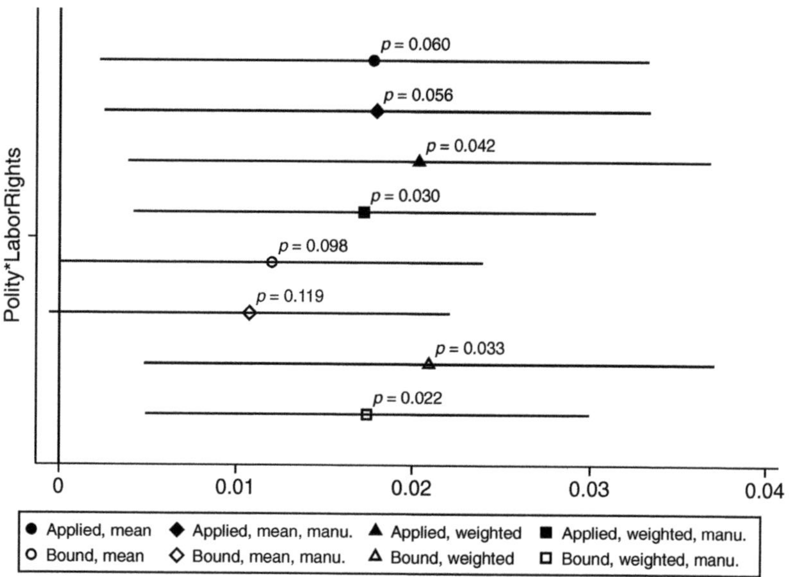

FIGURE 2.9. Interaction of democracy and labor rights with alternative tariff measures

tariff measures constructed using weighted means rather than simple means. Last, I used union density (*Union*) – rather than respect for labor rights – as an alternative measure of labor union influence on trade policy. Similar to the main regression results, the coefficient for the interaction between democracy and labor union density is positive and statistically significant (0.024; p = 0.004). Across all of these robustness tests, the results are substantively similar: an increase in democracy is associated with a decrease in tariffs when respect for labor rights (or labor union density) is low, but this relationship shrinks as respect for labor rights increases.

DISCUSSION

The regression results presented above provide strong support for my theory. Not only are the findings statistically significant, they also suggest that labor unions played a substantively important role in international trade policy in developing countries. In short, trade liberalization was associated with the combination of democracy and labor repression. Developing countries that became more democratic but continued to repress labor unions tended to lower their tariffs. In this vein, an increase in *Polity* was associated with a decrease in tariff levels only when the level of respect for labor rights was low. In contrast, developing countries that became more democratic and respected labor rights tended to maintain high tariffs; an increase in *Polity* was associated with no change in tariffs when respect for labor rights was high.

Between these two extremes, the level of respect for labor rights helped to determine the extent to which democracy was associated with trade liberalization. This was demonstrated by the positive and statistically significant coefficient on the interaction between *Polity* and *LaborRights*; the more labor rights are protected, the less an increase in democracy is associated with trade liberalization. Last, variation in respect for labor rights within established democracies also helps to explain trade policy outcomes. Holding democracy constant at a high level, labor rights were positively associated with tariff levels. This means that in democracies, an increase in labor repression was associated with a decrease in tariff levels.

These main results are robust to controlling for numerous alternative explanations and potential confounders including population, GDP per capita, WTO membership, the political party in power, welfare spending, a history of import–substitution industrialization, economic crises, and IMF pressure. The main regression model included country-level fixed effects, a time trend, and an AR(1) correction in order to address concerns about omitted variable bias and serial correlation, focus the analysis on variation over time within each country, and control for secular trends in tariff rates, democracy, and respect for labor rights. The results are also robust to alternative measures of the dependent and main independent variables. I found similar results when estimating the model using eight different measures of trade policy, labor unions density instead of labor rights, and binary measures of democracy from Polity, V-Dem, and UDS. Last, the regression results were similar when including a lagged dependent variable as an alternative method for addressing serial correlation, estimating a tobit model in order to address potential censoring of the dependent variable, using year-level fixed effects instead of a time trend, and estimating Newey–West standard errors to address potential autocorrelation among the residuals within each country.

The regression results also contain important findings regarding alternative explanations for trade liberalization in developing countries. The results challenge the common international political economy argument that democratization was sufficient for trade liberalization in developing countries.[44] In contrast, this chapter showed that the degree to which increases in democracy were associated with trade liberalization was conditional upon governments' level of respect for labor rights. My results suggest that transitions to democracy that were accompanied by high levels of respect for labor rights were actually associated with the maintenance of high tariffs. In other words, we cannot understand the relationship between democracy and trade policy without also thinking about how labor rights shape the political influence of labor unions.

The results also suggest that we should rethink the compensation hypothesis that forms the foundation for so much work on democracy and international

44 Milner and Kubota 2005; Eichengreen and Leblang 2008; Chaudoin et al. 2015.

trade policy.[45] This approach argues that democratic governments often maintain open economies by compensating "trade losers" with welfare programs. Without such compensation, democratic governments would face an anti-globalization backlash that would force elected leaders to maintain high tariffs. A pivotal assumption of this approach is that democracies offer welfare compensation to trade losers because they cannot exclude them from trade policymaking. However, the analysis above showed that democracy and respect for labor rights are barely correlated in developing countries; democracy is not a guarantee that governments will not use labor repression to reduce labor unions' political influence. Moreover, the regression results demonstrate that even when controlling for levels of government welfare spending, an increase in democracy is more likely to be associated with trade liberalization when the level of respect for labor rights is low. In other words, even when there was a generous welfare safety net for trade losers, democratization was more likely to lead to trade liberalization when governments used labor repression to weaken union demands for trade protection.

The quantitative analysis presented above has three key strengths as well as limitations that motivate additional research. First, the regression analysis permits me to examine the relationships between democracy, labor rights, and tariff rates while controlling for alternative explanations. This means that the link between labor repression and trade liberalization in democratic developing countries is unlikely to be a spurious correlation driven by welfare spending, political partisanship, IMF pressure, economic crises, the legacy of import-substitution industrialization or the other factors included in the model. Second, the regression analysis helps to reveal the relative importance of labor repression and other explanatory factors, a task that is much more difficult to accomplish in a small number of case studies. Third, the quantitative analysis helps to guard against unintentional selection bias that can easily influence the inferences drawn solely from qualitative analysis. While each of the case studies in the following three chapters has its unique historical details – different governments violated labor rights in idiosyncratic ways – the regression analysis establishes that the relationship between labor repression and trade liberalization is a generalizable dynamic across more than 100 developing countries.

The main limitation of the quantitative analysis is that it cannot reveal the causal mechanisms that may link labor repression to trade liberalization in democratic developing countries. What is it about labor repression that facilitates trade liberalization in democratic developing countries? How exactly does the process unfold? To answer these questions, I complement the quantitative analysis with qualitative case studies that illustrate the political processes through which labor repression influences trade policy outcomes. The case studies of Mexico, Argentina, Bolivia, Turkey, and India presented in

45 Cameron 1978; Ruggie 1982; Adsera et al. 2002.

the following three chapters use a structured-focused approach to illustrate the observable implications of my theory's causal mechanisms. More specifically, each case asks (1) whether democracy increased demands for trade liberalization; (2) whether labor repression decreased union mobilization against trade liberalization; and (3) whether union opposition influenced trade policy outcomes. In these ways, the qualitative case studies in the following chapters help to illustrate the mechanisms that produce the correlations identified using quantitative methods in this chapter.

3

Democracy Is Not Enough

Labor Rights and Trade Policy in Mexico, Argentina, Bolivia, Turkey, and India

On September 3, 1984 Argentina's main labor union confederation, *Confederación General del Trabajo* (CGT), launched a general strike against the economic reforms proposed by Raúl Alfonsín, the country's first democratic president after a decade of military rule.[1] The Argentine government respected workers' rights to protest in this manner, and the CGT went on to launch a total of thirteen general strikes that stymied Alfonsín's attempts to lower tariffs and open the economy.[2] When Mexico pursued similar trade policy reforms during the same period, the government of Carlos Salinas de Gortari also faced opposition from protectionist labor unions.[3] But in contrast to Argentina, Mexico's democratizing government used a series of repressive labor measures – interference in union elections, banned strikes, and police brutality – to overcome labor opposition and successfully implemented its move toward free trade.[4]

This chapter shows how such labor repression played a crucial role in the history of free trade in many democratic developing countries. While the regression analyses in the previous chapter showed that my argument is robust to alternative explanations and generalizable across more than 100 developing countries, this chapter begins to fill in the missing pieces – the causal mechanisms – that link democracy, labor repression, and trade liberalization. Drawing on qualitative case studies of Mexico, Argentina, Bolivia, Turkey, and

1 "Peronist Strike Brings Most Industry to Halt," *Los Angeles Times*, September 4, 1984.

2 Murillo 2001.

3 In 1990, the leader of CTM argued that trade liberalization would bring unemployment and the destruction of Mexico's industries; see "Apertura Commercial: Empezó el Desastre," *Proceso*, October 15, 1990; Kay 2011.

4 Middlebrook and Middlebrook 1995; Hathaway 2002. Mexico's Polity measure of democracy increased seven points from 1985 to 1994, the same period during which the country liberalized its trade policies.

India during the late twentieth century, this chapter tells the stories of labor unions that vehemently opposed trade liberalization, democratic governments that used mass arrests to break union-led strikes, and how government's found it easier to lower tariffs when unions were stopped from mobilizing workers.

To discipline my analysis, I adopt a structured-focused approach that presents each case study in three sections, each of which focuses on a different causal mechanism.[5] First, I begin each case by exploring whether democracy was associated with demands for trade liberalization, specifically from export-oriented business and the general public. Second, I examine whether labor repression decreased union mobilization. In cases where governments respected labor rights, I describe how such protections enabled unions to launch strikes and protests against trade liberalization. Last, I discuss whether union opposition influenced trade policy outcomes.

The most novel step of my argument is that democracies used labor repression to reduce union opposition to trade liberalization. I therefore carefully selected case studies that help me explore this main causal mechanism using a series of cross-case and within-case comparisons. The chapter begins with two "most similar" cases with different trade policy outcomes – Mexico and Argentina in the 1980s. A cross-case comparison illustrates how Mexico's trade liberalization was facilitated by labor repression that limited union opposition, just as Argentina's maintenance of high tariffs was made more likely by the government's respect for labor unions to launch general strikes. This case study of Argentina in the 1980s is revisited in Chapter 5, which presents an in-depth case study of Argentine trade liberalization in the 1990s. A within-case comparison of the two periods illustrates how Argentina's President Menem used labor repression to weaken labor union opposition and avoid the general strikes that hampered trade liberalization in the 1980s.

Next, this chapter presents case studies of two countries – Bolivia and Turkey – that both contain variation in my theory's dependent variable (trade policy) and key independent variables (political regime type and respect for labor rights) over time, thus allowing for two different within-case comparisons. The Bolivian case study compares the country's first two presidential administrations after the return of democracy: Siles (1982–1985) who maintained high tariffs and Paz (1985–1989) who drastically opened the economy. A within-case comparison illustrates how Siles' respect for labor rights enabled union-led general strikes that hampered economic reforms, while Paz used labor repression to break a general strike and facilitate trade liberalization. The Turkish case study compares two different democratic transitions separated by the 1980 coup: the 1961 democratic transition which was followed by high tariffs, and the 1983 transition which was followed by rapid trade liberalization. A within-case comparison illustrates how respect for labor rights during the 1960s and 1970s empowered labor unions to launch strikes that

5 George and Bennett 2005; Goertz 2017.

defended high tariffs, while labor repression in the 1980s (started by the military regime but continued after the return of democracy) squashed union opposition and helped to pave the way for trade liberalization.

Last, this chapter presents a case that is "most different" from the relatively new democracies analyzed in this chapter – the long-established democracy of India. The Indian case study illustrates how Prime Minister Rajiv Gandhi's attempts to lower tariffs between 1985 and 1987 were thwarted by union-led general strikes. Despite the numerous differences between India (1985–1987), Argentina (1983–1989), Bolivia (1982–1985), and Turkey (1961–1980), all of these countries maintained high tariffs after facing union-led general strikes that were enabled by high levels of respect for labor rights. This case study of India in the 1980s is revisited in Chapter 4, which presents an in-depth case study of Indian trade liberalization in the 1990s. A within-case comparison of the two periods illustrates how Prime Minister Narasimha Rao used labor repression to weaken labor union opposition and avoid the general strikes that helped to block trade liberalization in the 1980s.

The case studies presented in the following chapters purposefully include numerous cases of failed attempts at trade liberalization. Argentina, Bolivia, Turkey, and India all experienced periods during which democratic governments maintained high tariffs after labor unions protested against trade liberalization. Since each of these countries later lowered their tariffs, within-case comparisons provide clear tests of my main causal mechanism: did democratic governments use labor repression in order to overcome union opposition? When scholars only study positive cases of trade liberalization it is easy to conclude that labor unions – frequently silenced by labor repression – played an insignificant role in trade policy making. But absence of evidence is not evidence of absence; the following three chapters demonstrate that the relative lack of union mobilization against trade liberalization was often the product of strike bans, mass arrests, and other forms of labor repression. A summary of the case studies presented in the next three chapters is displayed in Figure 3.1

MEXICO AND ARGENTINA

This section presents a cross-case comparison of trade policy in Mexico (1980–2000) and Argentina (1983–1989). These countries represent "most similar" cases in the sense that both countries started the period with authoritarian governments facing economic crises, subsequently democratized, witnessed governments propose trade liberalization, and had protectionist labor union confederations that opposed the reforms.[6] Despite these similarities, the levels of labor union mobilization and trade liberalization in these countries were very different. In Argentina, respect for labor rights harbored a series of general strikes that helped convince the government to maintain high tariffs

[6] George and Bennett 2005.

		Democracy	Labor Rights	Trade Policy
Mexico	1980–2000	Low → High	Low	Liberalization
Argentina	1983–1989	Low → High	High	Protection
	1989–1994	High	High → Low	Liberalization
Bolivia	1982–1984	Low → High	High	Protection
	1985–1989	High	High → Low	Liberalization
India	1985–1989	High	High	Protection
	1991–1995	High	High → Low	Liberalization
Turkey	1961–1980	Low → High	High	Protection
	1983–1985	Low → High	Low	Liberalization

FIGURE 3.1. Cases studies – Democracy, labor rights, and trade policy

throughout the 1980s. In Mexico, labor repression helped to weaken labor union opposition and thereby facilitated the government's success in lowering tariffs and joining the GATT and NAFTA. As my theory predicts, the degree to which an increase in democracy leads to trade liberalization depends upon the government's level of respect for labor rights.

Democracy and the Potential for Trade Liberalization

Argentina and Mexico both entered the 1980s with autocratic governments and high tariffs. Although their democratic transitions were distinct – Argentina's quick and led by labor unions, Mexico's gradual and led by business elites – such political regime change pushed governments in both countries toward trade liberalization.

Argentina's Democratic Transition

After a coup in 1976, Argentina was ruled by a military dictatorship for eight years. The struggle for democracy was led most prominently by Argentina's main labor union confederation, the CGT, which launched a wave of strikes that spread across the country starting in 1977. A year later, Saúl Ubaldini, Secretary General of the CGT, publicly declared that Argentina's problems could be solved "only through a government elected by the people" and demanded the establishment of a full democracy.[7] These strikes, combined with the military's defeat in the Falklands War, culminated in Argentina's transition to democracy in 1983.[8] As Collier explains, the CGT's strikes "prevented the military regime from consolidating power and finally led to its destabilization."[9]

When Argentina's newly-elected president, Raúl Alfonsín, entered office in 1983, the country's economy was collapsing under the weight of high inflation and a debt crisis inherited from the military. Argentina's transition from autocracy to democracy subsequently empowered the pro-trade preferences of consumers and export-oriented businesses and pushed Alfonsín toward trade liberalization. The general public was exhausted by inflation, and 80 percent of Argentines supported Alfonsín's sweeping 1985 reform package.[10] Although Alfonsín knew that labor unions would oppose his reforms, he hoped that stabilizing the economy would help attract working-class support away from the rival Peronist party.[11] In addition, a group of Argentina's leading "captains of industry" from the country's globally-competitive agro-industrial and manufacturing sectors supported Alfonsín's efforts to lower tariffs on capital goods, increase exports, and generate large trade surpluses.[12]

Mexico's Gradual Democratization

Mexican politics was dominated by one-party rule from 1929 until the country gradually democratized at the end of the twentieth century. Starting in the early-1980s, disagreements over economic policy led Mexico's internationally-oriented businesses to abandon the ruling *Partido Revolucionario Institutional* (PRI) in favor of the more economically liberal opposition party, *Partido Acción Nacional* (PAN).[13] The rise of the PAN contributed to a competitive presidential election in 1988, the PRI's loss of the lower house of parliament in 1997, and Mexico's transition to democracy in 2000 with the election of PAN candidate Vicente Fox in a free and fair election.[14]

Mexico's gradual democratization shifted the balance of political power away from import-competing industries and toward the pro-trade preferences of export-oriented businesses and consumers. Starting in the 1980s, the PRI feared that the loss of business support would lead to electoral defeats and therefore began to pursue trade liberalization and other policies "that could have been lifted straight from the PAN's platform."[15] The same group of "outward-looking, multinationally-linked, big business elite" that backed the PAN also organized the *Consejo Coordinador Empresarial* to lobby for lower tariffs.[16] During this period, PRI leaders also argued that trade liberalization

[7] Collier 1999, 122. [8] Munck 1989. [9] Collier 1999, 124.

[10] "Wide Support Seen for Economic Reform Program," *Los Angeles Times*, June 20, 1985.

[11] Schamis 1999. [12] Smith 1990. [13] Thacker 2000.

[14] Shirk 2005. Between 1985 and 1994, Mexico's Polity score increased by 7 points, from negative 3 to positive 4.

[15] Thacker 2000, 123. [16] Thacker 2000, 9.

would improve overall economic competitiveness and thereby attract popular support; President Salinas' reforms of the late 1980s reduced inflation, increased economic growth, and by 1991 over 60 percent of the population approved of his performance.[17]

Labor Rights and Labor Opposition

In Argentina, labor unions led the struggle for democracy and the country's democratic transition was accompanied by high levels of respect for labor rights. In turn, these rights empowered labor unions to launch a series of powerful strikes against Alfonsín's economic reforms. In Mexico, business elites led the struggle for democracy and the country's gradual democratic transition saw a steady erosion of respect for labor rights. In turn, the government used such high levels of labor repression to co-opt and weaken labor union opposition to trade liberalization.

Argentina's Respect for Labor Rights

Argentine labor unions were powerful and openly launched strikes at the end of the military junta; when democracy returned to Argentina in 1983, it was accompanied by high levels of respect for labor rights.[18] Labor unions successfully demanded laws that acknowledged workers' rights to organize and collectively bargain, as well as union control over social services – all of which were similar to laws that had been repealed by the military government in the 1970s.[19] When strikes began to spread across Argentina early in Alfonsín's term, *La Razón* explained that "less fear of punishment" was the main reason for the "expansion of the labour struggle."[20] By 1986, Argentina received a perfect score on Mosley's labor rights index, suggesting that it protected 37 different categories of workers' rights endorsed by the ILO.[21]

Argentina's respect for labor rights empowered the CGT to aggressively resist Alfonsín's economic reforms. Throughout this period, the CGT clearly articulated its opposition to trade liberalization, demanding the continuation of "a process of import substitution to generate currency savings and a greater integration of the national economy."[22] In an effort to block Alfonsín's reforms, the CGT launched a series of thirteen general strikes that paralyzed the economy and destabilized Alfonsín's rule.[23] During one general strike against Alfonsín's reforms in 1986, CGT Secretary General Saúl Ubaldini told 200,000 workers rallying in Buenos Aires that, "anyone who doesn't want to speak with the leaders of organized labor will speak with the workers in the streets."[24] Such "thunderous denunciations of government economic policies"

17 Murillo 2001. 18 Madrid 2003.
19 Palomino 2000, 22. 20 "Más Huelgas en Respuesta a la Crisis," *La Razon*, October 13, 1984.
21 Mosley 2011. 22 Confederacion General del Trabajo 1989b, 13, author's translation.
23 Murillo 2001. 24 Confederacion General del Trabajo 1989a, 10, author's translation.

made these general strikes the main arena of opposition in Argentine politics, more important than the party system or legislature.[25]

Despite the effect of such labor opposition, Alfonsín's government permitted these strikes to continue without resorting to labor repression.[26] When Alfonsín's vice president denounced one of the CGT general strike as "inopportune" and cautioned that "the defeat of the economic plan would not mean the defeat of the Government, but the defeat of all Argentinians," he carefully clarified that "of course we respect the right to strike."[27] On the eve of a general strike in 1987, Argentina's Minister of Labor announced that "the government will not take any measures to limit the scope of the CGT's strike ... we have not even considered the possibility."[28] As one Argentine journalist noted, Alfonsín "made no attempt to deal with such outbreaks. He sat back and let them happen."[29]

Mexico's Labor Repression

Mexico's respect for labor rights decreased throughout its gradual transition to democracy. Although many Mexican workers were unionized, most belonged to "official" labor unions, such as the *Confederación de Trabajadores de México* (CTM), that were coopted and controlled by the PRI through the use of labor repression. CTM leaders frequently worked alongside the Mexican government to sign "protection contracts" with foreign investors, which guaranteed low wages, no strikes, and the absence of independent unions that might more faithfully represent the interest of rank-and-file workers.[30] If workers demanded union elections, it was common for CTM thugs to intimidate and

[25] McGuire 1992, 46.

[26] There is one possible exception to this characterization of Alfonsín's record regarding the CGT's general strikes. The CGT's twelfth general strike, on September 9, 1988, devolved into a violent brawl that left roughly one hundred civilians and police officers injured. While the government and the CGT made conflicting claims about who was responsible, *Crónica* reported that violence in the *Plaza de Mayo* did not break out until six policemen were hurt by rocks and bottles thrown by protestors. Although Alfonsín's government may have used this provocation to unleash police brutality against protestors, it quickly returned to respecting labor rights. When the CGT announced a thirteenth general strike, Alfonsín's Minister of Labor explained that "the Government will keep on guaranteeing, as it has done so far, the unrestricted observance of human rights, union freedom, and the entire system of liberties and guarantees that are inherent to the republican system." The government did not prohibit the general strike, and the protest proceeded without any disturbances. See, "Refriegas, Graves Enfrentamientos y Congoja Popular," *Crónica*, September 10, 1988; "Repudia el Pais Toda Violencia," *Crónica*, September 12, 1988; "No Hubo Incidentes," *Crónica*, September 13, 1988.

[27] "Paro y Concentración de la CGT," *Clarín*, November 3, 1987.

[28] "Masivo Acatamiento al Paro de la CGT," *Crónica*, November 4, 1987.

[29] This quote is from Santiago Senén González, *The Review of the River Plate*, October 31, 1990.

[30] Hathaway 2002.

beat workers that supported an independent union.[31] The rise of electoral competition from the PAN led the PRI to adopt more business friendly policies and labor rights restrictions that weakened labor unions. According to Davis, this period "witnessed a fundamental transformation in the structure of power within the PRI which, among other things, reduced labor's say in national policy making."[32]

The CTM, long co-opted by the PRI, obediently supported the negotiation of NAFTA despite their traditional opposition to trade liberalization.[33] As Kay explains, opposing NAFTA "would have been seen as a betrayal, and quite likely would have resulted in severe sanctions," and therefore "the CTM fell into lockstep with the PRI government to actively endorse and pave the way to its passage."[34] While some "progressive CTM leaders" secretly opposed NAFTA, rigid union hierarchy's made it extremely difficult "to openly oppose the policies of the national leadership."[35]

In contrast, Mexico's largest independent labor union, the *Frente Autentico del Trabajo* (FAT), argued that free trade would only benefit internationally-oriented companies while maintaining cheap labor in Mexico.[36] Although the FAT played a unique role in Mexico's domestic opposition to NAFTA, years of repression relegated the union to a minority status within the country's broader labor movement.[37] When FAT members protested against NAFTA in Mexico City in 1991, for example, they were met by police barricades that stopped them from marching into the *Zócalo*, the city's central square and most popular location for rallies.[38]

Trade Policy Outcomes

Argentina's Maintenance of High Tariffs

There is broad scholarly consensus that the CGT's general strikes were a crucial factor in the failure of Alfonsín's reforms.[39] Levitsky and Way conclude that the CGT "protests contributed in an important way to the failure of the austerity programs," and Murillo explains that, "labor opposition, business distrust, and the erosion of political credibility contributed to the failure of this program."[40] Or, as CGT head Ubaldini boasted in 1986, "when the people say enough,

31 Hathaway 2002, 433. 32 Davis 1992, 16.

33 On CTM protectionism, see Davis 1992, 661. In 1990, the leader of CTM argued that trade liberalization would bring unemployment and the destruction of Mexico's industries; see "Apertura Commercial: Empezó el Desastre," *Proceso*. October 15, 1990.

34 Kay 2011, 71 & 241. 35 Kay 2011, 242. 36 de la Garza Toledo 1994; Davis 1992.

37 de la Garza Toledo 1994; Hathaway 1997; Kay 2011.

38 "Independent Groups Marched in Complete Disorder Yesterday," *El Nacional*, May 2, 1991; "Dissident Marchers Disappointed," *The News*, May 2, 1991.

39 Levitsky and Way 1998; Anderson 2016. 40 Murillo 2001, 133.

there is no government that can bear it."[41] When Alfonsín left office in 1989, Argentina's average tariffs stood at 25 percent, only three percentage points lower than they had been in 1982, the last year of the military regime.[42] In short, Argentina's transition to democracy was associated with high levels of respect for labor rights, powerful union opposition to trade liberalization, and the maintenance of high tariffs.

Mexico's Trade Liberalization

The Mexican government initiated limited trade liberalization in 1985, joined the GATT in 1986, began to negotiate NAFTA in 1990, and joined the new trading bloc with the US and Canada in 1994. From 1988 to 1993, the increasingly democratic Mexican government lowered its average tariff rate from 34 percent down to 4 percent. As Thacker concludes, "over this relatively short period of time, a strong free trade coalition coupling public and private sector elites managed to take and consolidate control over the apex of the trade policy-making apparatus, guiding Mexico into the new world of North American free trade."[43] Although CTM leaders believe that trade liberalization would hurt their rank-and-file members, they acquiesced to the PRI's reforms.[44] According to Hathaway, "only independent unions such as the FAT were able to openly oppose government policy" and years of repression relegated that union confederation to a weak and minority status within the country's broader labor movement.[45] In short, increases in democracy empowered export-oriented businesses to demand lower tariffs while labor repression weakened labor union opposition and thereby facilitated trade liberalization.

Cross-Case Comparison of Argentina and Mexico

A cross-case comparison of Argentina and Mexico illustrates how democracy empowered groups that favored trade liberalization, as well as how the level of respect for labor rights shaped unions' ability to counterbalance those demands. Argentina's 1983 democratic transition and Mexico's gradual democratization during the 1980s both increased the political influence of pro-trade business and publics exhausted by economic crises. In both countries, labor union confederations made clear that they opposed trade liberalization. In Argentina, respect for labor rights enabled the CGT to launch 13 general strikes that paralyzed the economy and helped to block Alfonsín's reforms. In Mexico, in contrast, the government used labor repression to squash the FAT and to co-opt leaders of the CTM into acquiescing to trade liberalization. When respect for labor rights was high (Argentina), an increase in democracy was followed by general strikes that helped to maintain high tariffs; when respect for labor

41 "Ubaldini: Se Terminó la Paciencia," *Crónica*, January 17, 1986.

42 Tariff data from World Bank. 43 Thacker 2000, 9. 44 Murillo 2001; Kay 2011.

45 Cook 1994, 14; Hathaway 2002, 433.

rights was low (Mexico), an increase in democracy was followed by trade liberalization over which labor unions had little influence.

Although Argentina and Mexico represent "most similar" cases, they still vary in numerous ways besides their level of respect for labor rights. For example, Mexico gradually democratized over the course of the 1980s and 1990s while Argentina rapidly transitioned from military rule to democracy in 1983. In addition, Mexico's close proximity and large land border with the United States may have made trade liberalization a more attractive option than it was for Argentina. It is therefore not possible to conclude definitively that variation in respect for labor rights explains the difference in labor union mobilization and trade policy outcomes across these two cases. In order to better control for such inevitable difference across even two very similar cases, the following section presents a within-case comparison of trade politics in Bolivia, another Latin American country that democratized and opened its economy during the 1980s.

BOLIVIA

This section presents a within-case comparison of trade policy in Bolivia under President Siles (1982–1985) and President Paz (1985–1989), the country's first two presidents after the return of democracy in 1982. During both periods, Bolivia's democratic governments faced economic crises, business demands for trade liberalization, and labor union demands for continued trade protection. Despite these similarities, the levels of labor union mobilization and trade liberalization in these two periods were very different. Under Siles, respect for labor rights enabled strikes and protests that helped to convince the government to maintain high tariffs. Under Paz, in contrast, labor repression squashed Bolivia's labor unions and facilitated the government's dramatic decrease in tariffs. As my theory predicts, Bolivia's transition to democracy in 1982 was accompanied by high levels of respect for labor rights and led to the maintenance of high tariffs. My theory's second path toward free trade also correctly predicts Bolivia's eventual trade liberalization in 1985: while maintaining a high level of democracy, Bolivia's government facilitated trade liberalization by increasing labor repression.

Bolivia and President Siles: 1982–1985

Democracy and the Potential for Trade Liberalization

Bolivia's labor unions played a pivotal role in the country's circuitous democratization struggle and eventual transition to democracy.[46] Bolivia's main labor union confederation, *Centrál Obrera Boliviana* (COB), led nation-wide protests that led the military to agree to elections in 1979. When those elections were

[46] Collier 1999, 143–149.

followed by a military coup, the COB launched a general strike that ended with the military agreeing to another election in 1980. After those elections were followed by yet another coup, the COB threatened an indefinite general strike that demonstrated widespread support for democracy and ultimately led to a negotiated exit for the military regime.[47] When Siles was inaugurated President in October 1982, he knew that his UDP coalition government "largely owed its restoration to power to the COB."[48] In turn, Bolivia's labor unions therefore "exercised veto power over Siles' successive stabilization programs."[49]

While the COB used its influence to demand high tariffs and other policies associated with import-substitution industrialization, the transition to democracy also empowered Bolivian businesses that favored trade liberalization and more market-oriented reforms. The *Confederación de Empresarios Privados de Bolivia* (CEPB), became the "voice of a capital class seeking to reassert itself" and launched a multi-faceted lobbying, research, and public relations campaign meant "to shift elite and public opinion away from the state-centered and populist formula that dominated policy making since the 1950s."[50]

Bolivia's private mine owners and commercial farmers called for lower tariffs on capital goods and pushed for a 48-hour CEPB-led business strike that demanded lower wages and an end to Siles' export controls.[51] Although import-competing manufacturers favored continued trade protection, Bolivia's business leaders built a "consensus within the CEPB on the need for an orthodox restructuring of the Bolivian economy."[52] The CEPB often argued that such reforms were necessary to satisfy international investors and the IMF, which since the 1950s had "envisioned Bolivia's economic growth as resting on free trade the reduction of public spending, and the encouragement of foreign capital investment."[53]

Labor Rights and Labor Opposition

Siles entered office at the end of 1982 with Bolivia facing an economic crisis inherited from the military regime, a crisis which included massive amounts of foreign debt, hyperinflation, and a collapse of export earnings. To address the crisis, the COB proposed an 18-point plan that included delaying the country's debt payments, channelling financial resources to "strategic areas of the economy," and creating a foreign trade institute that would further reduce

47 Dunkerley 1990; Malloy 1991, 47. 48 Dunkerley 1990, 14.

49 Conaghan and Malloy 1995, 122.

50 Conaghan 1995, 117. In English, the CEPB is known as the Bolivian Confederation of Private Entrepreneurs.

51 Jenkins 1997; "Businessmen to Protest COB-Government Agreement," *Paris AFP*, February 1, 1984. This newspaper article, translated from Spanish to English, is available from the Foreign Broadcast Information Service. For all subsequent references from this archive I include [FBIS] after the name of the original source.

52 Conaghan 1995, 119. 53 Dunkerley 1990; Kofas 1995, 217.

imports.[54] The COB also demanded a sliding minimum wage scale linked to inflation and co-management of the country's mines.[55]

In defense of their demands, Bolivia's labor unions launched nation-wide protests and strikes whenever Siles proposed alternative economic policies. At times, just the threat of a strike was sufficient. When Siles initially resisted these proposals, Bolivia's powerful mineworkers' union responded by announcing a 48-hour deadline, after which they would launch an indefinite general strike.[56] Before the deadline passed, Siles issued a supreme decree officially confirming that the government would co-manage the Mining Corporation of Bolivia with the mineworkers' union.[57]

Other times, the COB crippled the national economy with general strikes until winning major policy concessions. When Siles announced wage restraints, cutbacks on public spending, and drastic price increase for government-subsidized foods in April 1984, the COB started a 72-hour general strike that closed banks, factories, mines, and public offices.[58] There was an average of fifty-three strikes, marches, or road blockades each month of Siles' presidency, including nine general strikes launched by the COB.[59] With Bolivia's economic crisis worsening in 1985, Siles announced new austerity measures that sought to increase food, transportation, and gasoline prices by 450 percent.[60] The COB immediately launched a general strike that lasted sixteen days and included miners blocking traffic and setting off dynamite around the capital of La Paz.[61]

Siles repeated decreed stabilization plans meant "to satisfy the IMF and the United States internationally and the CEPB domestically" only for the COB to respond with strikes and demonstrations that forced the government to "modify the program to the point of annulling its effectiveness."[62] Despite the obstacles that Bolivia's labor unions posed to economic reforms, Siles committed to "maintaining order without resort to violence" and developed a reputation for having a "notable respect for human rights" as well as broader labor rights.[63] According to Conaghan and Malloy, the "Siles government was unable to sustain any of the orthodox packages" at least in part because it

54 "COB Proposes Political, Economic Changes," *La Paz Radio Illimani Network* [FBIS], April 15, 1983; "Labor Federation Demands Submitted to President," *La Paz Cadena Panamericana* [FBIS], August 11, 1983.

55 "COB Proposes Political, Economic Changes," *La Paz Radio Illimani Network* [FBIS], April 15, 1983.

56 "Government Granted 48-Hour Deadline," *La Paz Cadena Panamericana* [FBIS], September 8, 1983.

57 "Government Issues COMIBOL Decree," *La Paz Cadena Panamericana* [FBIS], September 10, 1983.

58 "Unions in Bolivia Strike to Protest Austerity Plan," *New York Times*, May 1, 1984.

59 Conaghan 1995, 116.

60 "Bolivia – The Inflation Fever Cools," *Los Angeles Times*, May 1, 1984.

61 "Bolivian Unions Accept Wage Rise and End Strike," *New York Times*, March 24, 1985; "Hyper-Inflation Traumatizes Bolivia," *New York Times*, April 8, 1985; "Bolivian Unions Accept Wage Rise and End Strike," *New York Times*, March 24, 1985.

62 Gamarra 1991, 8.

63 Dunkerley 1990, 2, 15.

was "unwilling to use force against the opposition and unable to withstand the demand to maintain consumption."[64]

Trade Policy Outcomes

With the COB launching strikes "at the slightest hint of back-sliding" from Siles, the government eventually conceded most of the COB's eighteen policy demands, including continued trade protection.[65] In a speech to factory workers in La Paz, Siles promised "preferential treatment to the production of goods and services of general consumption" and asserted that the country's growth "will not rely, as in the past, on trade expansion."[66] In 1984, Siles announced "strict control of nonessential or luxury imports" that would provide "favorable treatment" for industrial enterprises that "invest in the country, create jobs, and supply Bolivians with goods and services."[67] In response to CEPB and IMF calls for privatization, austerity, and trade liberalization, Vice President Jaime Paz Zamora explained that "if we had practiced IMFism here, we would have had to dismiss half the public administration employees and close 80 percent of the factories because they are not profitable."[68]

Siles openly acknowledged that his protectionist economic policies were influenced by a mix of labor union mobilizations and his administration's commitment to respect labor rights. During a radio address to the nation in 1984, Siles explained this dynamic in terms strikingly similar to this book's main argument; he stated that his policies were often "agreed upon under pressure, threats, stoppages, and strikes that the democratic government has had to tolerate *in order not to stain the clean image of democracy with repression*."[69] Vice President Zamora put it even more forcefully when he claimed that, "the dictatorship knew how to resolve conflicts: bring tanks onto the streets, exiles the leaders, kill them. . .the democratic state still does not know how to tackle conflicts and does not have the instruments for doing so."[70] In short, Bolivia's high level of respect for labor rights enabled unions to launch strikes that contributed to the government maintaining high tariffs and other union-favored economic policies.

Bolivia and President Paz: 1985–1989

Democracy and the Potential for Trade Liberalization

With inflation reaching an annual rate of more than 50,000 percent and strikes paralyzing the economy, Siles called for elections in 1985, a year ahead of

64 Conaghan 1995, 110. 65 Conaghan 1995, 116.

66 "President Siles Zuazo Addresses Factory Workers," *El Diario* [FBIS], May 19, 1983.

67 "President Siles Addresses Nation on Economy," *La Paz Domestic Service* [FBIS], April 7, 1984.

68 "Paz Zamora Discusses Government's Problems," *El Pais* [FBIS], June 5, 1984.

69 "President Siles Addresses Nation on Economy," *La Paz Domestic Service* [FBIS], April 7, 1984, italics added.

70 "Paz Zamora Discusses Government's Problems," *El Pais* [FBIS], June 5, 1984.

schedule.[71] The combination of economic crisis and social upheaval led to a landslide loss for Siles' party, and a first place finish for Hugo Banzer Suárez (32.8% of the vote), Bolivia's military dictator from 1971 through 1978. However, since Bolivia's constitution requires a candidate to receive a majority of the vote in order to be directly elected as President, Banzer's ADN party formed a pact with Paz Estenssoro's MNR party and the Congress elected Paz as the next President of Bolivia. This "pacted democracy" excluded Siles' MIR party, created a two-party legislative coalition to support subsequent government policy, and greatly diminished the COB's influence.[72]

Banzer had campaigned on a clear platform of neoliberal reforms proposed by the CEPB, and Paz's campaign also hinted at the need for austerity to improve Bolivia's economy; these two candidates, and their opposition to Siles' center-left economic policies, garnered 63 percent of Bolivia's electorate.[73] While scholars caution that the election of 1985 should not be "facilely interpreted as a popular mandate for neoliberalism," it is clear that the hyperinflation, real wage decreases, and unemployment of the early 1980s "had undermined the public's belief in leftist prescriptions."[74] Paz was inaugurated on August 6, 1985 and quickly hired CEPB members that had previously planned Banzer's neoliberal reform package.[75] On August 29 Paz decreed a "New Economic Policy" (NPE in Spanish) that sought to halt hyperinflation by curtailing public spending, increasing the price of fuel, freezing government wages, privatizing industries, and decreasing tariffs.[76]

Labor Rights and Labor Opposition

The proposal to privatize Bolivia's tin mines was particularly threatening to Bolivia's mineworkers' union, which dominated the COB. Trade liberalization also posed a direct threat to labor unions in the textile factories that produced clothing for the domestic market. According to one estimate, 29,000 industrial jobs were eliminated in the three years following the government's reduction of trade barriers in 1985 – the equivalent of 1.5 million job losses in the United States today.[77] As Jenkins explains, "trade liberalisation was therefore a central feature of the adjustment package...Not surprisingly, organised labour was strongly opposed to the government's economic policies which led to a sharp reduction in real wages and increased unemployment."[78]

Within days of the NPE announcement, the government's Planning Minister warned that the government would declare any COB strikes to be illegal and that "this government is not willing to be crucified as President Siles Zuazo's

71 "Hyper-Inflation Traumatizes Bolivia," *New York Times*, April 8, 1985; "Bolivian Unions Accept Wage Rise and End Strike," *New York Times*, March 24, 1985

72 Malloy 1991, 51; Cyr 2015. 73 Stokes 2001.

74 Conaghan et al. 1990, 12; Conaghan 1995, 123; Sturzenegger 1995.

75 Conaghan et al. 1990, 12; Dunkerley 1990. 76 Pop-Eleches 2008.

77 Conaghan and Malloy 1995, 17. 78 Jenkins 1997, 313.

administration was. It will not yield its position on this crisis."[79] According to *Agencia EFE*, "the government has not bothered to disguise its fear of the protests of the workers against the economic policy."[80] Despite such warnings, the COB voted to launch a general strike aimed at "paralyzing all labor activities for 48 hours, or indefinitely if the government does not positively answer [our] demands."[81] The COB explained that the strike was called "over the total liberalization of the economy" including "the freedom to import" and the "decentralization of the main state enterprises."[82]

Paz's government then launched an escalating, month long campaign of labor repression that eventually broke the general strike and actively dismantled the COB.[83] One week into the general strike, two COB meetings were targeted with dynamite explosions, leading a union leader to accuse "the government of causing these attacks with the purpose of threatening the union leaders…this is the government method of dialogue, via terrorism."[84] The following week, Bolivian police officers surrounded the COB headquarters during a national meeting, resulting in a Bolivian human rights organization to denounce that "basic individual and social rights are being violated through a policy of repression and intimidation."[85] In a formal complaint sent to the ILO, the COB lamented that the Paz administration had "unleashed a repressive policy against workers and union leaders" that included heavily armed military and police forces violently occupying labor centers.[86]

When the COB announced a national hunger strike to "radicalize the measures of pressure to demonstrate the workers' rejection of the government's economic policy," Paz declared a "state of siege" that suspended Bolivia's constitution.[87] In the pre-dawn hours of September 19, police occupied the union building where COB leaders were leading their hunger strike and detained 1,500 workers, including the top leadership of the COB.[88] The following day, the government announced that COB Secretary General Juan Lechín Oquendo and other COB leaders had been banished to the Amazon jungle in the country's far north.[89]

79 "Government Unwilling to Negotiate Economic Policy," *Madrid EFE* [FBIS], September 3, 1985.
80 "State of Siege Rumored," *Madrid EFE* [FBIS], August 30, 1985.
81 "COB Votes to Strike," *Paris AFP* [FBIS], September 3, 1985.
82 "Further Report," *Paris AFP* [FBIS], September 5, 1985.
83 Cyr 2015, 293.
84 "COB Central Office in Teachers Club Dynamited," *Paris AFP* [FBIS], September 10, 1985.
85 "Police Surround COB Headquaters," *Paris AFP* [FBIS], September 16, 1985.
86 "Denounces Government Policy," *Paris AFP* [FBIS], September 7, 1985.
87 Nazmi 1995; "President Condemns Strikes," *La Paz Cadena Panamericana* [FBIS], September 18, 1985.
88 "COB Rejects State of Siege," *La Paz Cadena Panamericana* [FBIS], September 19, 1985.
89 "CBO Goes Underground," *Paris AFP* [FBIS], September 20, 1985; "Labor Union Chiefs Held as Bolivia Declares Siege," *Los Angeles Times*, August 28, 1986.

The Bolivian government's labor repression was clear to contemporary observers; according to Amnesty International, "there is evidence of violations of human rights; that the workers' right to strike has been ignored; that the government has not considered the very poor situation of the relatives of the people who have been banished; and that the Bolivian press does not report what is really happening in the country."[90] In an absurd response, Bolivia's Information Minister argued that, "the state of siege is a right recognized by the Constitution; therefore, it is logical that there cannot be any violation of human rights if the government acts within the Constitution and the law."[91]

With the Bolivian Congress approving Paz's "state of siege," the COB feared that the government would further "increase its repressive measures against the labor movement."[92] When the COB contacted the government to begin negotiations, the Interior Minister insisted that "the state of siege will be maintained. We also will not hold talks under pressure of a strike."[93] With few remaining options, the COB decided to concede; on October 2, the COB joined the government to jointly announce the end of the hunger strike and the general strike that was first launched almost a month earlier. There can be little doubt that Bolivia's democratic government used labor repression to squash union opposition to trade liberalization and the NPE; as the COB's executive committee concluded, workers suffered "an onslaught of fascist repression *despite* the democratic system prevailing in the country."[94] One member of Paz's cabinet, looking back on the government's repressive methods, admitted that they had "behaved like authoritarian pigs."[95]

Trade Policy Outcomes

After violently breaking the general strike, Paz implemented his NPE – "opening up the economy quite fully to foreign trade" – with relatively little domestic opposition.[96] The NPE eliminated almost all quantitative restrictions

90 "Minister 'Surprised' by Amnesty International Report," *La Paz Cadena Panamericana* [FBIS], September 30, 1985.

91 Ibid.

92 "COB, Government Begin Dialogue, Situation Evaluated," *Madrid EFE* [FBIS], September 26, 1985.

93 "Barthelemy Respondes," *La Paz Cadena Panamericana* [FBIS], September 28, 1985; "Minister Comments on Status of Talks with COB," *La Paz Cadena Panamericana* [FBIS], October 1, 1985.

94 "COB Elects Executive Committee," *La Paz Cadena Panamericana* [FBIS], September 20, 1985; "COB to Continue Strike," *La Paz Cadena Panamericana* [FBIS], September 21, 1985; "COB Reports Strikes Continue," *Madrid EFE* [FBIS], September 24, 1985, italics added.

95 Quoted in Conaghan and Malloy 1995, 149.

96 Morales 1996, 36.

and lowered tariffs from a high of 150 percent to a low uniform rate near 20 percent.[97] With business demanding further trade policy reforms, Paz granted tariff exemptions for agro-industry inputs and capital goods, offered tax rebates to stimulate exports, and lowered tariffs to a uniform 10 percent.[98] Although import-competing industries argued that such "indiscriminate opening of the internal market to foreign goods" was "unfair and destructive," they failed to win support from the other business represented by the CEPB.[99] After all, as Jameson concludes, "the program adopted by his [Paz's] government came directly out of the CEPB."[100]

The only concession the COB received for ending its general strike (besides the release of labor leaders) was the creation of a joint commission through which unions and the government would analyze Paz's economic reforms. The terms of the agreement clarified that this commission could discuss the new economic model "but without changing its essential features."[101] Just as Siles' governments acknowledged that his protectionist economic policies were heavily influenced by labor-led strikes, Paz's government explicitly boasted that labor repression was a crucial part of its reform strategy. Just four years after Paz broke the COB's general strike, Bolivia's Planning Minister, Gonzalo Sánchez de Lozada ("Goni"), travelled to Buenos Aires for the inauguration of Argentina's new President, Carlos Menem. When asked how the government could reform the Argentine economy – a story told in the next chapter – Goni explained that "the only stabilisation plan worth its salt was one accompanied by a state of siege, under which recalcitrant trade unionists could be packed off to Patagonia for a while."[102]

Within-Case Comparison of Bolivia Under Siles and Paz

A within-case comparison of Bolivia under Siles (1982–1985) and Paz (1985–1989) illustrates how democracy empowered groups that favored trade liberalization, as well as how the level of respect for labor rights shaped unions' ability to counterbalance those demands. In both periods, democracy gave pro-trade businesses political influence that they had lacked under military dictatorship.[103] Under Siles, CEPB demands were counterbalanced by the protectionist demands of labor unions; respect for labor rights enabled the COB to launch nine general strikes that forced the government to maintain high tariffs and other policies favored by Bolivia's unions. Under Paz, in contrast, CEPB demands for trade liberalization were safeguarded by a government

97 Morales 1995, 12; Jenkins 1997, 308.

98 Jenkins 1997, 314. In 1990, the tariff on capital goods was further reduced to 5 percent.

99 Dunkerley 1990, 31; Conaghan and Malloy 1995, 156. 100 Jameson 2019, 96.

101 "Government, COB Reach Agreement; Strike Ends," *Madrid EFE* [FBIS], October 3, 1985.

102 Dunkerley 1990, 1. 103 Conaghan 1995, 115.

"state of siege" that broke a COB general strike with dynamite and mass arrests. When respect for labor rights was high (Siles), an increase in democracy was followed by general strikes that helped to maintain high tariffs; once Bolivia had a stable democratic government (Paz), an increase in labor repression weakened union opposition and paved the way for Paz to open the Bolivian economy.

The case studies of Argentina, Mexico, and Bolivia all illustrated how variation in respect for labor rights influenced the ability of labor union to mobilize workers against trade liberalization. In order to show that this dynamic was not limited to Latin America, the following section presents a within-case comparison of trade politics in Turkey from the 1960s through the 1980s. Beyond illustrating the mechanisms of my theory in another region of the world, Turkish politics during this period also offers the unique opportunity to explore two very different democratic transitions. In 1961, Turkey transitioned from military dictatorship to democracy and maintained high levels of respect for labor rights. After a military coup in 1980 and three years of dictatorship, Turkey again transitioned to democracy in 1983, but this time continued the high levels of labor repression practiced by the military. A within-case comparison of these two democratic transitions in Turkish therefore serves as a sort of natural experiment, illustrating how the effect of democracy on trade policy depends on a country's level of respect for labor rights.

TURKEY

This section presents a within-case comparison of trade policy in Turkey before and after the military government that ruled from 1980 to 1983. The first period, from 1961 to 1980, was a period of democracy, respect for labor rights, and high tariffs that harbored powerful protectionist labor unions in import-competing industries. Amidst a worsening economic crisis in the late 1970s, however, Turkey's democratic government proposed trade liberalization and other economic reforms endorsed by the country's export-oriented industries. In response, labor unions launched protests and a nationwide general strike that helped to block the reforms. This first period ended on September 12, 1980, when Turkey's military overthrew the democratic government, heavily repressed the country's labor unions, and ruled the country for three years. Although the military devalued the Turkish lira, suppressed wages, and subsidized exports, it maintained the country's high tariffs.

The second period, from 1983 to 1989, started with the return of democracy. However, this period was fundamentally shaped by the legacy of the military's labor repression. Although Turkey's democratic government did not kidnap and torture union leaders like the military had, it did leave in place the military's ban on strikes and other anti-labor restrictions. During this period, Turkey's democratic government faced renewed demands for trade liberalization from export-oriented businesses, but high levels of labor repression weakened the ability of unions to mobilize against such reforms. As my theory predicts, Turkey's 1983 increase in democracy while respect for labor rights was low led to rapid trade liberalization.

Turkey: 1961–1980

Democracy and the Potential for Trade Liberalization

Turkey first democratized in 1946 and then held regular multi-party elections until a coup overthrew the government in 1960. A military junta then ruled Turkey for sixteen months, before giving way to a new constitution and democratic elections in 1961. The subsequent period from 1961 to 1980 is often considered a "golden era" for Turkey's labor movement – a period of democracy, respect for labor rights, and the high tariffs associated with import-substitution industrialization. However, the democratic governments of this period also faced pressure from Turkish businesses – represented by the Turkish Industrialists and Businessmen's Association (TÜSİAD) – that supported trade liberalization and a shift toward an outward-oriented economy. At the heart of this coalition were large family-controlled conglomerates that dominated Turkey's manufacturing sector and had come to see the ISI model as unsustainable; as one World Bank study explained, "TUSIAD [sic] formed the core of the interests that would ultimately benefit from open-economy policies."[104]

Demands for trade liberalization were especially strong following the oil shock of 1973, when the Turkish economy began to struggle with inflation, a growing trade deficit, and a debt crisis. Not only did the price of imported oil increase, but foreign lenders cut off credit, and Turks working abroad reduced their remittances.[105] During this period, TÜSİAD launched a mass media campaign against the government's continued trade protection, announcing that "ISI was in a bottleneck and should be replaced with an export-oriented economic model."[106] When the social democratic government at the heart of TÜSİAD's critiques collapsed in 1979, it "helped to create a powerful image of TUSIAD in the public mind as an organization that was so influential that it pushed democratically elected governments out of office."[107] In addition to TÜSİAD's pressure, Turkey's worsening economic crisis may have increased public support for economic reforms; according to the World Banks, "the experience of a winter in Ankara without heat or coffee…made Turks willing to take the economic and political risk of measures to open the economy."[108]

In November 1979, a right-of-center coalition led by Suleyman Demirel took control of Turkey's government and brought in a new economic team led by Turgut Özal. Özal had worked at the World Bank during the early 1970s, an experience that he later described as strongly influencing his views on economic policy.[109] After the World Bank, Özal worked with TÜSİAD, with whom he

104 Öniş et al. 1992, 32. 105 Öniş et al. 1992, 4. 106 Doğangün 2005.
107 Öniş and Türem 2002, 443. 108 Öniş et al. 1992, 28–29. 109 Öniş et al. 1992, 33.

published a 1978 article that advocated for trade liberalization and other liberal economic reforms.[110] In an effort to stabilize the economy in 1980, Özal proposed a package of neoliberal economic reforms known as the "24 January measures," which included trade liberalization, privatization, and devaluation of the Turkish lira. As Ahmad explains, "the program, a radical departure from earlier policies, was designed to create a new economy based on export rather than the home market."[111] These reforms, however, were vehemently opposed by Turkey's labor unions, which immediately launched strikes and protests to try and stop the government from opening the Turkish economy.

Labor Rights and Labor Opposition

Turkey's labor unions were able to mobilize workers against trade liberalization, at least in part, because of the country's constitution and pro-labor legislation. After the return of democracy in 1961, Turkey adopted a new constitution that recognized workers' basic rights to act collectively, but required that new legislation be passed to secure specific rights. Turkey's two main political parties had supported the right to strike during the 1950s, and the countries first labor union confederation, Türk-İs, led a series of protests demanding pro-labor legislation in the early 1960s. The country's Minister of Labor, Mustafa Bülent Ecevit, endorsed such legislation and argued that respecting labor rights would reduce union militancy and guard against communism; in 1962 he predicted that "if strikes and collective bargaining are allowed, I am certain that workers will not resort to demonstrations," and the following year he argued that the passage of pro-labor legislation would mean that "the last bridge between communism and the Turkish people who are essentially immune to communism in various ways will have been burned."[112]

In 1963, Turkey's democratic government then passed a new body of labor laws that guaranteed the rights to organize, collectively bargain, and strike. This legislation built upon ILO Conventions and "placed labour, for the first time in the Republic's history, on a more equal footing vis-à-vis the state and employers."[113] Turkey's labor unions were also strengthened by the government's pursuit of import-substitution industrialization, which fostered the industrial sectors of the economy in which Turkey's unions were concentrated. Turkey's two main labor union confederations, Türk-İs and DİSK, grew dramatically and union membership exceeded one million by 1971.[114] Over the course of the 1970s, overall union density rose from 16 per cent to 27 per cent.[115] The new constitution, pro-labor legislation, and the high tariffs of ISI "paved the way for workers' emergence as a powerful social class" and led to a "golden era" for the Turkish labor movement.[116]

110 Öniş et al. 1992, 32. 111 Ahmad 1993, 178. 112 Kaya 2018, 57, 64.
113 Özkiziltan 2020, 734.
114 Dinler and Büro 2012. Turkey also has two smaller labor union confederations, MISK and HAK-IŞ, that represent right-wing and Islamic union, respectively Nichols et al. 2002, 25.
115 Nichols et al. 2002. 116 Özkiziltan 2020, 739.

Turkey's labor unions vehemently opposed Özal's 1980 reforms and launched a series of protests and strikes that rocked the country for nine months. The first strike began almost immediately, when 500 textile workers occupied a factory in Izmir to protest layoffs caused by the government's economic reforms. The leaders of Turkey's radical labor union confederation, DİSK, then announced the beginning of a general strike that would spread across Turkey.[117] By March 1980, unions were striking in 77 textile mills and 108 metal factories throughout the country, and in Ankara and Istanbul journalists reported that "mounds of garbage line the streets and potholes in roads go unrepaired" as the general services unions joined the growing strike wave.[118] As DİSK's secretary general warned, "large-scale strikes have begun. They will be followed by other strikes and work stoppages. . .Let us be prepared for it."[119]

Trade Policy Outcomes

Demirel's government proposed to remove "the subsidies and protectionism that hobble a low-growth economy" and lead a "wholesale reorientation of policy toward a market-based economy."[120] As *The Economist* crooned, "the days of attempted autarky are over."[121] However, rather than implement all of Özal's "24 January measures" in a sudden shock, Demirel first focused on increasing Turkey's exports by devaluing the lira and decreasing workers' real wages. In the face of nationwide strikes and growing political violence, Demirel's government left office – removed by a military coup in September 1980 – having only made what Celasun and Rodrik call "small adjustments" to Turkey trade policies.[122]

There is a broad consensus among scholars of Turkish politics that union-led strikes contributed to the failure of the "24 January measures." For example, Yadirgi argues that, "the inexhaustible activities of the left and the unions, particularly DİSK, made it impossible for Özal to execute the neoliberal economic package."[123] From the very beginning of the reform process, unions frustrated the government efforts to fight inflation by limiting wage increases. Türk-İs and DİSK both threatened to launch strikes against legislation that would curtail collective bargaining and limit wage increases to a cost-of-living index – pressure that forced Demirel to withdraw the bill from parliament.[124] With inflation increasing and nationwide strikes suggesting that there was "widespread opposition" to the government's reform proposals,

[117] "Military Surround Mill," *Anatolia* [FBIS], February 14, 1980; "General Strike," *Anatolia* [FBIS], February 14, 1980.

[118] "1,500 Turkish Workers Arrested As Unrest Is Reported Spreading," *New York Times*, March 14, 1980.

[119] "DISK Leader Criticizes Government Wage Proposals," *Anatolia* [FBIS], March 23, 1980.

[120] "Turkey's Turn," *New York Times*, July 5, 1980; Öniş et al. 1992, 5.

[121] Quoted in Ahmad 1993, 178. [122] Sachs and Collins 2019, 719. [123] Yadirgi 2017, 217.

[124] Özkiziltan 2013, 237; "DISK Leader Criticizes Government Wage Proposals," *Anatolia* [FBIS], March 23, 1980.

Demirel's coalition government began to break apart.[125] According to the *New York Times*, a coalition partner of Demirel's government "virtually paralyzed" the government by threatening to withdraw from the coalition unless the government abandoned its economic reforms.

Union-led strikes also contributed to the worsening of political violence; terrorism associated with rival political parties claimed over 2,000 lives during Demirel's short government.[126] When the leader of the DİSK-affiliated metal workers' union was assassinated, former Prime Minister Ecevit warned that the killing was "no doubt, an open provocation" to more bloodshed. With this type of political violence in mind, Ecevit introduced a no-confidence motion against Demirel's leadership, citing the government's "failure to control inflation and terrorism."[127] As Özkiziltan explains, Turkey's government found itself "caught between two wildfires" with the pro-liberalization demands of TÜSİAD and the IMF on one side and the protectionist demands of Turkey's labor unions on the other.[128] According to Onder, "there was a strong opposition in society centered on the labor-union movement. . .the opposition was strong enough to frustrate the implementation of the new economic strategy"[129]

Prime Minister Demirel acknowledged that such social unrest and political instability threatened his reforms and "made it impossible to deal with the future of the country."[130] Similarly, Özal recognized that the "24 January measures" would trigger union resistance, and that such opposition would make it difficult to implement the reforms. As Ahmad explains, Özal knew his reforms would "cause much social turmoil. . .[and] asked that he be given five years of political and social harmony in which to accomplish his task of restoring the economy to a healthy state."[131] There can be little doubt as to whom Özal was appealing to for a chance to reform Turkey's economy without facing domestic opposition: on September 12, 1980, Turkey's military launched a coup, established a military dictatorship, and appointed Özal as Deputy Prime Minister and the head of the government's economic team.

Turkey: 1983–1989

Democracy and the Potential for Trade Liberalization

After three years of dictatorship, Turkey's military agreed to hold elections in 1983 and peacefully returned the government to civilian control. Understanding the prospects for trade liberalization after the return of democracy

125 Yadirgi 2017, 217.

126 "Military in Turkey Ousts Government of Premier Demirel," *New York Times*, September 12, 1980; Öniş et al. 1992.

127 "No-Confidence Debate in Turkey," *New York Times*, June 25, 1980.

128 Özkiziltan 2020, 742. 129 Önder 1998, 48-49.

130 "Demirel: Government to Ask Assembly for Martial Law Extension," *Ankara Domestic Service* [FBIS], June 13, 1980.

131 Ahmad 1993, 178.

requires a brief examination of Turkey's three years of military rule (1980–1983), which radically altered domestic politics in two key ways. First, the military government violently repressed labor unions, ostensibly removing them from the policymaking process. Second, the military worked closely with TÜSİAD to implement economic reforms that reduced inflation, secured financial support from the IMF and increased public support for further economic liberalization. Although TÜSİAD advocated for trade liberalization during the military dictatorship, the junta feared that such reforms would reduce national industrial production and lead to politically damaging bankruptcies. In short, the military regime crushed protectionist labor unions, strengthened pro-trade business, and returned to the country to democracy with high tariffs still in place.

As soon as the military took over in September 1980, it brutally repressed Turkey's labor movement, suspended the constitution, outlawed the labor union confederation (DİSK) that sponsored the general strike, jailed union leaders, banned strikes, and suspended collective bargaining.[132] The military closed union offices, banned all union activities, ordered workers who were on strike to return to their jobs, and placed Army units in key factories so as to ensure a lack of labor unrest.[133] The military sought to crush every manifestation of dissent from the left, including labor unionists, and openly acknowledged that policemen were torturing prisoners.[134] For Turkey's labor unions, the result was "an environment where any potential resistance against the impending institutional reforms was ruthlessly crushed."[135] Many of Turkey's employers welcomed this labor repression; for example, the president of the Confederation of Employers' Union announced that "the end of strikes would be an important step in Turkey's economic development."[136]

Crucially, the military did not just repress Turkish labor unions, it also changed Turkish law so as to permanently undermine the ability of labor unions to influence politics in the future. In 1982, the military rewrote the Turkish constitution to restrict the labor rights that had been granted in the 1961 constitution, including the right to strike. They also passed new labor laws that made it more difficult for workers to join unions, limited collective bargaining, prohibited strikes under most circumstances, and provided prison sentences and fines for unlawful strikes. The military coup therefore marked a critical break with the past two decades, a period during which unions "experienced a glorious period of development."[137]

While labor unions were repressed, the military gave TÜSİAD special permission to continue its operations. Just nine days after the coup, the military's Council or Ministers issued a decree that defined TÜSİAD as "an organization working for public interest" that could continue to advocate for

[132] Dogan 2010. [133] Şener 2004, 11–12. [134] Ahmad 1993, 184. [135] Özkiziltan 2020, 743. [136] Ahmad 1998. [137] Özkiziltan 2020, 743.

economic reforms.[138] A founding member of TÜSİAD sent a letter to the head of the military junta pledging support, and the business organization secured cabinet-level positions for several members. Özal and TÜSİAD became closely associated with the military's economic reforms, which helped to stabilize the Turkish economy.

When the military permitted a "guided" general election in November 1983, it banned all previous political parties but allowed Özal to run for Prime Minister as the head of the Motherland Party (ANAP). After Özal's party won a plurality of the 1983 vote, as well as municipal elections the following year, many concluded that "a key part of ANAP's political appeal was the success of the economic program."[139] After the return of democracy, "TUSIAD continued to occupy significant public space" and pushed for the trade liberalization that was first proposed as part of the "24 January measures" back in 1980.[140]

Labor Rights and Labor Opposition

Despite the return of democracy, Özal's newly-elected government left the military's constitution and repressive labor laws in place for years to come. Unions were prohibited from pursuing political activities or establishing relationships with political parties and politically motivated strikes, general strikes, and sympathy strikes were all illegal. Lawful strikes over wages could be suspended by the government for sixty days and settled by compulsory arbitration.[141] Özal's government continued the military's ban on DİSK, the social democratic union confederation that had led most of the strikes against the 24 January measures in 1980. The new government also continued trials against most of DİSK's top leaders, who in 1981 had been charged with offenses punishable by death. The trial hung over Turkey's return to democracy and did not conclude until 1986, when 264 trade union members received prison sentences that ranged from five to fifteen years.[142]

Özal's government permitted only one labor union confederation, Türk-İs, to continue representing workers. Türk-İs had publicly welcomed the 1980 coup, its Secretary General served as the military government's Minister of Social Security, and the union developed a reputation for having autocratic leaders that ignored the concerns of rank-and-file union members.[143] As the Secretary General of the Turkish Communist Party lamented in the opening month's of Özal's administration, "the Turkish trade union movement is experiencing one of its most difficult periods. DISK is still closed down–TURK-IS is dominated by a reactionary gang."[144] Throughout the 1980s and 1990s Turkish workers

138 Dogan 2010, 78.

139 Öniş et al. 1992, 6. Ahmad (1993, 190) argues that patronage also played a significant role in ANAP's 1984 electoral victory; "No other politician in Turkey has exploited patronage with quite the same skill as Turgut Ozal."

140 Öniş and Türem 2002, 443. 141 Nichols et al. 2002, 32. 142 Nichols et al. 2002, 34.

143 Nichols et al. 2002.

144 "Part Seven," *(Clandestine) Voice of the Turkish Communist Party* [FBIS], February 21, 1984.

found that Türk-İs "effectively denies them a voice" in union decision-making and that the union leaders' lack of accountability "stems from the past practice of the Turkish state, most especially from the consequences of the 1980 coup."[145]

With political activity and most strikes banned, Türk-İs aimed to establish good relations with the government and to request a dialogue regarding its economic reforms. However, unlike the pro-labor governments of the 1960s and 1970s, with Özal as Prime Minister "the attitude of government was no longer a tolerant one."[146] In the opening days of Özal's administration, his Minister of Labor addressed the Turkish Confederation of Employers' Unions and promised that the military's restrictions on labor rights would stay in place because "we are determined not to permit disruption of the labor peace through ideological acts."[147] One month later, a journalist asked Özal when martial law and bans on labor union activities would be lifted. Özal responded that "martial law is not a permanent system of administration. It is a temporary measure." When the journalist pressured Özal to "identify a period during which martial law might be lifted," Özal simply said "No, I cannot."[148]

With DİSK banned, union leaders standing trial, strikes prohibited, and the leaders of Türk-İs easily coopted by the state, there was little chance of organized labor opposition to Özal's economic reforms. As Özkiziltan explains, "little has changed, if anything, with regards to the policies and practices implemented in the domain of industrial relations by the successive governments after Turkey's transition to multi-party democracy with the elections held towards the end of the 1983."[149] As a report by the World Bank explains, the violent "persecution of labor leaders virtually stopped, but it had in any case become unnecessary for curtailing union power ... the Turkish government chose direct exclusion of labor in the early 1980s."[150] The report goes on to say that when the military laid down the terms for the return of democracy, it "perpetuated the reduced status of union."[151]

Turkey's Left continued to oppose Özal's economic reforms, but from clandestine radio stations rather than crowded public squares. According to *Bizim Radyo* (Our Radio), "What has changed amidst the cries of a transition to democracy? Nothing has changed...the fascist regime maintains power through its oppressive constitution, its martial law, its bans, and its iron-fisted shadow government called the NSC." The radio program went on to oppose Özal's "24 January economic measures, that is, an economic policy of destruction" and warned that "Özal's past is the same as his future...[he]

[145] Nichols et al. 2002, 41. [146] Buyukuslu 1998, 72.
[147] "Labor Minister Addresses Employers' Union," *Ankara Anatolia* [FBIS], December 17, 1983.
[148] "On Aid, Martial Law," *Istanbul Cumhuriyet* [FBIS], January 11, 1984.
[149] Özkiziltan 2013, 16. [150] Öniş et al. 1992, 18–19. [151] Ibid.

will continue to be the enemy of the workers. He will continue to serve the imperialist World Bank where he once worked."[152]

Trade Policy Outcomes

After taking office in November 1983, Özal moved quickly to liberalize Turkey's international trade policies. Over the next two months, the government liberalized the import regime by reducing the number of good that required import licenses and by lowering tariff rates.[153] These reforms were celebrated by Turkey's Association of Chambers of Trade and Industry, an organization representing internationally-oriented businesses. Chairman Mehmet Yazar explained, "the economic program of the new government was based on goals and views which this organization had advocated for years" and that his association "stood for the free market economy, and believed the economy should function according to economic laws without state intervention."[154] DİSK, after the government permitted it to reorganize in 1992, lamented that trade liberalization shifted Turkey's industrial output and exports toward low-skilled jobs in the textile and apparel sectors, which relied on low-wage, non-union labor.[155]

There can be little doubt that repressive labor laws smoothed Turkey's move toward free trade. According to Karacan, "the adoption of neoliberal politics, and the implementation of the economic measures named the 24 January Measures, would not have been possible without oppressing the resistance movement in society."[156] The World Bank drew similar conclusions, albeit with different rhetoric; "Turkey's top-down institutions of decision-making continued to work well in the trade policy area during the second reform phase [1983–1987], because it was important to move quickly in order to take advantage of the honeymoon after the start of restoring democracy" – a romantic period during which strikes remained illegal and labor opposition was silenced.[157] Looking back, even Özal acknowledged that "I can say that had September 12 [the coup] not taken place, today's results would have been impossible to achieve."[158]

Within-Case Comparison of Turkey 1961–1980 and 1983–1989

A within-case comparison of Turkey from 1961–1980 and 1983–1989 illustrates how democracy empowered groups that favored trade liberalization, as well as how the level of respect for labor rights shaped unions' ability to

152 "Our Radio Criticizes New Ozal Government," *(Clandestine) Our Radio* [FBIS], December 14, 1983.

153 "Import, Export Regulations for 1984 Announced," *Ankara Domestic Service* [FBIS], December 29, 1983.

154 "Union of Chambers Welcomes Economic Measures," *Ankara Anatolia* [FBIS], January 1, 1984.

155 Önder 1998, 54. 156 Karacan 2015, 140. 157 Öniş et al. 1992, 38. 158 Şener 2004, 14.

counterbalance those demands. From 1961 until the military coup of September 12, 1980, Turkey was a democracy that respected labor rights. When the government proposed trade liberalization and other liberal economic reforms in January 1980, protectionist labor unions responded with protests and strikes that helped to block the reforms. A coup then ushered in three years of military rule that not only violently crushed the labor movement, but also revised the country's constitution and passed new laws that restricted workers rights to organize and strike. These repressive labor laws remained in place after the country returned to democracy in 1983, leaving Turkey a democracy that had little respect for labor rights. When Turkey's democratic government then proposed the same trade liberalization and other economic reforms that had been blocked by labor union protests and strikes in 1980, the reforms were implemented without substantial opposition.

INDIA

This section presents a case study of trade politics in India in the 1980s, a period during which Prime Minister Rajiv Gandhi proposed but failed to implement trade liberalization. India transitioned to democracy upon independence from Britain in 1947 and then maintained high levels of respect for labor rights as well as high tariffs for several decades. Gandhi's trade policy proposals in the 1980s were vehemently opposed by India's import-competing industries and labor unions, which launched multiple general strikes that helped to maintain high tariffs. This Indian case serves two purposes. First, cross-case comparisons with Argentina, Bolivia, and Turkey illustrate how respect for labor rights and labor union opposition helped to impede trade liberalization across very different cases. Second, this case study of India in the 1980s presents the beginning of a within-case comparison with India in the 1990s, which is presented in Chapter 4. In contrast to the 1980s, India's democratic government used labor repression in the 1990s to weaken labor union opposition and thereby facilitate trade liberalization.

Democracy and the Potential for Trade Liberalization

In the early twentieth century, Indian workers organized the All India Trade Union Congress (AITUC) and led the struggle for democracy and independence from Britain. After gaining independence in 1947, India's democratic government pursued import-substitution industrialization and was steadfastly committed to organized labor. As Kuruvilla explains, economic policymaking in "India was influenced by the close ties between political parties and the labor movement forged in the struggle for independence."[159] India's Trade Union Act made it easy for workers to organize and unions thrived in India's mixed economy with high tariffs and a large public sector.[160] India's tariffs were associated

[159] Kuruvilla 1996, 650. [160] Kohli 2012.

with higher wages for workers, and India's labor unions provided consistently and strong support for trade protectionism; as Teitelbaum explains, unions "are known for their strident opposition to neoliberal reforms that most directly threaten the interested of workers in organized manufacturing."[161]

However, declining economic growth rates in the 1970s led India's government to gradually shift its political allegiances away from labor unions and toward Indian business. In the 1980s, Prime Minister Indira Gandhi's Congress Party initiated a series a pro-business reforms that prioritized economic growth over redistribution. According to Kohli, these economic reforms represented a strategic political move meant to shore up electoral support, as Indira Gandhi recognized that "a realignment with big capital. . .may lead to higher growth and thus to lower inflation, an outcome that India's largely poor electoral may appreciate."[162] Indira Gandhi relaxed limitations on the entry and expansion of firms and loosened industrial price controls, but maintained the high tariffs supported by labor unions and "India's well-established indigenous capitalist."[163]

By the time Indira Gandhi's son, Rajiv Gandhi, became Prime Minister in 1984, Indian businesses had begun to split regarding international trade policy, with "a significant, technologically modern faction willing to experiment with a more open economy."[164] Rajiv Gandhi believed that making the Indian economy more efficient would drive economic growth and the electoral prospects of the Congress Party, and "thought that the best way to do so was to open India's economy to the world."[165] After winning a landslide electoral victory in 1984, Gandhi described his economic approach as involving a "judicious combination of deregulation, import liberalization, and easier access to foreign technology."[166] Although the majority of India's industries continued to support trade protectionism, the combination of democracy and broad public demands for economic growth appear to have convinced Rajiv Gandhi to pursue trade liberalization.[167]

Labor Rights and Labor Opposition

Despite labor's relative decline in the 1970s and 1980s, India's labor unions remained sufficiently powerful to mobilize opposition to government policy by launching one-day general strikes, the turnout for which is widely seen as a barometer of working class public opinion. As Teitelbaum explains, Indian unions can "draw attention to an issue by calling a general strike – a very powerful weapon in India."[168] Similarly, the editors of *Economic and Political Weekly* explain that "one must not be too sceptical of the results that an action like the one-day strike can achieve. The public sector employees are part of the intermediate classes which are numerically large and are thus able to exercise

161 Dutta 2007; Teitelbaum 2011, 30. 162 Kohli 2006, 1255. 163 Kohli 1989, 308–310.
164 Kohli 2012, 36. 165 Kohli 2012, 34. 166 Quoted in Kohli 1989, 312.
167 For studies of trade liberalization in India that focuses more on ideology and the influence of technocrats, see Shastri 1997; Mukherji 2013.
168 Teitelbaum 2017, 11.

power in a parliamentary system."[169] Previous research suggests that such labor union-led strikes forced the Indian government to adopt a gradual pace for its privatization efforts in the 1990s.[170]

Union-led general strikes were especially important in the mid-1980s, when Prime Minister Rajiv Gandhi proposed lowering India's tariffs. In India, trade policy changes are traditionally announced in the early months of each calendar year during a Budget Speech delivered by the government's finance minister. In 1985, Gandhi's government announced a "New Fiscal Policy" that replaced import quotas with tariffs and also lowered tariffs on electronics and capital goods.[171] As Gandhi explained, "where import substitutes are not cost effective, India should opt for imports, especially of technology."[172] Gandhi's economic reforms also included substantial tax concessions on corporations and the upper-middle class, the relaxation of licensing regulations for domestic industry, and the loosening of India's anti-monopoly regulations.[173]

India's labor unions clearly preferred the maintenance of the protectionist status quo and opposed Rajiv Gandhi's trade reforms. Such labor opposition was clearly voiced during the pre-budget discussion between trade union representatives and the Finance Minister – a meeting traditionally held before the annual budget is finalized. The Secretary of AITUC used his allotted time to draw attention to unemployment and opposed the government's "import liberalisation policy." The Secretary of CITU, the union affiliated with the Communist Party of India – Marxist, lamented that India was "moving towards a free market economy" and warned that the government had "liberalised imports [thus] giving the policy of self-reliance an unannounced burial."[174] The CITU saw trade liberalization as a direct threat to employment in India's manufacturing industries and joined import-competing capitalists in voicing opposition to Rajiv's reforms; according to the CITU's monthly journal, *The Working Class*, "already voices of protest are coming from Indian industrialists against import liberalisation and the facilities given to multinationals…They offer a challenge to the trade union movement which must accept it, if it wants to protect the jobs of those who are already at work."[175]

At the pre-budget discussion of 1987, the CITU Secretary warned the Finance Minister that "the so-called import liberalisation has also caused a great damage to indigenous industries. The machine manufacturing industry has already shown a decline up to 14 percent."[176] During the CITU's national convention of 1987, the union's President explained that "Rajiv Gandhi's New Economic Policy of destabilizing the public sector, free competition from abroad and import liberalisation is not only adding to the distress of the people but undermining self reliance of the economy."[177] The CITU's protectionist

169 Raj 1987. 170 Uba 2005; Candland 2007. 171 India 1985.
172 Quoted in Kohli 1989, 313. 173 Kohli 1989.
174 "CITU Assails Govt's Economic Policies," *The Working Class*, February 1986.
175 "Unemployment and the Working Class," *The Working Class*, July 1986.
176 "Trade Union Assails Government's Economic Policy," *The Working Class*, February 1987.
177 "Presidential Address," *The Working Class*, June 1987.

trade policy preferences were shared by a clear majority of Indian labor unions; a coalition of union confederations representing two-thirds of all union members in India called on the government to stop the "import of technology and goods detrimental to indigenous development."[178] While INTUC, the labor union confederation affiliated with Rajiv's Congress Party did not formally join this coalition of labor unions opposed to the reforms, it did ask "its constituents not to adopt a confrontationist stand" against other protesting unions.[179] Summing up this broad labor union opposition to Rajiv's reforms, *The Times* concluded that "Gandhi's dilemma is that he cannot assuage public opinion without jettisoning the most important of his reforms."[180]

India's labor unions joined peasants, students, and intellectuals and launched a series of general strikes against Gandhi's reforms. The first general strike, launched on February 26, 1986, was organized by an all-India committee of labor unions around several policy demands, including protecting domestic goods against imports.[181] A convention of labor unions meeting before the strike passed a resolution that "protested against the government's policy of modernisation which amounted to increasing unemployment [and] was part of the pro-rich framework" being followed by Rajiv Gandhi's government.[182] Although Gandhi had been elected at the end of 1984 with an overwhelming majority of seats in the Parliament (404 out of 533), this strike signaled, according to one opposition leader, that "Mr. Gandhi's honeymoon with the people was over."[183]

A second general strike was launched on January 21, 1987 with broad support from India's central labor unions, including CITU, AITUC, BMS, and HMS. Although the Congress-aligned INTUC did not formally support the strike, it again asked its constituent not to adopt a confrontationist stand. Among the main concerns of the striking unions was that the Government stop the importation of technology and goods that were "detrimental to indigenous development."[184] Import-competing firms also registered their opposition to the trade policy reforms: according to the head of FICCI, a peak lobbying association for Indian firms, "after three decades of highly protective industrialization, liberalization cannot be taken up simultaneously on all fronts – it has to be phased."[185] With these general strikes and protectionist demands from Indian businesses "the society ... hit back: the state lost the temporary autonomy it had gained."[186]

178 "21st January Strike," *The Working Class*, February 1987. These policy demands were included in a nationwide strike notice supported by CITU, AITUC, BMS, and HMS. Based on union membership data from 1989, these unions represented 67 percent of Indian union members.

179 Raj 1987, 107.

180 "Why Gandhi's Reforms Could Falter," *Times of London*, May 22 1986.

181 Kohli 1989, 321.

182 "City Meetings to Organise Bandh," *Times of India*, February 23, 1986.

183 "Bandh Partial and Peaceful," *Times of India*, February 27, 1986.

184 Raj 1987, 107. 185 Quoted in Kohli 1989. 186 Kohli 1987, 316.

Trade Policy Outcomes

Despite the potential threat that such labor opposition posed to Gandhi's reforms, the government did not seek to repress these general strikes; according to the *Times of India*, "barring stray incidents of stone throwing on municipal buses and a mild lathi-charge, the bandh was peaceful."[187] Neither the major Indian newspapers, nor the CITU's *The Working Class*, mention instances of labor repression leading up to our during the strike. Instead of repression, the government responded with trade policy concessions. During the 1986 Budget Speech – delivered just two days after the general strike – Finance Minister V.P. Singh acknowledged the "importance of providing adequate support to our capital goods industry which is pivotal for self reliance" and increased the tariff on general machinery by 10 percent.[188]

Similarly, Rajiv's government did not seek to repress the second general strike launched on January 21, 1987. Again, neither India's newspapers nor the CITU's journal record any preventive arrests used to break the strike. Two million public sector workers throughout India's industrial sectors joined the strike, as the CITU warned that "a government sensitive to public opinion will definitely respond to such a protest and have second thoughts about its policy."[189] In an article published that week by the editor of *Economic and Political Weekly*, he declared that, "from all accounts, the one-day token strike on January 21 of employees of public sector undertakings was a success."[190]

Less than five weeks passed before the government began to make compromises and reverse more of the previously implemented reforms. In the budget speech on February 28, 1987, India's Finance Minister, V. P. Singh, reversed the governments trade policy liberalization by increasing tariffs on capital goods. According to Singh, "the capital goods industry needs special support" since the recently lowered tariff rate for machinery had "provided a strong encouragement for unnecessary imports."[191] The final two budgets of Gandhi's government, in 1988 and 1989, continued this policy reversal, as Rajiv concluded that "there seems little room for too many more concessions."[192] In these ways, Rajiv's government chose not to squash general strikes with preventive arrests, even when such opposition was helping to derail his economic agenda. According to Kohli, "what strikes like this make clear...is the type of opposition the government may expect if it ever really gets down seriously to privatize and to modernize the public sector" by deregulating the domestic economy and opening it to foreign competition.[193] Or, as Zagha concludes, "the main reason for this hesitant approach...is the strength of unions in the

187 "Lathi-charge" is a common tactic used by the Indian police to disperse crowds, and includes charging demonstrators with "lathi" or long wooden sticks. "Bandh Partial and Peaceful," *Times of India*, February 27, 1986. Bandh is a Hindi term for a general strike.

188 India 1986, 31. 189 "21st January Strike," *The Working Class*, February 1987.

190 Raj 1987, 106. 191 India 1987, 15. 192 Quoted in Varshney 1998, 318.

193 Kohli 1989, 321.

public sector...where unions are particularly strong, and reforms have hence been particularly gradual."[194]

Cross-Case Comparison of India, Argentina, Bolivia, and Turkey

In India (1984–1989), Argentina (1983–1989), Bolivia (1982–1985), and Turkey (1961–1980), democratic developing countries proposed but failed to implement trade liberalization. Despite the many differences across these cases, respect for labor rights and opposition from protectionist labor unions played important roles in blocking trade liberalization in each case. In Argentina, Alfonsín's government respected labor rights and the CGT launched thirteen general strikes that paralyzed the country and helped convince the government to maintain high tariffs. In Bolivia, President Siles' government was committed to protecting workers' rights and the COB launched general strikes that led the government to accept union demands for high tariffs and other protectionist policies. In Turkey, the constitution and pro-labor legislation guaranteed workers' rights, and DİSK led strikes that blocked the government's attempts to liberalize trade and implement other neoliberal economic reforms. In India, democratic governments protect labor rights that fostered a powerful labor movement, and unions launched strikes that helped convince Rajiv Gandhi to reverse his initial attempts to open India's economy. In short, these four very different cases all illustrate that when labor rights were protected, democratic governments that attempted trade liberalization met fierce opposition from labor unions that launched influential strikes and protests.

Comparing these different case studies also helps to address two important alternative explanations for trade liberalization and labor repression. First, these cases show that while economic crises played an important role in governments proposing trade liberalization, they were not sufficient for the implementation of such reforms.[195] Argentina (1983–1989), Bolivia (1982–1985), and Turkey (1980) all faced debts crises and hyperinflation, and these economic difficulties may have increased public support for trade liberalization and other structural reforms. In each of these cases, however, government proposals for trade liberalization were blocked by opposition that included labor union strikes and protests.

Second, these cases suggest that labor repression was often aimed at limiting union opposition to economic reforms, not simply a crisis-induced means to reduce wages for the sake of austerity or export competitiveness.[196] In Bolivia, for example, Paz's breaking of the COB's general strike was clearly meant to weaken union opposition to his NPE reforms, not simply to increase labor market flexibility.[197] Similarly, Turkey's government decided to maintain high levels of labor repression after the 1983 return to democracy, at least in

[194] Zagha 2000, 168. [195] Rodrik 1992; Blyth et al. 2002. [196] Kuruvilla 1996.
[197] Nazmi 1995; Cyr 2015.

part, in order to limit union opposition to its economic reforms.[198] The next two chapters document a comparable dynamic in India and Argentina, where democratic governments clearly used labor repression to try to limit the general strikes that impeded their predecessors' attempts at trade liberalization.

CONCLUSION

This chapter presented cases studies of trade politics in Mexico, Argentina, Bolivia, Turkey, and India in order to illustrate the causal mechanisms that link democracy, labor repression, and trade liberalization. More specifically, these cases showed how democracy increased the potential for trade liberalization, how the level of labor rights shaped the ability of unions to oppose trade liberalization, and how the presence or absence of union-led strikes and protests influenced trade policy outcomes. When democratic governments respected labor rights, labor union opposition helped to maintain high tariffs, as we saw in Argentina under Alfonsín from 1983 to 1989, Bolivia under Siles from 1982 to 1985, Turkey under Demirel in 1980, and India under Gandhi from 1984 to 1989. In contrast, when democratic governments did not respect labor rights, union opposition was weakened and tariffs fell, as we saw in Mexico under the PRI during the 1980s and 1990s, Bolivia under Paz in 1985, and Turkey in the mid-1980s.

Beyond illustrating my theory's causal mechanisms, these cases also demonstrated my theory's two pathways toward free trade. The first path predicts that an increase in democracy leads to trade liberalization if respect for labor rights is low. This was the case in Mexico during its gradual transition to democracy in the 1980s and 1990s, as well as in Turkey after its transition to democracy in 1983. In contrast, when respect for labor rights was high, an increase in democracy led to high tariffs. This was the case after democratic transitions in India (1947), Argentina (1983), Bolivia (1982), and Turkey (1961). The second path predicts that at high levels of democracy, governments can facilitate trade liberalization by increasing labor repression. This was the case in Bolivia, where Paz used a state of siege in 1985 to weaken labor union opposition to his reforms. As the next two chapters now demonstrate, India and Argentina both followed this second path toward free trade, as well. During the 1980s, both countries had democratic governments, high levels of respect for labor rights, and witnessed general strikes that helped maintain high tariffs. In the 1990s, new political leaders in both countries – Prime Minister Narasimha Rao in India and President Carlos Menem in Argentina – increased labor repression on their way to opening their countries' economies.

The case studies presented in this chapter generally agree with previous scholarship on each specific country. For example, prior studies of Mexico in the 1980s highlight how labor repression decreased union opposition to

[198] Öniş et al. 1992.

trade liberalization, just as studies of Argentina in the 1980s highlight how respect for labor rights enabled general strikes that helped to maintain high tariffs.[199] One of this chapter's main contributions was therefore to present these cases in a comparative perspective that hints at the generalizability of these dynamics around the globe. In contrast, the subsequent chapters on India and Argentina in the 1990s explicitly disagree with conventional explanations for how democratic governments overcame labor union opposition to trade liberalization. In these ways, my deductive theory and original empirical research combine to show how labor repression shaped trade policy outcomes even in cases where scholars explicitly deny its importance.

[199] e.g. Kay 2011; Murillo 2001.

4

India's Middle Path

Preventive Arrests and General Strikes

In the mid-1980s, Prime Minister Rajiv Gandhi attempted to lower India's tariffs and open the country's economy to global competition. As discussed in Chapter 3, Gandhi's trade policy proposals led India's protectionist labor unions to launch a series of general strikes that helped to block these reforms; Gandhi left office in 1989 with India's average tariff still above 80 percent. This chapter continues this story into the 1990s, when Prime Minister Narasimha Rao launched a new attempt at trade liberalization. By 1996, Rao managed to lower India's average tariffs to 37 percent – a major success compared to Gandhi's efforts, but relatively gradual liberalization compared to many other democratic developing countries.[1] Trade politics in India under Gandhi and Rao therefore offers a within-case comparison that further illustrates how democratic developing countries used labor repression to facilitate trade liberalization.

Given India's gradual trade liberalization in the 1990s, my theory predicts that Rao's labor rights violations would have been worse than Gandhi's, while still being relatively moderate compared to democratic developing countries that liberalized more rapidly. The basic contours of the story are clearly visible in Figure 4.1, which displays India's levels of democracy, labor rights, and tariffs using the quantitative measures analyzed in Chapter 2.[2] The first panel shows that India's level of democracy was high and nearly constant across Gandhi and Rao's administrations. The second panel shows that India's level of respect for labor rights was relatively high during Gandhi's administration but then briefly dropped in 1992, the first full year of Rao's administration.

[1] Tariff data from the World Bank.

[2] Gandhi's administration ended in December, 1989 and Rao's began in June, 1991. In the intervening 18 months, Vishwanath Pratap Singh served as Prime Minister for less than one year and Chandra Shekhar served as Prime Minister for roughly seven months.

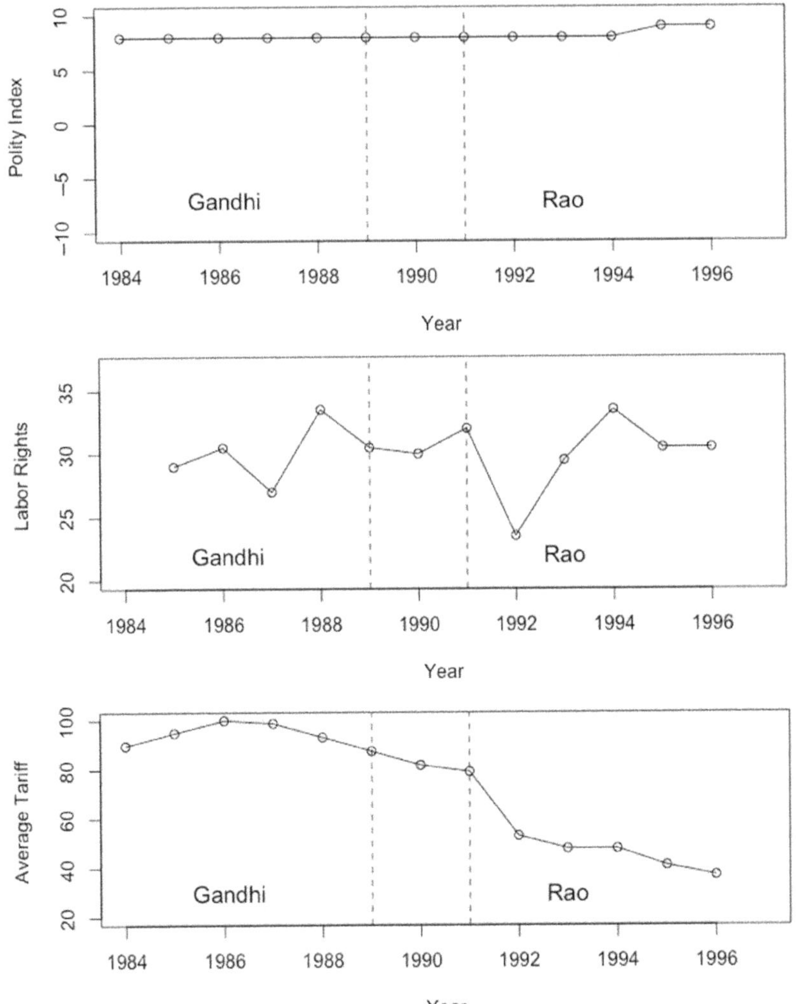

FIGURE 4.1. Democracy, labor rights, and tariffs in India

While Rao violated labor rights more than Gandhi ever had, India's labor repression never reached the depths of Mexico's squashing of independent unions or Turkey's complete ban on union activities.[3] The third panel shows that India's tariffs were extremely high and stable during Gandhi's

3 India's average *Collective Labor Rights* score during Gandhi's administration was 30, but dropped to 23.5 under Rao in 1992. When Mexico signed NAFTA in 1994, its *Collective Labor Rights* score was 14; when Turkey transitioned to democracy and lowered its tariffs in 1985, its score was just 3.25.

administration, dropped significantly at the beginning of Rao's administration, and then gradually declined throughout the rest of his time in office.[4]

India's 1992 decrease in this quantitative measure of labor rights was driven by specific labor rights violations including the firing of strikers, police brutality against protestors, and the preventive arrest of union members before a general strike.[5] This chapter draws on archival research to demonstrate that these were not isolated incidences, but rather part of a larger campaign of labor repression aimed at weakening union mobilization against Rao's economic reforms.[6] While Rao's labor rights violations did not squash all union activity, they nonetheless played an important role in the process through which India's democratic government overcame union opposition to trade liberalization.

To discipline my analysis, I present the story of Indian trade liberalization in three sections, each of which explores a different question related to my theory's causal mechanisms. First, did labor union opposition pose a threat to Rao's reforms? When Rao announced his plans to open India's economy in 1991, the country's labor unions clearly demanded the maintenance of high tariffs; as Teitelbaum explains, unions in India are "known for their strident opposition to neoliberal reforms that most directly threaten the interests of workers in organized manufacturing."[7] In an effort to block Rao's reforms, unions representing 55 percent of India's union members created the Sponsoring Committee of Indian Trade Unions (SCITU), which coordinated protests and strikes around the country.[8] When SCITU launched a general strike that mobilized more than twelve million Indian workers, contemporary journalists warned that "the path of such reforms therefore tends to be seriously imperiled by the possibility of

4 In 1996, India's average tariff rate was more than double the mean tariff rate across developing countries. Author's calculation using data from the World Bank. Sinha (2016) argues that India had a relatively closed economy until the early 2000s.

5 These labor rights violations are included in the 1993 *Annual Survey of Violations of Trade Union Rights* by the International Confederation of Free Trade Unions, which is one of three sources that was used to compile the *Collective Labor Rights Dataset*.

6 I analyzed primary documents and newspapers from numerous archives in India and the United States, including the Delhi offices of INTUC and CITU and the Library of Congress in Washington, D.C. My analysis of labor union opposition relies heavily on the CITU's monthly journal, *The Working Class*. I also draw upon national newspapers such as *Times of India*, *Hindustan Times*, and the *Indian Express*, as well as regional papers that provide more in-depth coverage on local news, such as Tamil Nadu's *The Hindu*. I thank Aparna Ravi for her research assistance, including visits to union archives in India.

7 Teitelbaum 2011, 30.

8 Author's calculation based on data from Aswathappa 2005, 539 For a summary of SCITU's activities, see Swamy and Singh 1994. Bharatiya Mazdoor Sangh (BMS) did not join SCITU, but organized its own protests against Rao's reforms. Between SCITU and BMS, unions representing roughly 75 percent of all Indian union members openly opposed Rao's reforms.

labour unrest. Once labour becomes seriously aroused, it becomes necessary to resort to repression if the reforms are not to be abandoned."[9]

Second, did Rao's government use labor repression to overcome labor union opposition? Prior research correctly highlights how Rao used partisan ties and tripartite committees to gain support from the Indian National Trade Union Congress (INTUC), a large labor union confederation affiliated with Rao's Congress Party.[10] While such co-optation was important, it was not sufficient to stop labor union opposition; INTUC represented only 25 percent of India's union members.[11] Just days before the first general strike, Rao promised SCITU leaders that he would invite them to tripartite committees if the unions would call of the mobilization.[12] When SCITU rejected the offer, Rao's administration turned to labor repression; in order to limit SCITU-led mobilizations the government banned demonstrations, broke up protests with tear gas, and preventively arrested tens of thousands of union members on the eve of general strikes.

Third, did labor union opposition slow trade liberalization in India? Despite the shocking nature of Rao's preventive arrests, Indian labor unions still managed to launch protests and general strikes that mobilized tens of millions of workers. As Kohli explains, India's long history of democracy and powerful labor unions limited the extent of labor repression and meant that "mercifully, labor could never be fully tamed."[13] Rao's trade policy reforms therefore "had to slow down due to trade unions' unity and resistance–[which] resulted in the government's adoption of the middle path."[14] India's labor union leaders and government officials both embraced the idea that domestic opposition led to gradual trade liberalization, and an analysis of industry-level tariffs suggests that the government was careful to maintain higher tariffs on industries with more powerful unions. Despite the labor repression discussed throughout this chapter, India's labor unions contributed to Rao's trade policy reforms being implemented more gradually than they otherwise may have been. If India's democratic government had maintained greater respect for labor rights, unions may have slowed Rao's trade liberalization even further. With less labor repression, general strikes and protests would likely have been larger, signaling broader public opposition and putting even greater pressure on India's government to maintain higher tariffs.

9 "Squeeze on Labour Already on," *The Hindu*, June 21, 1992.

10 Jenkins 1999; Candland 2007; Teitelbaum 2011.

11 Author's calculation based on data from Shenoy 2006, 75. Data published in the *Financial Express* on June 6, 1992 (reproduced in Aswathappa 2005, 539) suggests that INTUC represented only 21 percent of Indian union members.

12 Mathur 1993. 13 Kohli 2012, 106. 14 Masilamani 1995, 20–21.

THE THREAT OF UNION OPPOSITION

Narasimha Rao was elected prime minister in 1991 amidst worsening economic conditions. The collapse of the Soviet Union led to the loss of India's main export market, the Gulf War dramatically increased the cost of imported oil, and India found itself in a balance of payments crisis. Pro-market reform in China, domestic demands for higher economic growth rates, a loan from the IMF, and growing pressure from the United States all pushed India toward trade liberalization and the opening of its economy.[15] In response, Rao proposed his New Economic Policy (NEP), a broad reform agenda that included devaluation of the rupee, dismantling of the industrial licensing regime, privatization of the public sector, opening of capital markets, labor law reforms that would ease the firing of workers, and trade liberalization.[16]

Rao's government frequently claimed that there was a broad societal consensus in favor of its economic proposals; Finance Minister Manmohan Singh, for example, declared that there was "a great convergence of opinion about the Government's reform programme."[17] But India's labor unions were deeply critical of Rao's NEP, as well as his decision to announce the reforms before consulting with union leaders.[18] India's labor unions represented 20 million public sector workers, many of whom were employed in the import-competing manufacturing industries that were most threatened by trade liberalization.[19] As the *Times of India* reported, "all major trade union leaders anticipate a period of labour unrest precipitated by the new economic moves."[20] Similarly, contemporary journalists warned that "organized industrial workers [are] the only force that can thwart the government's dreams of an industrial revolution."[21]

In India, the labor movement has long been divided between several labor union confederations, most of which are affiliated with specific political parties.[22] India's first labor union, the All India Trade Union Congress (AITUC), led the country's fight for independence and still maintains a close affiliation with the Communist Party of India. After gaining independece in 1947, India's main political party, the Indian National Congress, launched its own labor union confederation, the Indian National Trade Union Congress (INTUC). Such partisan cleavages within the labor movement proliferated, with the formation of labor union confederations affiliated with the Communist Party of India – Marxist (CITU), the Hindu-nationalism Bharatiya Janata Party (BMS), and the independent Hind Mazdoor Sabha (HMS).[23] Although partisan differences within India's labor movement often limited cooperation, union confederations affiliated with various left and center parties quickly came together to oppose Rao's economic reforms.

[15] Jenkins 1999; Candland 2007; Teitelbaum 2011; Kohli 2012; Mukherjee 2016. [16] Sinha 2016.
[17] Swamy and Singh 1994, 3. [18] Ibid. [19] Uba 2005; Ghosh 2006.
[20] "Discontent for the Working Class," *Times of India*, July 22, 1991.
[21] "India: Heads For Labor Trouble," *Inter Press Service*, August 2, 1991.
[22] Teitelbaum 2011. [23] Noronha et al. 2011, 167.

Within two months of the announcement of the NEP, CITU joined with five other union confederations to form the Sponsoring Committee of Indian Trade Unions (SCITU), a new organization tasked with coordinating union opposition. Together, this new coalition of labor unions opposed to Rao's reforms represented roughly 55 percent of all Indian labor union members. In their inaugural convention, the constituent unions announced their,

> Resolute opposition to the sweeping economic policy changes adopted by the Government of India in the interest of the Indian and foreign big business and multinationals under the pressure of the International Monetary Fund, which seriously endangers India's goal of building a self-reliant economy and exposing the country to neo-colonial exploitation. It is reprehensible that the Government did not disclose the conditionalities of the IMF to the Parliament, nor consulted the working class before announcing these policy measures.[24]

India's two largest union confederation – INTUC and BMS – refused to join SCITU due to political partisanship.[25] INTUC was affiliated with Rao's Congress Party, and as Teitelbaum argues, such partisan ties often help Indian politicians to restrain union militancy. BMS was affiliated with the rightwing, Hindu-nationalist Bharatiya Janata Party (BJP), and as Masilamani explains, the "basic differences between the Leftist trade unions and the BMS...[meant that] the BMS could not become a party to that."[26] Although INTUC and BMS remained outside of SCITU, both had clear misgivings about trade liberalization and Rao's NEP. Just six months before Rao's election, INTUC declared that lowering tariffs "went against our national interest as it would retard our efforts towards self-reliance by facilitating unfettered import of even indigenously available technology and our indigenous industrial efforts."[27] In July 1991, INTUC openly promised their full cooperation and help to other labor unions in case of any nationwide strikes.[28] In September 1991, BMS observed a "Boycott Multi-National Corporation Products Day" to demonstrate its opposition to Rao's plan to open India's economy.[29] Between the protests launched by BMS and SCITU, unions representing roughly 75 percent of Indian union members actively resisted Rao's efforts to open India's economy.[30]

24 "All India T.U. Convention Against Economic Policies of the Government, 17th September 1991," *The Working Class*, September 1991.

25 INTUC, BMS, and the labor union confederations associated with SCITU did briefly collaborate to launch a joint strike against the privatization of the India Iron and Steel Company (IISCO). CITU and other unions argued that this public sector enterprise would have been more profitable if not for trade liberalization that exposed India's steel industry to cheaper imports. See, Masilamani 1995 and "The Steel Workers' Strike on 7th September," *The Working Class*, October 1993.

26 Masilamani 1995, 18.

27 Indian National Trade Union Congress 1990, 7.

28 "Acid Test for Centre: TUs Strike Plan," *Economic Times*, July 29, 1991 quoted in Masilamani 1995, 16.

29 Masilamani 1995, 18.

30 Author's calculation based on data from Shenoy 2006, 75.

Despite INTUC and BMS remaining outside of SCITU, the "unprecedented cohesion" of India's labor unions was "potentially explosive politically and exposed the vulnerability of [Rao's] minority government."[31] Just as opposition to the NEP was uniting the Indian labor movement, SCITU announced a general strike for November 29, 1991. In a jointly published appeal, all SCITU-affiliated unions "urged the workers all over the country to prepare themselves for a long drawn and intense agitation in the coming months to compel the government to change its anti-working class policies."[32] With the government concerned that INTUC might join the general strike, "the potential of a united workers' movement assumed disturbing proportions."[33]

Consultation and INTUC

Although Rao had originally announced the NEP without first consulting with union leaders, the mounting threat of labor opposition led him to change his approach. Less than two weeks before the scheduled general strike, Rao arranged a meeting between national labor union leaders and Minister of State for Labour P.A. Sangma, that was "aimed at defusing the potential escalation of conflict."[34] Rao had announced the NEP without first reviewing the reforms with union leaders, and this meeting was the first consultation between unions and the government during Rao's administration. At the meeting, labor union leaders associated with SCITU vented their frustration concerning the NEP, while Sangma promised regular dialogue and consultation from that point on.[35] In particular, Rao's government offered to establish tripartite committees through which the government, business representatives, and union leaders could review future economic reforms. Such tripartite committees were convened annually in the early years of the republic, but only one such negotiation was held throughout the entire decade of the 1980s.[36] In exchange for these future consultations, the government requested that all unions call off the general strike.

The Congress-affiliated INTUC accepted this quid pro quo and agreed not to join the strike.[37] The day after the meeting, the front page of INTUC's weekly newspaper, *Indian Worker*, announced a "call to workers *against* the Nov. 29 strike"; INTUC President Shri G. Ramanujam explained that "with the formation of the tripartite committee that has brought about a material change in the situation [there is] no reason for a strike."[38] Soon after, INTUC would boast that it was responsible for the government creating tripartite committees to discuss the NEP.[39] In India, there is a long history of union leaders restraining worker protests and strikes in order to support the broader

31 Mathur 1993, 9. 32 Masilamani 1995, 15. 33 Mathur 1993, 8. 34 Ibid.
35 Masilamani 1995. 36 Mathur 1993. 37 Mathur 1993, 8.
38 "Call to Workers Against Nov. 29 Strike," *Indian Worker*, November 18, 25 & December 2, 1991.
39 Masilamani 1995, 28.

political goals of the political parties with which they are affiliated.[40] In this way, Rao's government used non-repressive tactics – the creation of tripartite committees – to reduce opposition from INTUC, a large union that represented between 20 and 25 percent of Indian union members. The much larger coalition of unions that created SCITU, however, rejected the government's offer and left the meeting prepared to go through with their general strike later that month.

Scholars of India's economic reforms tend to overlook this continued opposition from the majority of India's labor unions. Jenkins influential work on this period argues that Rao overcame domestic opposition with a strategy of "reform by stealth," which was ultimately able to "disrupt and complicate the utility-calculating capacity of interest groups." With regards to labor union opposition, Jenkins argues that Rao's creation of tripartite committees "reduc[ed] the possibility that more strident versions of trade union resistance would spread to and overwhelm other institutions, such as legislatures and political parties."[41] While Jenkins is correct that Rao's tripartite committees helped to reduce resistance from INTUC, this strategy was insufficient to avoid "strident" resistance from the rest of India's labor movement. Although SCITU launched four general strikes during Rao's administration, one of which mobilized as many as 25 million workers, Jenkins' discussion of union opposition fails to even mention these events.[42]

General Strike of November 29, 1991

On November 29, 1991, an estimated 12 million workers participated in the general strike, "crippling industry" throughout the country. According to contemporary journalists, the general strike was the biggest industrial strike in India since 1978, with coal, steel, ship-building, and several other industries coming to "an almost complete halt."[43] Following the strike, labor unions and the Indian government began a public debate regarding the meaning of the nationwide demonstration. The General Secretary of CITU, M. K. Pandhe, declared that the mobilization was an "unprecedented and historic strike" and promised that "the trade unions would intensify their protest against the Centre's economic policies."[44] The general secretary of AITUC told reporters that the general strike was "a strike against the policies of the government. It exposes the government claims that there is a consensus...the working class has given a fitting reply, and it is only the beginning."[45]

In contrast, Minister of Labour Sangma announced that the "one-day nation-wide industrial strike led by left unions had fizzled out, with no real

40 Teitelbaum 2011, 58–60. 41 Jenkins 1999.

42 "Mixed Response to Bharat Bandh," *Hindustan Times*, September 10, 1993.

43 "Walkout Crippled Industry," *Hong Kong AFP* [FBIS], November 29, 1991; "Partial Response to Strike," *Times of India*, November 30, 1991.

44 "Partial Response to Strike," *Times of India*, November 30, 1991.

45 "Walkout Crippled Industry," *Hong Kong AFP* [FBIS], November 29, 1991.

support from the workers."[46] He went on to thank INTUC and BMS for not supporting the strike and claimed that only 15 percent of workers throughout the country joined the strike. According to contemporary journalists, however, the unions' claims were closer to the truth; for example, the *Times of India* explained that "claims and counterclaims made by the government and the striking unions have both been exaggerated to suit their viewpoints. But by and large the strike was successful, disrupting normal life partially in many places."[47] Another journalist argued that the strike's spread across heavy industries and other sectors of the economy "points to the discontent among a broad spectrum of workers. There is obviously a feeling that a disproportionately large part of the cost of structural adjustment is being demanded from the relatively less privileged in society."[48] They also noted that while consultation may have convinced INTUC to abandon the strike, such offers were not sufficient to overcome broader union opposition; "the setting up of a tripartite body to discuss issues of industrial relations...has had sub-optimal results in convincing the trade unions about the government's promise of an adjustment with a human face."[49]

Turnout for the November 1991 general strike – roughly 12 million – also set a clear benchmark by which to measure subsequent strikes. As soon as SCITU announced a second general strike for June 1992, unions and the government began publicly debating whether the upcoming strike would be bigger or smaller than the last. CITU General Secretary Pandhe, for example, predicted that "many more workers are likely to join the strike this time as compared to the November 29 strike which was supported by over 12 million workers."[50] The day before the general strike, Pandhe called a news conference to announce that "over 12.5 million workers are expected to participate in the strike."[51] In contrast, Sangma told journalists that the upcoming strike would surely have lower turnout than the previous strike, citing a decrease in the number of labor unions that have given strike notice.[52] In other words, union and government leaders disagreed about how big the second general strike would be, but agreed that relative turnout could be used to gauge whether union opposition was gaining or losing momentum.

What might growing labor union opposition mean for the future of Rao's economic reforms? Rao and his Congress Party, of course, were well aware that Prime Minister Rajiv Gandhi had proposed similar reforms in the mid-1980s, only to backdown in the face of mounting opposition from protectionist businesses and labor unions. Back then, unions launched two general strikes before the government started to make major concessions; a month after the

46 "Partial Response to Strike," *Times of India*, November 30, 1991.
47 Ibid. 48 "Striking a Warning," *Times of India*, November 30, 1991.
49 Ibid. 50 "1000s Held Over Strike Call," *Times of India*, June 14, 1992.
51 "Unions Gear Up to Take on Govt.," *Times of India*, June 16, 1992.
52 "Sangma Plea to Boycott Stir," *Hindustan Times*, June 15, 1992.

second strike in 1987, the Gandhi government announced that it would reverse course and increase the tariffs that it had previously cut.[53] With this recent past in mind, the *Times of India* warned Rao that "in the past, no government was willing to take on organized labor...the time for fiction is now over" and adviced that the "necessary first step" would be "hitting the most obdurate unions on the head."[54] Although the fall of the Soviet Union, a balance of payments crisis, and other changes since the 1980s meant that unions were unlikely to completely block Rao's reforms, contemporary observers clearly believed that union opposition remained an important obstacle.

RAO'S REPRESSION OF SCITU

With the majority of India's labor movement actively mobilizing against the NEP, Rao's government began to use labor repression to weaken union opposition. This section describes how the Indian government violated labor rights to decrease the impact of three different mobilizations between the first general strike in November 1991 and India's joining the WTO at the end of 1994.

Before the second general strike in June 1992, the government threatened to fire strikers and "preventively arrested" tens of thousands of union members in order to reduce turnout. In the lead up to the third general strike in September 1993, the government again used preventive arrests to weaken the ability of unions to mobilize workers. When unions planned a march on Parliament in April 1994, the government banned the demonstration and used police brutality to suppress the mobilization. In these ways, Rao's government used labor repression to weaken labor union opposition to trade liberalization and other economic reforms during the 1990s in ways that Rajiv Gandhi did not during the 1980s.

General Strike of June 1992

With the June 1992 general strike fast approaching, the Indian government set out to ensure that it would be smaller than the strike of November 1991. Some government efforts were benign, like when Rao's cabinet members publicly called on workers not to join the general strike. Minister of Labour Sangma announced that labor unions had no alternative economic strategy, that the government was already consulting with union leaders, and that the "working classes have no reason to doubt our sincerity."[55] Minister of Finance

53 India 1987, 15.

54 "Curb Trade Union Excess," *Times of India*, June 12, 1991. The author went on to acknowledge that "this cannot be done just by sending the police to quell demonstrations...it requires a sustained political campaign to educate people on how the country will benefit in a dozen important ways from the reforms."

55 "Sangma Plea to Boycott Stir," *Hindustan Times*, June 15, 1992.

Manmohan Singh warned that workers should not be misled by "Marxist propaganda" and that the government's "new policy initiatives did not depart from the basic objectives of India's policy laid by Jawaharlal Nehru," the father of India's planned economy and state-led industrialization.[56] Similarly, Minister for Industry P. J. Kurien announced that "the new economic policy would not harm the interests of workers" and that "the Prime Minister was committed to protecting their interests."[57]

But Minister of Labour Sangma also went much further, threatening that workers joining the general strike could be punished by losing their jobs. With many of India's government-owned public sector enterprises facing financial difficulties, Sangma promised that public sector workers willing to break the strike would be rewarded with enhanced job security, as those public sector units would "certainly receive priority attention in revival schemes underway – we will reward those who work on that day."[58] Despite Sangma's efforts to dampen the threat, contemporary observers clearly recognized the unprecedented nature of what was happening; according to V. Krishna Ananth, a journalist focused on Indian labor politics, the government "held out a veiled threat that those units that go on strike might be penalised. Government funds for rehabilitation as well as retraining and redeployment of labour was linked up with the strike. In fact it was for *the first time* that such a threat had come on the eve of an industrial strike."[59] CITU General Secretary Pandhe lamented that the "Government was resorting to all means to sabotage the strike. Not only had it offered preferential treatment to workers not joining the strike but had also made it clear that the striking workers would be "punished."[60] A SCITU leader asserted that such threats were "a direct attack on the workers' right to strike."[61]

The government, however, was not content to rely on the power of persuasion and veiled threats; by the morning of the June 16, 1992 general strike, as many as 25,000 union members had already been arrested and jailed.[62] The government made these "preventive arrests" in order to decrease mass picketing, a popular union tactic used to shut down train and bus networks during general strikes.[63] If union members are detained in jail, they cannot picket, and if they cannot picket, then strike breakers (what Indian labour unions call "blacklegs") can more easily maintain normal economic activities. India's Constitution explicitly empowers Parliament to enact laws that grant the government the power to preventively arrest and detain people for a broad

56 "Manmohan Criticises Strike Call," *Hindustan Times*, June 15, 1992.
57 "TUs to Go Ahead with Nationwide Agitation Today," *Hindustan Times*, June 16, 1992.
58 "Sangma Plea to Boycott Stir," *Hindustan Times*, June 15, 1992.
59 "Industrial Unrest Simmering," *The Hindu*, June 21, 1992, italics added for emphasis.
60 "TUs to Go Ahead with Nationwide Agitation Today," *Hindustan Times*, June 16, 1992.
61 "Strike: T.U.s War Against Centre," *Statesman*, June 14, 1992.
62 "Magnificent Response to General Strike on 16 June," *The Working Class*, July 1992.
63 In India, these picketing tactics are known as *rail roko* and *rasta roko*, respectively.

set of activities connected with "the security of a State, maintenance of public order, or maintenance of supplies and services essential to the community."[64] In 1980, India enacted the National Security Act, which established "special powers" to allow for the detention of persons without trial on the suspicion that the detainee posed a threat to "public order."

Similarly, India's Criminal Procedure Code, established in 1973, granted police officers wide discretion; as one scholar of India's police explains, "it is not imperative that arrests should be made only on the commission of an offense. Police have been given authority to arrest even to *prevent* the occurrence of an offense."[65] As one journalist explains, "detainees in such sweeps are often placed in India's overcrowded prisons or kept guarded at police stations or even at large stadiums. Since most of those arrested are held under preventive detention laws, they are usually released the day after the protest without being charged."[66] Although India is the world's largest democracy and has a reputation for pro-labor legislation and strong unions, the government has legal standing to arrest and detain workers that *may* go on strike in the near future. And while the legal authority to make preventive arrests preceded Rao's administration, it is important to clarify that Rajiv Gandhi's administration did not preventively arrest union members before the general strikes launched against his reforms in 1986 and 1987.[67]

Although we do not know exactly how Rao's government decided which union members to preventively arrests, the archival record suggests a clear strategy. First, the government was most concerned with reducing picketing in the public transportation sector, as a general strike that would shut down city buses and trains would quickly multiply the number of people staying away from work and, for all intents and purposes, joining the strike. Transportation services in India were therefore widely seen as "the barometer to gauge the success or failure of a bandh or strike call."[68]

Second, India's federal system granted the power of preventive arrest to each state's Chief Minister (the equivalent of US governors), rather than to the central government. This meant that preventive arrests were not made, for example, in West Bengal, where Chief Minister Jyoti Basu was a member of the Communist Party of India and vocally supported the SCITU-led general strike.

64 Jinks 2000, 323. It was this constitutional provision that infamously permitted Indira Gandhi to declare the Emergency that suspended democratic rights in India from 1975 to 1977.

65 Verma 1997, 68.

66 "Anti-Gandhi Strike Grips Much of India," *New York Times*, March 16, 1988.

67 Gandhi's administration did oversee preventive arrests before a 1988 general strike, which was launched to demand the Prime Minister's resignation amidst the infamous "Bofors scandal" and growing controversy over political repression in Punjab. The important contrast between Gandhi and Rao, however, is that Gandhi did not use preventive arrests to weaken general strikes launched against his economic reforms, while Rao did. See Kohli 2012, 53; "Opposition Rallying to Resist Bill on Punjab," *The Hindu*, March 14, 1988.

68 "Partial Response in Capital," *Hindustan Times*, June 17, 1992. Bandh is a Hindi term for a general strike, while bharat bandh refers to a nationwide general strike.

As a result, preventive arrests leading up to the 1992 general strike, as well as the 1993 general strike discussed below, were only made in states with Chief Ministers that were members of Rao's Congress or affiliated parties.[69]

Third, the government's preventive arrests were concentrated in two states – Kerala and Tamil Nadu – that had large concentrations of the SCITU unions that were planning the general strike. 88 and 51 percent of all union members in Kerala and Tamil Nadu, respectively, were associated with SCITU. The only other state with a similar concentration of SCITU union members was West Bengal (72 percent), but the states's Chief Minister from the Communist Party would never have agreed to coordinate preventive arrests with Rao's Congress Party government.[70] In short, India's government arrested (1) transportation workers in states where (2) local political leaders were willing to collaborate with Rao's central government, and (3) the general strike was likely to be most successful.

Keeping the Busses Running in Tamil Nadu

These dynamics were on clear display in Madras City, Tamil Nadu, where the state's Chief Minister and police made preventive arrests in order to "leave nothing to chance." According to *The Hindu*, the "main thrust of the police would be on the smooth operation of PTC [public transportation] services."[71] The police and state government assured smooth operation by preventively arresting 8,000 road transportation workers who may otherwise have picketed bus terminals during the day of the general strike.[72] In addition to these arrests, the government offered a bonus of 200 rupees to all transportation workers willing to break the strike. In order to further guard against labor union picketing, "armed reserve and local police personnel would be posted in front of all [bus] depots." Police were stationed at central bus terminals in the early morning to ensure that the "lift service" that brought bus drivers to their routes would not be disrupted by picketing. The Inspector General of Police announced that "there was no need to panic...[because] prohibitory orders banning procession and rallies were in force all over the state."[73]

The union members arrested in the days before the general strike were detained in overcrowded jails until after the strike passed.[74] Salem Central

69 "1000s Held Over Strike Call," *Times of India*, June 14, 1992; "Centre Gears Up for Bandh," *Hindustan Times*, September 9, 1993; "Mixed Response to Bharat Bandh," *Hindustan Times*, September 10, 1993; "Bharat Bandh on 9th September," *The Working Class*, October 1993.

70 Authors calculation based on union state-level union membership in states with more than 400,000 registered union members in 1989 from P.D. Shenoy, *Globalization: Its Impact on Industrial Relations in India*, 2006.

71 "Police Leave Nothing to Chance," *The Hindu*, June 16, 1992.

72 "Unprecedented Repression in TN: Union Leaders," *Indian Express*, June 17, 1992.

73 "Normal Rail, Bus Services Today," *Indian Express*, June 16, 1992.

74 *The Working Class* (July 6, 1992) reports that DSP along with AIDMK MLA entered the CPI(M) office and arrested all the activists present.

Jail, which could only accommodate a total of 2,000 prisoners, held an additional 4,000 political prisoners on June 16. According to a local newspaper, *The Hindu*, "there was commotion in the jail since morning because of the crowd and the inability of the authorities to serve food on time."[75] The political prisoners protested against the delay into the evening, when "darkness enveloped the jail" following a power outage. Authorities alleged that the prisoners then attacked the jail guards, who responded with a lathicharge that injured 10 political prisoners.[76] Elsewhere in Tamil Nadu, in the regional city of Tirpur, a union member arrested in connection with the strike died in police lock-up.[77] The bulk of the political prisoners in Tamil Nadu were held until June 20 – four days after the general strike ended – when Chief Minister Jayalalitha finally "directed the Director General of Police to release all those taken into custody in connection with the recent agitations."[78]

On the day of the strike, an additional 1,400 union workers were arrested in Madras, "in front of the transport corporation depots after they attempted to obstruct loyal workers from reporting for duty."[79] The government's actions drew immediate condemnation from labor union leaders, as well as the press. According to the President of the DK, a political party in Tamil Nadu, "the State Government was adopting anti-democratic and repressive measures to prevent Opposition parties from going ahead with the proposed all-India bandh on June 16."[80] The CPI(M) demanded the immediate release of the prisoners and decried that the "basic democratic right" to protest "had been denied with the preventive custody of volunteers belonging to different parties and trade union members."[81] The day after the strike, the leaders of the main labor unions that organized the strike gave a press briefing in which they denounced "the unprecedented repression by the state government."[82] An editorial in the *Times of India* decried the Central government's "confrontationist attitude," as well as the "conduct of some state governments, e.g., Tamil Nadu and Kerala, which vindictively arrested close to 20,000 workers before June 16, although the strike was legal and preceded by adequate notice."[83]

The government's efforts – the preventive arrest of SCITU-affiliated bus drivers and bonuses for striker breakers – successfully kept the buses running during the general strike of June 16. According to the Madras Transportation Corporation, of the city's 2,210 buses, all but ten operated the day of the

75 "Lathicharge in Jail," *The Hindu*, June 15, 1992.

76 "Lathicharge" is a common tactic used by the Indian police to disperse crowds, and includes charging demonstrators with "lathi" or long wooden sticks.

77 "Strike Hits Banks, Airlines," *Times of India*, June 17, 1992.

78 "CM Orders Release of Agitators," *The Hindu*, June 21, 1992.

79 "Normal Life Unaffected, Claims Govt.," *The Hindu*, June 17, 1992.

80 "10,000 Taken into Preventive Custody," *The Hindu*, June 15, 1992.

81 Ibid.

82 "Unprecedented Repression in TN: Union Leaders," *Indian Express*, June 17, 1992.

83 "After the Strike," *Times of India*, June 18, 1992.

strike.[84] *The Hindu* reported that the "strike evoked poor response" in part because "elaborate security arrangements were made to ensure that normal life was not affected."[85]

Debating the June 1992 General Strike

In the days after the general strike, leaders from the Indian government, as well as India's labor unions, attempted to claim victory. India's Minister of State for Labor, P. A. Sangma, quickly proclaimed that "today's strike was meant to protest against the new economic policy of the Government and thus its failure meant that the people supported the Government policy."[86] In direct contrast, SCITU claimed that "the overwhelming response to their call for a countrywide strike by the industrial workers was a clear proof of their rejection of the government's new economic policy and restructuring."[87] Addressing a press conference in Madras City, labor unions leaders claimed that "the impact of the strike was more than the previous strike observed on November 29 last year and this showed that the workers were concerned over the liberalisation policies of the Centre."[88] Similarly, Pandhe announced that,

> Notwithstanding false propaganda by the official media and statements made by the Union Labour Minister P. A. Sangma, the working class all over the country responded magnificently to the call of general strike given by the Sponsoring Committee of Indian Trade Unions. The sweep of the strike was much wider than the last general strike.[89]

Many of India's newspapers, even those originally critical of the general strike call, sided with the unions' assessment of growing working class turnout. An editorial in the *The Times of India* explained that "whatever the truth in the claims and counter-claims about success of the June 16 strike, it should be plain that participation in the action far exceeded the relatively limited strength of the Left and the National Front-led trade unions that had organised it...It shows that large numbers of ordinary people are uncomfortable." The editors went on to explain that the strike demonstrated broad labor union opposition to the NEP, even though the INTUC and BMS did not officially endorse the strike; "Remarkably, there was virtually no opposition to the industrial action from the Congress and BJP-led unions ... On the contrary, there was sympathy, rooted in shared misgivings about the new economic policies." An editorial in *The Hindustan Times* faulted the government for insisting that its economic reforms would not harm Indian workers; "the truth, however, is that in some cases, workers may have to suffer and the Government's attempt should be to make their suffering bearable for them."[90]

84 "Normal Life Unaffected, Claims Govt.," *The Hindu*, June 17, 1992. 85 Ibid.

86 "Industrial Strike Near-Total," *Hindustan Times*, June 17, 1992.

87 "Overwhelming Response, Say Left Unions," *Indian Express*, June 17, 1992.

88 "Normal Life Unaffected, Claims Govt.," *The Hindu*, June 17, 1992.

89 "Magnificent Response to General Strike on 16 June," *The Working Class*, July 1992.

90 "The Strike and After," *Hindustan Times*, June 17, 1992.

Questions also arose concerning the central government's role in the preventive arrests and labor repression throughout the country. When Sangma was asked about these arrests – "25,000 in Tamil Nadu, 1,000 in Kerala, and several hundred in some other states" – he said that he was unable to confirm reports of large-scale arrests of industrial workers, as he lacked full details in the matter. Regardless, Sangma insisted that "the Central government could not be blamed for what the state government of Tamil Nadu or others had done with strikers. The maintenance of law and order was a state subject."[91] For their part, labor union leaders asserted that "despite repressive measures the strike was near total in many industries."[92]

Just as the Indian government limited preventive arrests before the second general strike of June 1992 to a small number of states, it also permitted some union mobilizations to proceed without intervention. On November 25, 1992, for example, the SCITU held a rally in New Delhi that the Central government and Delhi police chose not to repress. The "Workers March to Parliament" attracted a million union members from around the country. According to the CITU's, *The Working Class*, "the workers came from Jammu & Kashmir, Himachal Pradesh, from Andaman Nicobar, from Goa and from Tripura representing the four extremes points in the country."[93] The workers marched from New Delhi's Red Fort to the Boat Club, before holding a demonstration in front of the nation's Parliament, the *Sansad Bhavan*.

During the rally, Pandhe warned that public sector workers were preparing an industrial strike to "safeguard the self-reliance economy" from external pressure from the "U.S. imperialists." He lamented that the U.S. was utilizing the IMF, World Bank, and GATT to "blackmail third world countries" to open their economies. The rally culminated in a main declaration that "analysed the economic and industrial policies, pointed to their dangerous facets as prescribed by the IMF, which undermined the economic sovereignty of the country and posed a threat to its independence and freedom." The union organizers considered the march a "red letter day in the history of working class struggle in India...[which] broke all previous records of trade union gatherings" and did not report a single instance of government or police repression.[94]

General Strike of September 1993

After the second general strike of June 1992, the unions associated with SCITU branched out to a form a broad-based coalition that included organizations representing peasants, agricultural workers, students, lawyers, women, and cultural groups. Seven thousand delegates from these organizations met in

91 "Industrial Strike Near-Total," *Hindustan Times*, June 17, 1992.

92 "Normal Life Unaffected, Claims Govt.," *Hindustan Times*, June 17, 1992.

93 "Forward to Bharat Bandh," *The Working Class*, December 1992. 94 Ibid.

New Delhi's Talkatora Stadium on April 15, 1993 and created the National Platform of Mass Organisations against the Government's Economic Policies (NPOMO).[95] The NPOMO's first Declaration expressed "grave concern over the threat posed to the self reliance of the country due to the economic policies pursued by the Narasimha Rao Government" and called on the the government to "reject the anti-national Dunkel proposal" that laid the groundwork for the formation of the World Trade Organization.[96]

The SCITU and NPOMO then jointly announced a third general strike for September 9, 1993, against the "economic and industrial policies being pursued by the Narasimha Rao Government."[97] Facing its third general strike in less than two years, Rao's government was clearly concerned that such union opposition posed an ongoing threat to their economic reforms. The day before the strike, Minister of Finance Singh lamented that SCITU general strikes were "destabilising the political system and jeopardising the economic reforms programme."[98] Speaking at the annual meeting of one of the India's main manufacturers' association – the Associated Chambers of Commerce and Industry – Singh warned that "the country is now at a critical pass and if the economic restructuring *is not allowed to go through*, India will enter the twenty-first century as the poorest Asian nation."[99]

In order to limit the scope of the general strike, Rao's Chief Minister of Home Affairs, S.B. Chavan, carefully coordinated security measures between the central and state governments. Chavan convened a cabinet-level meeting with the Ministers of Commerce, Labour, Information and Broadcasting, and Steel in order to discuss his personal efforts at "supervising the measures to meet the situation arising out of the bandh [general strike] call."[100] Chavan also personally spoke with several Chief Ministers to "review the arrangements to tackle the situation" and "sent detailed instructions to all the Chief Secretaries regarding the measures to be taken."[101] The *Hindustan Times* reported that Chavan was "keeping the Prime Minister posted on the situation" and that the Central Government "offered to send more forces on request" to different State governments.[102]

As the government "beefed up security measures to ensure that there was no serious disruption of normal life," Chavan explained that he was "keen to ensure that public transport was not affected in any way in all urban centres."[103] An article in *The Hindu* reported that "In Bombay, police personnel on bandobust duty were seen in every nook and corner."[104] According to the

95 Swamy and Singh 1994. 96 "Bharat Bandh on September 9," *The Working Class*, May 1993.
97 "To Bharat Bandh and Industrial Strike on September 9," *The Working Class*, September 1993; "Massive Countrywide Court Arrest," *The Working Class*, September 1993.
98 "Instability Will Ruin Reforms: Manmohan," *The Hindu*, September 10, 1993.
99 Ibid, italics added. 100 "Centre Gears Up for Bandh," *Hindustan Times*, September 9, 1993.
101 The Chief Secretary is a high-level political appointee chosen by each state's Chief Minister.
102 "Centre Gears Up for Bandh," *Hindustan Times*, September 9, 1993. 103 Ibid.
104 "Bandh Hits Roads, Rail Traffic," *The Hindu*, September 10, 1993.

Times of India, "security has been beefed up throughout the country to foil any attempt to disrupt normal life during the bandh."[105] The CITU, for their part, "warned the Government against any repressive measures against the bandh organisers and supporters, and said these would be unitedly resisted."[106]

The central and state governments then made a fresh round of roughly 10,000 preventive arrests.[107] There were reports of 3,000 preventive arrests in Tamil Nadu, 1,206 in Kerala, and the rest in Maharashtra, Haryana, Madhya Pradesh, and Delhi.[108] Similar to the general strike of 1992, all states that made preventive arrests were controlled by the Congress Party.[109] Workers' efforts to spread the strike were closely suppressed by police. In the industrial belt outside New Delhi, "several vanloads of burly Haryana police kept vigil" while workers adorned factory gates with red flags. Large factories in the area were reported to have "doubled their private security guards to prevent gate meetings by trade unions."[110] When workers attempted to hold such meetings, policemen cordoned off the factory gates and "were seen persuading trade union leaders to clear the area." When workers turned such meetings into small processions in nearby Ghaziabad, they were followed by mobile police vans.[111] According to the *Hindustan Times*, workers around New Delhi "made stray efforts in the morning to take out processions and force the closure of industrial units, adequate police presence thwarted their plans."[112] Senior officials from the district government explained that "all-out efforts were made to ensure the bandh was a flop."[113]

In Tamil Nadu, thousands of preventive arrests were followed up by police efforts to disrupt picketing that could still disrupt the transportation system. *The Hindu* reported that "police personnel were posted at railway stations and bus deports and terminii to ensure that there was no disruption in the operations."[114] These police removed 1,500 strikers that attempted to block traffic or squat on the roads throughout the state. With such police measures in place, the press reported that "the number of buses on road was marginally less as a section of the crew members abstained" and that the general strike "evoked a poor response in Tamil Nadu.[115]

105 "State Gears Up for Bandh," *Times of India*, September 9, 1993.

106 "Centre Gears Up for Bandh," *Hindustan Times*, September 9, 1993.

107 "Partial Response," *Times of India*, September 10, 1993.

108 "Mixed Response to Bharat Bandh," *Hindustan Times*, September 10, 1993; "Bharat Bandh on 9th September," *The Working Class*, October 1993.

109 Tamil Nadu was ruled by the ADMK, which was aligned with the Congress. Madhya Pradesh was under "President's rule," which meant Rao's Central Government directly ruled the State. The Delhi police were controlled by the Central Government's Chief Minister of Home Affairs. Kerala, Maharashtra, and Haryana all had Chief Ministers from the Congress Party.

110 "Bandh Impact in Faridabad Partial," *Hindustan Times*, September 10, 1993.

111 "Response to Bandh Poor in Ghaziabad," *Hindustan Times*, September 10, 1993.

112 "Mixed Response to Bharat Bandh," *Hindustan Times*, September 10, 1993.

113 "Bandh Impact in Faridabad Partial," *Hindustan Times*, September 10, 1993.

114 "Poor Response in T. Nadu," *The Hindu*, September 10, 1993. 115 Ibid.

Police lathicharged workers in nearly fifty places throughout the country, injuring over 150 activists, including women and children.[116] The leadership of the CPI-M "condemned the widespread police repression against those who participated in the bandh" as well as the "deployment of police outside the CPI-M State Committee office in New Delhi.[117] In Maligaon, Assam, workers picketing in front of the Northeast Frontier Railway headquarters were attacked by police wielding batons – over a dozen were injured and four were hospitalized in critical condition.[118] Such police measures helped limit the spread of the strike, permitting a spokesperson of the Assam State Government to announce that the strike "had little impact in the State."[119]

Similar to previous general strikes, the September 1993 general strike was also followed by competition between government officials and union leaders to spin the turnout in their favor. The *Hindustan Times* reported that the strike's "sponsors claimed this evening that more than 20 millions workers took active part in today's actions. All this was in the face of repression let loose by the administration and false propaganda by the electronic media."[120] According to the CITU, "despite these repressive measures millions of people all over country magnificently responded to the call of bandh."[121] Jyoti Basu, the CPI-M Chief Minister from West Bengal, said that "the Narasimha Rao Government should take a lesson from the people's overwhelming protest against the new economic and industrial policies."[122]

In contrast, a spokesman for the Congress Party denounced the strike as "a total flop" and announced that "we congratulate the working class for not responding to the politically motivated bandh."[123] Other Congress officials declared that the Bharat bandh was a failure, and that "the lukewarm response to the bandh call given by trade unions and left parties in protest against the Government's economic policies...showed that the people were in favour of the policies of Prime Minister P.V. Narasimha Rao."[124]

March to Parliament, April 1994

Following the general strike, labor unions and other organizations affiliated with the NPOMO planned a march to Parliament in New Delhi on April 5th, 1994, where they demanded that the Indian government not sign the Dunkel Draft that would form the WTO. When the day came for the NPOMO march to Parliament, it was heavily repressed by the central government and the

116 "Bharat Bandh on 9th September," *The Working Class*, October 1993.
117 "Bandh a Success: CPM, CPI," *Hindustan Times*, September 10, 1993.
118 "Many Leaders Held in Assam," *The Hindu*, September 10, 1993.
119 Ibid. Assam was also ruled by a Chief Minister from the Congress Party.
120 "Mixed Response to Bharat Bandh," *Hindustan Times*, September 10, 1993.
121 "Bharat Bandh on 9th September," *The Working Class*, October 1993.
122 "Congress (I) Terms Bandh a 'Flop,'" *The Hindu*, September 10, 1993. 123 Ibid.
124 "Endorsement of Policies: Cong," *Hindustan Times*, September 10, 1993.

Delhi police. While some details differ between the accounts of labor unions, the NPOMO, government officials, and various newspapers, the basic contours of the day are clear: roughly 150,000 demonstrators were banned from protesting in front of the Parliament and were dispersed with police brutality that included rubber bullets, water canons, steel barricades, barbed wire, mounted police on horseback, and an "unprecedented number of teargas shells." According to the CITU, "All over the world the people do have the right to demonstrate before the Parliament. In India, the Boat Club, the traditional place for demonstrations before Parliament, where the 25th November '92 one-million rally was also held, was banned for entry by the Fund-Bank imposed 'democracy.'"[125]

With the demonstration banned by the government and New Delhi's Boat Club sealed off with 8-foot high steel barricades, barbed wire, and the help of an additional twenty-two companies of police, the NPOMO demonstrators searched for a new location to assemble. The other traditional place for demonstrations in New Delhi – the Red Fort, where India's independence was declared in 1947 – was booked by Hindu nationalists that refused to coordinate their opposition with the NPOMO.[126] With these two popular protest locations unavailable, as many as 200,000 demonstrators filled the busy, two kilometer Ring Road from the Red Fort to Raj Ghat, a large park and memorial to Mahatma Gandhi.

The organizers of the march denounced the Delhi police for their "gross denial of democratic rights by using excessive force and denying permission for the protest march."[127] The NPOMO demonstrators decided on "asserting the right to march to Parliament," and according to the CITU's *The Working Class*, "marched on to break the impregnable cordon" erected by the Delhi police. Accounts differ of the ensuing violence, with blame variously attributed to the police and the protestors. According to India's *The Telegraph*, "the peaceful grounds of Raj Ghat turned into a battle arena with the police lobbying teargas shells for over two hours to disperse the protestors." The *Times of India* told of how "mounted police rode through the lawns of the Vir Bhumi and Shakti Sthal [memorials to Rajiv and Indira Gandhi] to strike at the demonstrators." *The Pioneer* claimed that "the anger of the common man against the Dunkel proposals was at full display at Raj Ghat."

Although the police chief of Delhi "clarified that the softer option was exercised and firing not resorted to," he also acknowledged that the nearly 1,000 teargas canisters used to disperse the crowds was "the maximum since 1971."[128] In explaining his methods to *Reuters*, the police chief blithely

125 "April 5 Marks the Start of Militant Battle," *The Working Class*, May 1994.

126 "Endorsement of Policies: Cong," *Hindustan Times*, September 10, 1993; "April 5 Marks the Start of Militant Battle," *The Working Class*, May 1994.

127 "100 Hurt as Protestors, Police Clash in Delhi," *The Hindu*, April 6, 1994. The following quotes from *Telegraph*, *Times of India*, and *The Pioneer* are available in the May 1994 issue of *The Working Class*.

128 "April 5 Marks the Start of Militant Battle," *The Working Class*, May 1994; "Leftists' Rally," *Hindustan Times*, April 6, 1994.

commented that "we have used tear gas canisters and a little bit of caning."[129] According to *The Telegraph*, this "little bit of caning" looked more like "the police resorting to massive lathicharge and teargassing to disperse the two-lakh [200,000] protestors."

The CITU claimed that it "was the most brutal onslaught by the police since independence on the democratic aspirations of the people...it was as if a pre-planned war exercise by the Government on its own people."[130] Looking back on the day's events, one Member of Parliament, S.R. Pillai, concluded that "this is the cruelest attack on the people during the last 20 years...the Government is mounting an attack on the people to suppress their views on the new economic policy and the Government's drive to sign the GATT treaty."[131] Pillai's comparison of police brutality in 1994 to state repression during the Emergency of the mid-1970s was particularly powerful, given that he was arrested and jailed for a year during that period.[132] The night after the protest, two left-wing political parties issued a statement that "condemned the brutal lathicharge on peaceful demonstrators," and claimed that "the incident confirmed the government's economic sellout with growing authoritarianism."[133] Reflecting on the Indian government's efforts to pass the NEP over labor opposition, the CITU reflected that,

> As a part of the new economic policy formulated and pursued by the government at the behest of World Bank and IMF, the working class and the common masses are sought to be totally disarmed of their trade union and democratic rights so as to contain the increasing mass protest movements against the policy and its disastrous fall out.[134]

The government's repression of the march attracted international attention and led journalists to note widespread opposition to trade liberalization and India's joining the WTO. The *Washington Post* reported that "police blasted protestors with water cannon, charged them with bamboo canes and batons and fired more than 740 rounds of tear gas to prevent them from marching across town to the parliament building."[135] The *Los Angeles Times* wrote that "the clashes were yet more evidence that Rao's government has done a poor job of making the case for the agreement to India's rank-and-file

129 "Thousands of Indian Leftists Riot in Protest of World Trade Pact," *Los Angeles Times*, April 6, 1994.

130 "April 5 Marks the Start of Militant Battle," *The Working Class*, May 1994.

131 "Leftists Rally Against Dunkel Lathicharged," *Hindustan Times*, April 6, 1994.

132 "Nearly 24 MISA Detainees Still Active in Politics," *New Indian Express*, June 26, 2015.

133 "Anti-Dunkel Rallyists Clash with Police," *Indian Express*, April 6, 1994.

134 "Report of the General Secretary," *The Working Class*, April 1994.

135 "Demonstrators in New Delhi Demand That India Reject Trade Accord," *Washington Post*, April 7, 1994.

citizenry."[136] Similarly, a study published by India's Public Interest Research Group in 1994 – aptly titled *Against Consensus* – concluded that "the activities of opposition parties and their affiliated organisations [labor unions] in the past three years (July 91–September 94) clearly demonstrate that there is no consensus on [the] adjustment programme."[137]

In summary, India's government periodically used labor repression to contain labor union mobilizations against trade liberalization and Rao's other economic reforms. When labor unions announced their first general strike against Rao's reforms in 1991, the government permitted the strike to proceed without labor repression. But when unions announced a second general strike for June 1992, and boasted that growing turnout would demonstrate growing opposition to Rao's reforms, the government turned to labor repression. In the days before the general strike, Rao's government oversaw the preventive arrest of tens of thousands of labor union members. These preventive arrests helped to ensure that picketing did not shut down the transportation systems in Tamil Nadu and Kerala, two states in which the general strike might otherwise have been much larger. The government also threatened to fire public sector workers who joined the strike, an ultimatum that contemporary journalists decried as unprecedented on the eve of a general strike. With rising unemployment and public sectors workers worried about losing relatively well-paid jobs, such threats also helped to decrease turnout for the general strike.

Although the government then permitted unions to launch a million man march to Parliament in November 1992, it cracked down again with preventive arrests when unions launched a third general strike in September 1993. These preventive arrests occurred across five states and the capital city of Delhi, and again limited the ability of workers to picket and increase turnout for a general strike. And when unions tried to recreate their march on Parliament in 1994, Rao's government banned the demonstration and broke up the rally with tear gas and police brutality. Such labor repression not only limited the ability of workers to peacefully demonstrate that day, but also likely deterred turnout for subsequent union-led protests. While Rao's government sometimes permitted unions to mobilize against his economic reforms, it also frequently used labor repression to limit the size of these demonstrations. Most importantly, Rao's use of preventive arrests in the 1990s marked a clear increase in labor repression from the 1980s, when Gandhi respected unions' rights to launch general strikes against his economic reforms.

136 "Thousands of Indian Leftists Riot in Protest of World Trade Pact," *Los Angeles Times*, April 6, 1994.

137 Swamy and Singh 1994, 3.

INDIA'S GRADUAL TRADE LIBERALIZATION

Between 1991 and 1996, Rao's administration lowered India's average tariff from roughly 80 percent down to 37 percent. Although this trade liberalization marked the beginning of "an emphatic break from the closed, state-led strategy of economic development," Rao's time in office ended with India's economy still relatively closed.[138] As Montek Ahluwalia, a key economic advisor during the reform period, explained, "although India's tariff levels are significantly lower than in 1991, they remain among the highest in the developing world."[139] Did opposition from protectionist labor unions contribute to the slow pace of India's trade policy reforms?

Previous studies of India's economic reforms frequently conclude that labor union opposition helped to slow the implementation of Rao's NEP. For example, Masilamani writes that "it has become clear that the government does not want to face the opposition of unions. Hence, the reform measures have slowed down. The unions' resistance, such as all-India strikes and bandhs, have, thus, slowed down the reform processes."[140] Similarly, Candland notes that "according to World Bank officials, organized labor remains the greatest obstacle to the full implementation of India's IMF structural adjustment program."[141] India's labor unions also believed that labor union opposition had slowed down Rao's reforms, even if they were ultimately disappointed with the end result: "Although the massive countrywide protest action since the last three years have slowed down the economic reforms, the Government has refused to reverse the reforms and is going ahead with the anti-national and anti-people policies by ruthlessly suppressing the democratic struggles."[142]

The potential impact of labor unions on India's trade policy reforms can also be seen in the evolution of the government's rhetoric about the pace of liberalization. Finance Minister Singh first announced Rao's economic reforms during the July 1991 budget speech, when he warned that "we do not have time to postpone adjustment and stabilisation. We must act fast and act boldly."[143] When over 12 million workers joined a general strike against Rao's reforms in November 1991, the government quickly changed its tune. At the next budget speech, just three months later, Singh announced a new approach to trade liberalization: "the process of reform should be gradual, so as to moderate the impact of the adjustment ... and the pace at which domestic industry is exposed to competition."[144]

138 Banga and Das 2010; Teitelbaum 2011, 30; Sinha 2016.

139 Ahluwalia 2002, 74. 140 Masilamani 1995, 31. 141 Candland 2007, 108.

142 "Call of the National Convention All India General Strike and Hartal on September 29," *The Working Class*, July 1994.

143 India 1991. 144 India 1992.

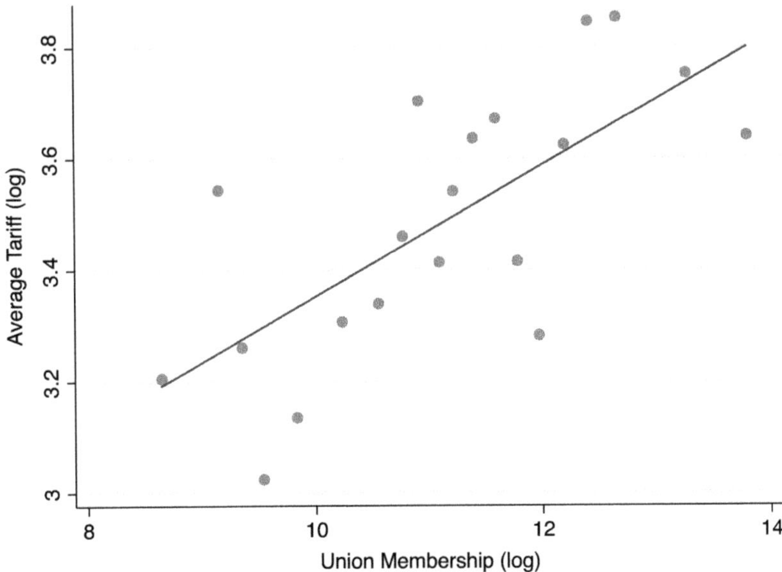

FIGURE 4.2. Indian tariffs and union membership, 1990–2007

Beyond rhetoric, Rao's government also appears to have carefully lowered tariffs more slowly in industries with more powerful unions. Since union protests and strikes inform politicians about the possible electoral consequences of implementing unpopular policies, this is precisely how we would expect union opposition to influence industry-level tariffs. At the beginning of Rao's term, India's highest tariffs protected the industries with the most labor union members; the four industries with the most union members had average tariffs of 97 percent, while the four industries with the fewest union members had average tariffs of only 51 percent.[145] By the end of Rao's time in office, tariffs had come down across the board, but they decreased more gradually on the industries with more union members. From 1990 to 1996 tariffs for industries with the fewest union members dropped by 58 percent, while tariffs for industries with the most union members decreased by only 48 percent.

Figure 4.2 shows that this positive association between industry-level union membership and tariffs held throughout India's reform process, as successive

145 Author's calculation using tariff data from the World Bank and union membership from the Indian Labour Year Book. Data is available for sixteen industries, and this calculation compares tariffs for industries in the top and bottom quartile of union membership. The analysis uses the number of labor union members as a measure of industry-year level labor power, rather than the percentage of workers that are unionized. All else being equal, lowering tariffs on an industry with a large number of protectionist union members is more politically difficult than lowering tariffs on an industry with a smaller number of union members.

governments slowly opened the economy.[146] Even when taking into account numerous industry-level covariates and other confounders, a 10 percent increase in union membership was associated with a 1 percent increase in tariffs.[147] Although labor union protests and general strikes usually denounced trade liberalization across the board, the government may have responded to such mobilizations by slowing the rate of tariff reductions in industries with the most union members.

CONCLUSION

How did Prime Minister Rao open India's economy in the early 1990s? Just a few years earlier, Prime Minister Gandhi had proposed similar trade policy reforms, but backed down in the face of domestic opposition that included two union-led general strikes. This chapter argued that part of Rao's relative success was rooted in his use of labor repression to weaken union opposition to his reforms. When India's labor unions announced a general strike against Rao's reforms in 1991, the government first attempted to overcome union opposition through conciliation; Rao offered to created tripartite committees in exchange for unions calling off the strike. When the majority of India's labor movement rejected Rao's offer and announced a second strike, the government turned to more repressive measures. As described above, the Indian government used the little-known power of "preventive arrest" to detain union members before and during general strikes in June 1992 and September 1993. The government arrested tens of thousands of workers in an effort to reduce picketing that could disrupt transportation networks and further spread the strike. The preventive arrests before the June 1992 strike came at a potential critical juncture when government and union officials were engaged in a public debate about whether

[146] In this binned scatter plot, observations are grouped into bins based on similar values of union membership and the mean tariff value within each bin is calculated and plotted. Annual tariff data for sixteen industries is available from the World Bank's World Integrated Trade Solution. Data on labor union membership for these industries is available from the Indian Labour Year Book, which is produced annually by India's Ministry of Labour and Employment. Since less than 25 percent of registered Indian labor unions provide membership information in any given year, this data represents a low estimate of union membership. In order to address considerable variation from year-to-year within each industry, the analysis uses a three-year running average of union membership.

[147] This finding is based on ordinary least squares regression with panel corrected standard errors. Using data from the *Economic and Political Weekly* Research Foundation India Time Series, the model controls for industry-year-level employment, fixed capital, and profitability, includes a time trend to address the decline in tariffs over time, and uses an AR(1) correction to address concerns about serial correlation in tariff levels. For additional information, see the Appendix.

union opposition to Rao's NEP was increasing or decreasing. In the absence of preventive arrests, turnout for these general strikes would likely have been larger, creating additional pressure for the government to slow its trade policy reforms.

How are we to evaluate such counterfactual claims about the history of free trade? It is inherently difficult, perhaps even impossible, to say what would have happened to Rao's trade policy reforms if not for the preventive arrests and police brutality that weakened union opposition from 1992 through 1994. In some sense, the government's own actions provide compelling evidence in favor of my argument: Rao almost certainly used labor repression because he believed that union opposition would otherwise reduce his ability to implement trade liberalization and the rest of the NEP. Yet one of the tragedies of history is that the successful use of repression makes it difficult to establish that such violence played an important role in determining specific policy outcomes.

Another approach is to consider India's trade policy reforms in the broader global context of the late twentieth century. In Chapter 1, I developed a theory that explained why democratic developing countries during this period were more likely to lower their tariffs when respect for labor rights was low. With that framework in mind, India's trade policy reforms clearly fit my theory's second path toward free trade: increased labor repression by an established democratic government. In the 1980s, Gandhi's democratic government respected labor rights and union-led general strikes helped to block his attempts to lower India's tariffs; in the 1990s, Rao's democratic government used preventive arrests – an increase in labor repression – to limit general strikes launched against his reforms. In Chapter 2, I examined tariff levels across more than 100 developing countries and found that a democracy increasing labor repression was generally associated with decreases in tariffs. Rao's increase in labor repression while opening India's economy therefore clearly fits a general dynamic followed by many democratic developing countries.

In Chapter 3, I presented a series of case studies that illustrated how democracies used high levels of labor repression – such as Bolivia's "state of siege" – to squash union opposition and quickly open their economies. While Rao's preventive arrests in the 1990s represented a marked increase in labor repression compared to Gandhi's respect for labor rights in the 1980s, such labor repression was relatively mild compared to Bolivia. As expected, Rao's 'moderate' labor repression was associated with more trade liberalization than Gandhi managed to implement, while still being relatively gradual compared to Bolivia's rapid opening. In these ways, the story of Indian trade politics is part of a growing constellation of theory and evidence that collectively points to how democratic developing countries used labor repression to facilitate trade liberalization. Moreover, the Indian case demonstrates some of my book's most important theoretical and empirical contributions: the ability to deductively predict labor rights violations in cases where previous work ignores them, and then to use archival research to uncover how governments used labor repression to weaken union opposition to trade liberalization. To further test my theory, and continue demonstrating its ability to support revisionist accounts of the history of free trade, the next chapter turns to the puzzle of how Argentina overcome labor union opposition to trade liberalization in the 1990s.

5

Opening Argentina

Menem's Repression of the CGT

Argentina transitioned from military dictatorship to democracy in 1983 and elected Raúl Alfonsín as President. Alfonsín attempted to lower Argentina's tariffs and pass other neoliberal policies, but his economic reforms were blocked by a series of thirteen general strikes launched by the CGT, the labor union confederation led by Saúl Ubaldini. When Alfonsín left office in 1989, Argentina's average tariffs still stood at 25 percent, only three percentage points lower than they had been in 1982, the last year of the military regime. By 1991, however, Alfonsín's successor, President Carlos Menem, was able to lower tariffs to just 12 percent. This chapter tells the story of how Menem used labor repression to overcome union opposition and quickly open Argentina's economy. Trade politics in Argentina under Alfonsín and Menem therefore offers a within-case comparison that further illustrates my theory's second path toward free trade: increased labor repression in an established democracy.

The basic contours of the story are clearly visible in Figure 5.1, which displays Argentina's levels of democracy, labor rights, and tariffs using the quantitative measures analyzed in Chapter 2. The first panel shows that after Argentina's transition to democracy in 1983, the country's level of democracy was high and nearly constant across Alfonsín and Menem's administrations. The second panel shows that Argentina's level of respect for labor rights was high during Alfonsín's administration but then dropped sharply during Menem's administration.[1] The third panel shows that Argentina's tariffs were

[1] In Argentina, the Spanish word *represión* is commonly used to refer to acts of physical violence by the government against protestors and dissidents. For example, the museum at ESMA, a military base in Buenos Aires that was used to torture people during the junta, uses the word *represión* to describe the military's dirty war against its own citizens. While Menem did not implement this type of *represión*, his long list of labor rights violation – manipulating union elections, declaring strikes illegal, decertifying striking unions, and breaking a strike with the military – clearly fit this book's definition of labor repression, which is the violation of workers' basic rights to act collectively.

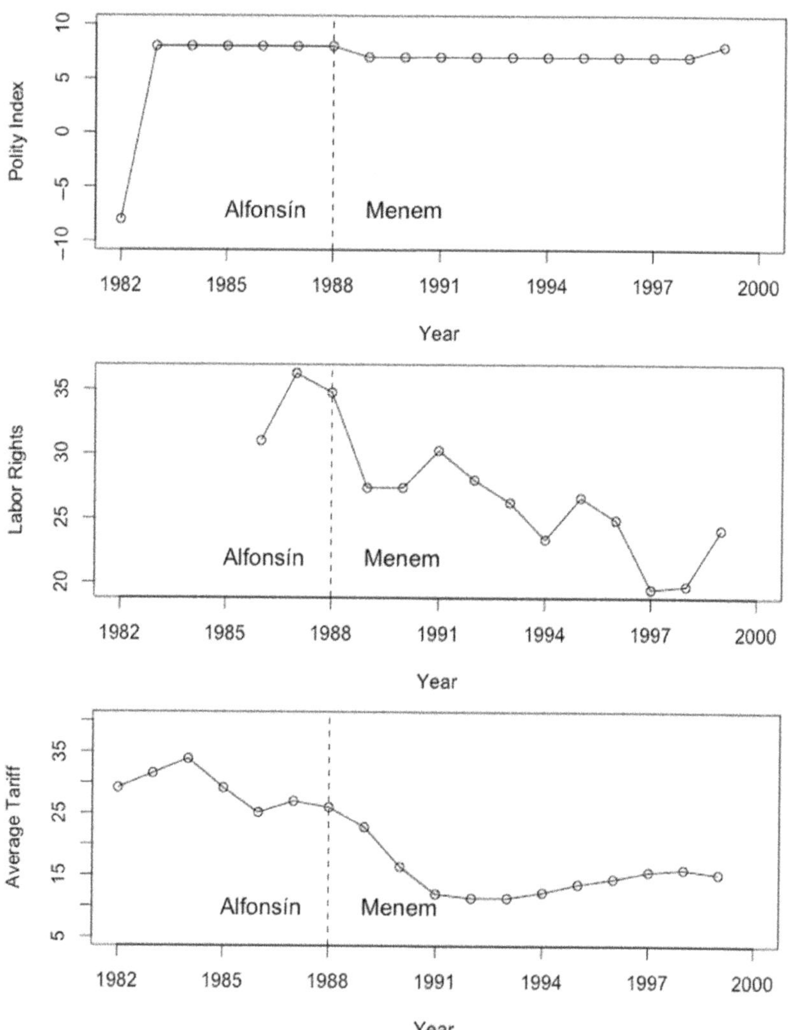

FIGURE 5.1. Democracy, labor rights, and tariffs in Argentina

relatively stable during Alfonsín's administration, but then fell quickly in the opening years of Menem's administration. As my theory predicts, Alfonsín's combination of democracy and respect for labor rights was associated with high tariffs, just as Menem's mix of democracy and labor repression was associated with trade liberalization.[2]

[2] The plot for democracy, labor rights, and tariffs are based on Polity, the *Collective Labor Rights Dataset*, and the World Bank, respectively. The plots for labor rights and average tariffs are based on a two-year rolling averages. The vertical line at 1988 divides the Alfonsín and Menem administrations, though Menem was inaugurated in July of 1989.

The decrease in this quantitative measure of labor rights is driven by specific labor rights violations including the prohibition of strikes, the decertification of striking unions, and the manipulation of union finances.[3] This chapter draws on archival research and fieldwork interviews to demonstrate that these were not isolated incidences, but rather part of a larger campaign of labor repression aimed at weakening labor union opposition to Menem's reforms.[4] Menem's labor repression is therefore an ideal illustration of the "second face" of power through which governments can change the "rules of the game" in ways that deter workers and unions from mobilizing against trade liberalization and other economic reforms.[5] As Carlos Tomada, Argentina's Minister of Labor from 2003 to 2015, explained "it was clear that the objective was to break the backbone of Argentine trade unionism; that was the objective of Martínez de Hoz [Economic Minister during the military dictatorship], and it was the same for Menem…that Menem destroyed the labor movement as if we were in a dictatorship, there can be no doubt."[6]

To discipline my analysis, I break the story of Argentine trade liberalization into two periods. In each, I explore the same two questions: did labor union opposition pose a threat to Menem's reforms, and did Menem's government use labor repression to overcome such union opposition?[7] The first period focuses on the opening four months of Menem's presidency (July–October 1989), a time during which the CGT was unified in opposition to his economic reforms, which included trade liberalization, privatization, and decreased public spending.[8] During this period, Menem was clearly concerned that CGT general strikes could block his reforms, just as they had done to Alfonsín's during the 1980s. When Menem called on the CGT to forgo strikes for two years, Ubaldini rejected the request, along with Menem's entire economic plan. Ubaldini was then re-elected as CGT secretary general.[9] In response, Menem launched a campaign of labor repression that included replacing dissident union leaders

3 The *Collective Labor Rights Dataset* is based on labor rights violations documented in the International Trade Union Congress' *Annual Survey of Violations of Trade Union Rights* and two other sources. The violations listed above are included in the 1990 Annual Survey, see International Confederation of Free Trade Unions 1990.

4 I analyzed primary documents and newspapers in several archives in Argentina and the United States, including CONICET, CEDINCI, Di Tella University, and the Library of Congress in Washington, D.C. I also draw on various Argentine newspaper articles that were collected and archived by the Foreign Broadcast Information Service, as well as major U.S. newspapers such as the *New York Times* and *Washington Post*. Although Saúl Ubaldini died in 2006, I spoke with several union leaders, rank-and-file union members, and government officials that worked closely with him, including the CGT's head labor lawyer, Ubaldini's assistant and chofer, three CGT organizers, one of Ubaldini's sons, and former Minister of Labor Carlos Tomada. The name of Ubaldini's son is also Saúl, and for the sake of clarity I refer to him as Saulito Ubaldini. I thank Rocío López Karababikian for her generous assistance with my fieldwork in Argentina.

5 Gaventa 1982; Lukes 2004. 6 Author interview with Carlos Tomada, December 19, 2019.

7 George and Bennett 2005; Goertz 2017. 8 Gerchunoff and Torre 1996.

9 "No Soy Obsecuente de Nadie, Aseguró Saúl Ubaldini," *Clarín*, July 27, 1989; Senén González 1999, 29.

and manipulating union finances. By October 1989, this labor repression helped Menem construct a coalition that included a slim majority of union leaders willing to abandon Ubaldini, support the government's economic reforms, and ultimately split the CGT into two separate confederations. The CGT–Azopardo, led by Ubaldini, continued to oppose Menem's economic reforms while the CGT–San Martin supported them.[10]

The second period of the story of Argentine trade liberalization focuses on the year after the splitting of the CGT (November 1989–November 1990). Although the CGT split weakened labor union opposition, contemporary Argentine journalists and politicians believed that the Ubaldini-led CGT–Azopardo still had the potential to block Menem's reforms.[11] In response, Menem used additional labor repression to weaken the CGT–Azopardo; the government ruled strikes by key CGT–Azopardo unions to be illegal, fired strikers and decertified unions that disobeyed, broke a "showdown strike" with military troops, and decreed a strike ban on the eve of a CGT–Azopardo general strike.[12] It was only at the end of this second period, following more than a year of labor repression, that the CGT–Azopardo finally crumbled, journalists pronounced the "decline of Ubaldini," and Menem slashed Argentina's tariffs.[13]

Throughout both periods, labor union opposition to Menem's economic reforms was concentrated in import-competing industries and the public sector. At the core of Ubaldini's coalition was Argentina's metalworkers union (UOM), which at that time was one of the largest and most powerful industry-level unions in the country.[14] The UOM knew that metal workers would lose hundreds of thousands of jobs if Menem lowered steel tariffs; as Antonio Caló, secretary general of the UOM, explained, "the market opened to the world and we cannot compete with the world, it's impossible ... the UOM was against it."[15] Many public sector unions were strongly opposed to Menem's

[10] The CGT–San Martin was named after the *Teatro San Martin*, where a meeting in October 1989 ended in the splitting of the CGT. The CGT–Azopardo was named after the street where its main office was located, *calle Azopardo*.

[11] "Alfonsín Warns of Threat to Congress," *Brazil and Southern Cone*, 19 April 1990; "CGT Muestra Las Uñas," *Página/12*, March 9, 1990.

[12] "Rally Strengthens Menem's Hand," *Latin American Weekly Report*, April 19, 1990; "Ratificaron la Continuidad del Paro Telefónico," *La Nación*, September 8, 1990; "The Right to Strike: the Decree and the Possible Bargains," *The Review of the River Plate*, November 14, 1990. pg. 294.

[13] "Ubaldini's Decline," *La Prensa* [FBIS], November 21, 1990.

[14] "The Collective Bargaining Time Bomb," *The Review of the River Plate*, April 28, 1989; "Mainly About Ubaldini," *The Review of the River Plate*, July 12, 1989.

[15] Author interview with Antonio Caló, December 26, 2019. Smaller unions from import-competing industries, such as ceramics, also joined Ubaldini's coalition. As Diego Moreyra, the secretary general of the ceramics union, recalled in an interview on December 16, 2019, "tariffs went down a lot – it was a terrible time of closing factories."

plans to privatize state-owned enterprises and decrease public spending. Unions representing government employees and public sector workers in industries such as oil, energy, banks, railroads, and telecommunications therefore also made up an important part of the coalition of unions that joined Ubaldini to oppose Menem's economic reforms.[16] In other words, unions opposed to trade liberalization joined unions opposed to privatization and decreased public spending to form a coalition of unions opposed to Menem's broad reform agenda.

This account of trade liberalization in Argentina differs from the conventional wisdom in three important ways.[17] First, scholars often argue that the CGT split because the overwhelming majority of Argentina's Peronist labor unions trusted Menem's Peronist party. Such partisan loyalty led union members to believe that Menem's proposed economic reforms must have been necessary. While such partisan ties certainly mattered, I show that Menem's labor repression also played a crucial role in splitting the CGT. Second, scholars frequently mention the CGT–Azopardo and Ubaldini only in passing as weak, unpopular, and unimportant. In contrast, I reconstruct a lost vision of Argentine politics in 1990, a year during which contemporary observers clearly viewed the CGT–Azopardo as a major obstacle to Menem's economic reforms. Third, scholars commonly see the lack of CGT–Azopardo general strikes as evidence that very few labor unions opposed Menem's reforms. Instead, I show that widespread labor union opposition to Menem's reforms did not translate into general strikes because of Menem's systematic campaign of labor repression.

In short, I present a revisionist history that explains how Menem systematically used labor repression to split the CGT and then to overcome the forgotten challenge posed by the CGT–Azopardo. Even in the face of labor rights violations, Argentine unions launched strikes that demonstrated the broad scope of public opposition, increased resistance from rival political parties, and even inspired leaders of Menem's own party to reject his reforms. If Argentina's democratic government had respected labor rights, rather than increasing labor repression, union opposition may have been powerful enough to slow or even block Menem's reforms. Although such counterfactuals are inherently difficult to evaluate, it is relatively easy to demonstrate how Menem repeatedly used labor repression to weaken union opposition and ensure that his reforms did not suffer the same fate as Alfonsín's.

16 Pozzi and Schneider 1994; "The CGT Split – And After?" *The Review of the River Plate*, October 27, 1989.

17 e.g. Ranis 1992; Levitsky and Way 1998; Murillo 2001; Levitsky 2003.

THE CGT AND MENEM: JULY–OCTOBER 1989

The Threat of the CGT

The CGT and Ubaldini played pivotal roles in Argentina's struggle for democracy against the military regime that governed the country from 1976 through 1983. In 1982, Ubaldini led one of the country's most important public protests against the military – a labor-backed rally for *"Paz, Pan, y Trabajo"* (Peace, Bread, and Work) that gathered 50,000 protestors outside the Casa Rosada.[18] After Alfonsín's election in 1983, Ubaldini became an important defender of Argentine democracy; following a failed military coup in 1987, Ubaldini joined Alfonsín and Cafiero – Argentina's main labor union leader, the President, and the leader of the main opposition party – on the balcony of the Casa Rosada to affirm that the labor movement stood behind Argentina's democratically-elected president. According to Carlos Tomada, this gesture of solidarity was "a great contribution to Argentina's democratic process;" while previous military coups had always had some support from civil society, "here they lined up–and there I think the Argentine tradition of democratic breakdown through military coups was broken."[19]

Ubaldini's popularity started with the democratization struggle in the late 1970s and early 1980s, but he rose to national fame through his leadership of thirteen general strikes against Alfonsín's economic reforms between 1983 and 1989. In Argentina, they track the *centimil*, or the number of square centimeters of newspaper stories published about a specific word or topic; from 1983 to 1986, the most popular subject was Alfonsín, and the second most popular was Ubaldini. From 1986 to 1989, the two switched places and Ubaldini became the most popular topic in the country.[20] Similarly, McGuire writes that "Ubaldini's power resided in his combative oratory and in the public's consciousness of this militant opposition to the dictatorship. The mass demonstrations and media attention that accompanied the general strikes gave Ubaldini an indispensable forum for calling on these power resources."[21] According to Tomada, the CGT general strikes made Ubaldini the most prominent Peronist leader, even more important than the leaders of the PJ, the Peronist political party; "on one side there was Alfonsín, and on the other side was Ubaldini – he fulfilled the place of the Justicialista Party. His leadership was so strong that the party had little to say and the confrontation ended up being Alfonsín with Ubaldini."[22]

Politicians and union leaders in Argentina talk about Ubaldini's charisma and popularity – especially before the battle with Menem – in nearly spiritual terms. Oraldo Britos, an Argentine senator and congressman who worked closely with union leaders throughout his twenty-five years in office, tells a

[18] "A 35 Años de la Marcha 'Paz, Pan y Trabajo,'" *Politica Del Sur*, March 30, 2017.
[19] Author interview with Carlos Tomada, December 19, 2019.
[20] Author interview with Saulito Ubaldini, whose estimate of the centimel was based on his own research that contributed to Lerena 2007.
[21] McGuire 1999, 200. [22] Author interview with Carlos Tomada, December 19, 2019.

particularly vivid story of traveling with Ubaldini. The two friends went to Britos' small hometown of Villa Mercedes – 400 miles from Buenos Aires – where workers were striking against the closure of a local meat-packing plant. On the long drive home, their car got struck in traffic behind a priest leading a procession of Catholics celebrating the day of the Virgin Mary. Ubaldini got out of the car, approached the procession, and crossed himself to pay his respects. As Ubaldini walked back to the car, Britos watched on as the faithful abandoned the priest and started a new procession behind Ubaldini. Britos concluded the story, a smile on his face many decades later, by telling me what he told Ubaldini: "You have already become a saint for all these people!"[23] Similarly, Ubaldini's driver told me that in the 1980s, "You couldn't go out into the street with Saúl. You'd go out and people would just embrace you, he was one of the most popular people in existence."[24]

Ubaldini's leadership of the CGT, constant media attention, and popularity – especially amongst Argentina's working class – made him a important ally for any Peronist running for president in 1989. Menem therefore invited Ubaldini to rallies around Argentina, where the two Peronists campaigned in favor of salary increases and a "productive revolution" based on trade protectionism, strong unions, and state involvement in the economy. The CGT endorsed Menem and published its own economic proposals that called for a continuation of import-substitution industrialization and an inward focus on the national economy.[25] During the election, Ubaldini travelled every weekend for campaign events in different provinces; according to his aid, Julio Mirogui, this was because "at that time he qualified as a star, a rock star. When we took him to the provinces he always spoke at the end, not the candidate."[26]

After Menem was elected, he quickly abandoned his promise of a "productive revolution" and embraced a series of pro-market reforms that included trade liberalization and privatization – a bait-and-switch that Stokes refers to as "neoliberalism by surprise."[27] As Argentine scholar Héctor Palomino explained, "This turn was incongruous with Menem's campaign promises and, obviously, contrary to the policies promoted by Ubaldini and the CGT."[28] Menem therefore faced two related problems with the CGT and Ubaldini. First, Ubaldini's popularity posed a threat to Menem's leadership of the Peronist movement – a threat that prominently flared up throughout the first year of Menem's presidency. Second, after the CGT's thirteen general strikes against Alfonsín's economic policies, Ubaldini was Argentina's clearest symbol of opposition to neoliberal economic reform. According to one of Ubaldini's CGT aides, the conflict started with the presidential campaign when audiences "applauded Saúl more than Menem, and there came a problem of envy,

[23] Author interview with Oraldo Britos, December 26, 2019.
[24] Author interview with Darío Nazar, December 2, 2019.
[25] Confederacion General del Trabajo 1989b.
[26] Author interviews with Julio Mirogui, December 17, 2019.
[27] Stokes 2001. [28] Author interview with Héctor Palomino, December 23, 2019.

of resentment." And the problem only worsened when Menem embraced neoliberal reform and appointed prominent business men to his cabinet: "when Ubaldini found out that they were going to put a Bunge & Born man as Minister of Economy...There it all started, with those two things."[29] Héctor Recalde, the CGT-Azopardo's head labor lawyer, recalled that "the romance with the government lasted very little...obviously, he [Menem] did his best to get him [Ubaldini] out."[30] As *El Pais* put it, "the militant Ubaldini, whom Menem invited to his electoral campaigns, now became an obstacle to the application of the already approved laws of Economic Emergency and State Reform" at the heart of Menem's economic plan.[31]

When Menem was inaugurated in July 1989, his new Minister of Labor, Jorge Triaca, announced that he "expected the unions to give the administration two strike-free years" in which to implement its economic reforms.[32] Although CGT leaders had campaigned for Menem and originally welcomed his Peronist government, they quickly clarified that continued support would depend on Menem's economic policies. Ubaldini, still the secretary general of a united CGT, flatly rejected the no-strike proposal and announced that "I am supportive of my government, but I am not submissive to anyone."[33] Lorenzo Miguel, the secretary general of the powerful metalworkers union (UOM) echoed Ubaldini's sentiment and warned that unions must not unconditionally support the new government; announcing a potential strike, Miguel reminded Menem that "we reserve the right to disagree."[34] With union leaders rejecting Menem's no-strike request, newspapers warned that Argentine unions were unifying against Menem's choice of cabinet members and economic policies.[35] Although organized labor was "traditionally one of the pillars of Peronism, President Carlos Menem appears to be heading for trouble with the labour movement."[36]

Although several important labor union leaders broke with Ubaldini and supported Menem's reforms, these union leaders only represented a minority of the CGT. A small group of union leaders known as "the 15" had long endorsed neoliberal reforms. These union leaders collaborated with the military government when it tried to reform the Argentine economy in the 1970s, supported Alfonsín's economic reforms in the 1980s, and actively campaigned for Menem during the 1989 presidential election.[37] After Menem's election,

29 Author interviews with Alejandro [surname unknown], December 17, 2019. Bunge & Born was a powerful multinational corporation based in Argentina.

30 Author interviews with Héctor Recalde, December 16, 2019.

31 "La Central Sindical Peronista se Divide en Dos Sectores, Pese a la Mediación de Menem," *El Pais*, October 17, 1989.

32 *Latin American Weekly Report*, July 6, 1989.

33 "No Soy Obsecuente de nadie, Aseguró Saúl Ubaldini," *Clarín*, July 27, 1989; Senén González 1999, 29.

34 Senén González 1999, 29.

35 "Disgruntled Unions Seek New Unity," *Latin American Weekly Report*, July 20, 1989.

36 "Menem Makes Bad Start with Unions," *Brazil and Southern Cone*, August 3, 1989.

37 McGuire 1992, 47.

many of these union leaders were rewarded with cabinet positions. Other union leaders from "the 15" formed a labor liaison committee (*Mesa de Enlace*) that actively coordinated the administration's efforts to increase labor union support for its economic reforms. As Mettenheim and Malloy explain, this committee's "main purpose was to unconditionally back the administration policies."[38] For example, Guerino Andreoni was a *Mesa de Enlace* leader who then served as the first secretary general of the CGT–San Martin, the confederation that supported Menem's reforms after the CGT split into two different organizations. Andreoni denounced Ubaldini's leadership and argued that "the CGT should change its role because we can't confront the government like what happened with the [Alfonsín's] Radicals."[39]

The minority status of these pro-Menem union leaders was on display in August 1989, when the *Mesa de Enlace* tried and failed to replace Ubaldini as the secretary general of the CGT. After Ubaldini rejected the government's call for a no-strike pledge, Menem offered Ubaldini a position as a foreign labor ambassador in Spain – an offer that he quickly rejected. Days later, Ubaldini turned down another Menem offer, this time to be Argentina's representative to the ILO in Geneva.[40] As Ubaldini told journalists, "I have a job to fulfill here, that of secretary general of the CGT, that the working class entrusted me with and I am staying to accomplish it."[41] As Darío Nazar, Ubaldini's assistant, later explained, "it entered one ear and left the other. He knew they wanted to get him out of the fight…but he didn't even evaluate it, nothing."[42] The gambit was straightforward and journalists noted that "Menem has been hard at work trying to persuade CGT boss Saúl Ubaldini to resign and take up a post abroad."[43] By the end of the month, *Clarín* would publish a political cartoon with a newsboy running through the street yelling, "This just in! Today they didn't offer Ubaldini a single ambassadorship."[44]

Menem's logic was clear to contemporary observers, who noted that "the CGT staged 13 strikes during the previous administration of President Raúl Alfonsín. Menem does not want to see the same thing happen to him. With the support of Menemista unionists, he is trying to oust Ubaldini from the CGT."[45] With Ubaldini refusing this "golden exile," Menem encouraged the *Mesa de Enlace* to demand a special meeting of the Central Confederal Committee, a body of the CGT's largest unions with the power to remove Ubaldini. The Committee met on August 11, 1989 and a majority of its delegates (126 of 229) quickly voted to keep Ubaldini "firmly entrenched at the helm of the CGT."[46]

38 von Mettenheim and Malloy 1998, 149.

39 "Ofrecen otra Embajada a Ubaldini," *Clarín*, August 2, 1989. 40 Ibid.

41 "Ubaldini Dijo que Seguir al frente de la Central Obrera," *Clarín*, August 3, 1989.

42 Author interview with Darío Nazar, December 2, 2019.

43 *Latin American Weekly Report*, July 6, 1989. Embarrassingly, Menem told reporters that Ubaldini had requested the position, a claim that Ubaldini publicly denied.

44 "Notición," *Clarín*, August 31, 1989, pg. 4.

45 *Noticias Aliadas*, Volume 21, 1989, Latinamerica Press.

46 "Ubaldini Holds on to CGT Top Job," *Latin American Weekly Report*, August 24, 1989.

Journalists noted that the *Mesa de Enlace* was "none too discreetly backed by the Menem government" and that the outcome of the vote "left the pro-Menem faction in a minority, pondering whether to lead a breakaway organisation of their own."[47] As *Latin News* reminded its readers, "it was generally agreed that organised labour could make or break government efforts to lift Argentina from its deep economic crisis."[48]

The Splitting of the CGT

Luis Barrionuevo stood at the window of Buenos Aires' Teatro San Martin on October 10, 1989, and waved to his supporters down below on Avenida Corrientes. With police barricades lining one of the city's busiest arteries, Barrionuevo watched as hired thugs attacked Ubaldini supporters with sticks, rocks, and broken glass bottles.[49] Inside the theater, Argentina's union leaders met to decide whether or not Saúl Ubaldini should continue on as secretary general of the CGT until his elected term expired at the end of 1990.[50] The official vote ended with 664 delegates in favor of Ubaldini and 719 opposed, along with 92 abstentions from union leaders previously loyal to Ubaldini.[51] Barrionuevo emerged, his fist raised in the air victoriously, to celebrate the culmination of a campaign to oust Ubaldini from his leadership of the CGT.[52]

This section tells the story of that victory, specifically how Menem's government violated labor rights in order to defeat Ubaldini and split the labor movement into two weakened factions.[53] As explained below, Menem's actions opened space for violence against union leaders, and his government violated labor rights by replacing dissident union leaders and manipulating union finances. The resulting split in the CGT was crucially important for the implementation of trade liberalization and other economic reforms; As Héctor Amichetti, an Argentine union leader, explained, "Menem's great success was to divide the labor movement. If he had not been able to divide the labor movement, his plan of privatization, of total opening of the economy, would not have succeeded."[54]

Ubaldini's Car Bomb

At the center of Menem's plan were Minister of Labor Jorge Triaca and Luis Barrionuevo, the head of ANSSAL, a government agency with control over a

47 Ibid. 48 *Latin News*, September 7, 1989.

49 "Ubaldinistas Dejaron al Congreso de la CGT," *Crónica*, October 11, 1989 pg. 3.

50 "Power, Politics and Economics – or Wages," *The Review of the River Plate*, October 11, 1989.

51 "Como se Voto," *Clarín*, October 15, 1989.

52 "Heridos y Procesados por los Disturbios," *Crónica*, October 11, 1989.

53 After the CGT split, Ubaldini led the CGT–Azopardo, a confederation of unions opposed to Menem's reforms, while a rival confederation, the CGT–San Martin, supported Menem's reforms.

54 Author interview with Héctor Amichetti, December 19, 2019.

portion of union finances. After Ubaldini won the August 1989 vote in the Central Confederal Committee for CGT leadership, Triaca and Barrionuevo held a brief "damage-assessment session" with other union leaders that were part of the pro-Menem, *Mesa de Enlace*. Menem's cabinet members proposed that union leaders call a new meeting the following week to revise CGT regulations in a way that would allow for yet another vote on Ubaldini's leadership. This open collaboration between Menem's government and union leaders to oust Ubaldini from the CGT was so blatant that Menem's own vice president tried to distance himself from the growing scandal, telling reporters that he was "very opposed to the offensive unleashed against the secretary general of the CGT, Saúl Ubaldini, especially from sectors that are linked to the Government in some way."[55] As Kleinfeld and Barham argue, when democratic governments target political rivals in these ways they should be seen as complicit in any subsequent political violence.[56]

The night before the meeting proposed by Menem's officials – when union leaders would decide whether to hold another vote on Ubaldini's leadership of the CGT – Ubaldini worked late and decided to spend the night in a small apartment maintained for him on the top floor of the CGT headquarters. After midnight, Ubaldini's assistant, Darío Nazar, went downstairs, got into Ubaldini's Ford Falcon, and headed out to find a late dinner for both himself and his boss. While Nazar searched for food, Ubaldini stood at his sixth floor window and watched a lunar eclipse high above Buenos Aires. Whatever Ubaldini was pondering as he stared at the moon, his train of thought was broken a few minutes before 2:00 AM by a loud explosion; his car, parked in front of the CGT office had just blown up.[57]

Although no one was ever held responsible for the attack, many contemporary observers saw a direct link between the car bomb and Menem's campaign to remove Ubaldini from the CGT. According to an Argentine member of Congress, "the episode can not be separated from the pressures and interference of the Government in the internal dispute of the CGT since it is evident that this has fostered the climate for this attack."[58] A prominent Argentine journalist, José María Pasquini Durán, warned that "the President should reflect very carefully on what is *being done in his name* by those who intend to decapitate the CGT."[59] An Argentine union leader claimed that the bomb was worse than the military's dirty war, as this attack had come "from within Peronism itself" – an accusation that ambiguously included the *Mesa de Enlace* union leaders as

55 "Duhalde, Enojada por la Ofensiva contra Ubaldini," *Clarín*, August 13, 1989.

56 Kleinfeld and Barham 2018.

57 This description draws on an author interview with Darío Nazar, as well as "La Noche Bomba de Saúl Ubaldini," *Página/12*, August 18, 1989.

58 Ibid. 59 "Debajo de la Alfombra," *Página/12*, August 18, 1989, italics added for emphasis.

well as President Menem.[60] Although Ubaldini announced that, "I do not want to blame anyone for this act that borders on madness," a prominent Argentine newspaper wrote that the attack was clearly a "warning to the principal leader of opposition to the Government's economic plan."[61]

Thirty years later, it is difficult to reconstruct the exact meaning or influence of the attack on Ubaldini. Surprisingly, this book is the first to discuss the car bomb, an event that was on the front page of Argentina's main newspapers but is completely absent from the voluminous literature on Argentine economic reforms. Many of the union leaders and government officials I spoke with in 2019 recalled the attack as having occurred in the distant past, during a period in which they remembered such political violence being very common. Of course, Argentine union leaders were implicated in the assassinations and political violence that dominated the presidency of Isabel Perón in the early-1970s, and a military junta then waged a "dirty war" from 1976 to 1983 in which thousands of union members disappeared.[62] Yet those who wrote about the car bomb back in 1989 were emphatic that this was not business as usual. For example, journalists referred to the bomb as a return of "the ghosts of the past" and warned that the attack on Ubaldini could be "*the beginning* of a spiral of violence."[63]

At the same time, some assert that the car bomb was not an actual assassination attempt. For example, Víctor De Gennaro, a militant union leader who joined Ubaldini in the CGT–Azopardo, downplayed the attack and explained that "if they want to kill you in this country, they kill you."[64] Palomino, a scholar of Argentine labor politics, explained that such a "failed" attack likely represented a threat meant to demonstrate "what opponents of Menem's new economic proposals might expect."[65] Recalde, the CGT lawyer who joined Ubaldini the morning after the car bomb to file a complaint at a local police station, concluded that "it's not free, of course. You pay for taking a stand. Evidently, they wanted to somehow water down the part of the labor movement that resisted against the government's economic plan. In an extreme way, no?"[66] In this vein, well-known Argentine journalist Rubén Furman wrote that "if this episode is imagined as a wedge placed in the workers' movement to divide and weaken it more than it already is, it seems to have achieved its goal. . .the seed of distrust has already begun to germinate."[67]

60 This quote is from one of hundreds of telegrams that Ubaldini received from union leaders, politicians, and citizens in the aftermath of the car bomb. These telegrams are held in the CGT archive in Buenos Aires, Argentina.

61 "La Noche Bomba de Saúl Ubaldini," *Página/12*, August 18, 1989. 62 Robben 2005.

63 "Los Fantasmas del Pasado," *Página/12*, August 18, 1989; "Debajo de la Alfombra," *Página/12*, August 18, 1989, italics added for emphasis.

64 Author interview with Víctor De Gennaro, December 9, 2019.

65 Author interview with Héctor Palomino, December 23, 2019.

66 Author interview with Héctor Recalde, December 16, 2019.

67 "Los Fantasmas del Pasado," *Página/12*, August 18, 1989.

The day after the car bomb, CGT union leaders met and decided that they would hold another vote on Ubaldini's leadership in October, just two months in the future. And two days before that October meeting, Argentines again woke to news of violence aimed at union leaders; the office of a pro-Ubaldini newspaper was fire bombed in the middle of the night. In the days before the attack, the newspaper received threatening phone calls that demanded the paper stop running op-eds by labor union leader aligned with Ubaldini. The group that claimed responsibility for the attack distributed fliers throughout the neighborhood explaining that the newspaper "was ignoring our warning" and was "poisoning the public with the disease that infects all communications media: the promotion of Ubaldinismo."[68]

Triaca and the Ministry of Labor

We do not know who planted the bomb in Ubaldini's car, or exactly how such threats influenced union leaders. However, it is clear that during the two months between the August car bomb and the October CGT leadership vote Menem's government violated labor rights in order to ensure Ubaldini's defeat. The first tactic was to use the government's sweeping powers to intervene into union affairs and replace dissident union leaders. This effort was led Minister of Labor Jorge Triaca, who intervened into several industry-level labor unions and installed new leaders that would oppose Ubaldini's leadership of the CGT and support Menem's reforms. In the days leading up to the October meeting in Teatro San Martin, Triaca installed new leadership in at least five unions that jointly accounted for roughly ten percent of all CGT delegates.[69]

After the October Teatro San Martin vote, Ubaldini allies immediately complained of "miscellaneous irregularities concerning the accreditation of delegates."[70] The CGT–Azopardo's head labor lawyer, Héctor Recalde, met privately with Menem to argue that the final CGT vote was unfairly influenced by the government's last minute replacement of several union leaders. But given that any formal challenge would be adjudicated by the Minister of Labor himself, Recalde lamented that their concerns "will not be the subject of a legal or judicial process."[71] A year later, the CGT–Azopardo sent an official complaint to the Director General of the ILO, noting that the Minister of Labor had used a "twisted interpretation" of Argentine labor law to replace the leadership of numerous industry-level unions right before the Teatro San Martin meeting. Importantly, the complaint notes that the

68 The group took the name Comando Libertadores de America, the same name used by far-right military deaths squads during Argentina's dirty war. *Noticias Argentinas*, "Group Threatens, Bombs Lanus Newspaper," October 9, 1989.

69 Author's calculation based on delegate counts available in "Como se Voto," *Clarín*, October 15, 1989. *The Review of the River Plate* ("The Last Ten Months," Novemmber 30, 1989) lists these intervened unions as Construction, Road workers, Newspaper Sellers, and Municipal Workers, while a CGT letter to the ILO adds the Bread-makers union.

70 "Gestión por la Unidad," *Clarín*, October 18, 1989.

71 Ibid.

timing of such interventions meant that the Minister of Labor had "meddled in the very heart of our labor confederation."[72]

Leading up to the October CGT meeting, Argentine journalists clearly recognized the potential for Triaca to tilt the balance against Ubaldini; in late August, *The Review of the River Plate* listed the many different unions coalescing around Ubaldini before noting that "possible ministerial intervention" could easily reshuffle the sides.[73] Looking back on the CGT split, union leader Víctor De Gennaro put it simply, "Menem named Triaca as Minister of Labor ... and they legally recognized the leadership of unions that the Minister of Labor interfered with. With this they won. With the union leaders that had been elected, our sector, that of Ubaldini, would have won."[74]

Barrionuevo and Union Finances

The second tactic that Menem's government used to split the CGT was to manipulate union finances, an effort led by Menem's head of ANSSAL, Barrionuevo. ANSSAL was a new government agency that centralized the collection and control of union welfare funds (*Obras Sociales*).[75] Before Barrionuevo took over ANSSAL, these funds were deducted from workers' paychecks, matched by employers, and delivered directly to each union's fund. The ILO explicitly warns that such government control over union finances threatens to undermine their independence and is therefore a violation of workers' freedom of association.

Barrionuevo, according to most Argentine union leaders I spoke with, represented the ILO's worst nightmare concerning government manipulation of union funds. Carlos Tomada reflected that, "I believe that I know almost all of the union leaders and I respect them all...but Barrionuevo, no. For me, Barrionuevo, is the exception in the sense that there are others as bad as him, but none that had the power that he had. No one has done the damage that he has."[76] Antonio Caló, the secretary general of the metalworkers union (UOM) explained that being the head of ANSSAL "is an enormous power. And what did Barrionuevo do? He divided the CGT."[77] Darío Nazar lamented that Barrionuevo used ANSSAL "to weaken Saúl's power because it was Saúl in the CGT with all the unions behind him. Menem decreased the money for *Obras Sociales* and took the votes away from Saúl." Nazar recalled meetings in which union leaders openly apologized to Ubaldini, saying that "I have to

72 "Letter from CGT to ILO Director General," November 27, 1990, CGT Archives. The same letter also complains that Barrionuevo's ANSSAL was withholding funds from dissident unions and in general "discriminates against trade unions that do not belong to the current official union [CGT–San Martin]."

73 "On the Labour Front: Divided Loyalties ...," *The Review of the River Plate*, August 25, 1989.

74 Author interview with Víctor De Gennaro, December 9, 2019.

75 ANSSAL controlled 10 percent of all money destined for unions' *Obras Sociales*.

76 Author interview with Carlos Tomada, December 19, 2019.

77 Author interview with Antonio Caló, December 26, 2019.

leave from your side because if I don't . . . they'll take this from me, and they'll take that, they'll cut this, and they'll cut that." According to Recalde, the head labor lawyer for the CGT–Azopardo, Barrionuevo's ANSSAL "was handled as a key to restrict the resources of rebel unions. They cut their resources, and that has its weight in union life. Because one of the roles of the union leader is to provide social and welfare benefits to its affiliates. They take away resources, they take away popularity. They cut away at your base of support. To co-opt and to threaten and intimidate."[78]

Since the pro-Menem *Mesa de Enlace* garnered 47 percent of the August vote to remove Ubaldini, Barrionuevo carefully focused his threats on a small number of union leader aligned with Ubaldini. In the lead up to the October vote, the Argentine press regularly reported on meetings between Barrionuevo and union leaders that previously supported Ubaldini but were now seen to be slowly drifting toward the pro-Menem faction.[79] In order to make sure that each union leader voted as expected in October, Barrionuevo worked with the *Mesa de Enlace* to successfully demand an unprecedented change in CGT voting procedure; rather than the traditional secret ballot, each delegate would be individually called by name and required to cast their vote publicly.[80]

Barrionuevo's manipulation of union finances was an open secret; *Clarín* skeptically reported that Barrionuevo met with union leaders to explain that he would use his personal control over union funds to "avoid unnecessary and bureaucratic obstacles."[81] Ubaldini publicly denounced Barrionuevo and lamented that "you can't play with funds from the *Obras Sociales* to pressure unions. . .you should be just with the social welfare funds because that is why compañero Carlos Menem appointed you, and not to squeeze workers."[82] According to *The Review of the River Plate*, "Menem's personal representative in the labour area, Luis Barrionuevo, made Ubaldini his special target, and the President has made his wish to get rid of Ubaldini public."[83] According to *Clarín*, "Barrionuevo's role was to force the breakup of the CGT."[84] Similarly a political cartoon published between Ubaldini's victory in August and defeat in October depicted Ubaldini as a chair with four legs, a much shorter Barrionuevo

78 Author interview with Héctor Recalde, December 16, 2019.

79 For reporting on Barrionuevo's meeting with Carlos Alderete, the secretary of *Luz y Fuerza*, see "Ratifican a Ubaldini y Piden el Gobierno Participación para la CGT," *Clarín*, August 12, 1989. For similar reporting on the Juan Jose Zanola, the leader of the bank worker (*Bancarios*), see "Ubaldini Amenaza con Remplazar a los Disidentes," *Clarín*, August 29, 1989; "La Mesa Rechaza el Llamado de Ubaldini," *Clarín*, September 2, 1989.

80 *Clarín*, October 7, 1989; author interviews with Héctor Amichetti and Antonio Caló. This change in voting procedure was determined by a small committee of union leaders, on which the *Mesa de Enlace* held a majority.

81 *Clarín*, September 21, 1989.

82 "Ratifican a Ubaldini y Piden el Gobierno Participación para la CGT," *Clarín*, August 12, 1989.

83 "The CGT Split – And After?" *The Review of the River Plate*, October 27, 1989.

84 "Menem's Leadership Style, Political Future Noted," *Clarín* [FBIS], November 25, 1990.

stands facing him, one hand on Ubaldini's knees, the other holding a saw that is cutting through his front legs.[85]

After weeks of speculation, three key Ubaldini-aligned unions – light and power workers (*Luz y Fuerza*), bank worker (*Bancarios*), and bus drivers (*Unión Tranviarios Automotor*) – surprised their colleagues by abstaining on the crucial vote of whether or not to keep Ubaldini as secretary general of the CGT. According to one journalist, at the moment that the leader of *Luz y Fuerza* announced his decision to abstain from the vote, Ubaldini's supporters visibly "twitched their faces" and Menem's supporters "sighed with relief."[86] Antonio Caló, a union leader who attended the Teatro San Martin meeting, remembers the scandal of these abstentions. Caló recalled that *Luz y Fuerza* abstained even though they had previously promised to vote for Ubaldini; "there were unions that all their lives they were next to Ubaldini, then when it was time to vote, well, he lost ... there were a ton of unions – I don't want to name names – companions who were on the other side."[87] The ninety-two delegates controlled by these three abstaining unions – all recent Ubaldini allies – were more than enough to swing the election, which Ubaldini lost by just 75 out of 1,475 votes. When combined with the votes from union leaders that Minister of Labor Triaca replaced, Menem's government left a direct mark on roughly sixteen percent of CGT delegates – an enormous influence on a vote ultimately decided 53 to 47 percent.[88]

THE CGT–AZOPARDO AND MENEM; NOVEMBER 1989–NOVEMBER 1990

The Threat of the CGT–Azopardo

On November 17, 1989, Carlos Menem stepped out onto the balcony of the *Casa Rosada*, the office of the President of Argentina, to address the public gathered below in the *Plaza de Mayo*. The speech – Menem's first since his inauguration four months earlier – had already been delayed over three hours in the hope that more people would show up to hear Argentina's new President discuss his economic reforms.[89] When Menem finally emerged, he "struggled to smile" as he was delayed yet again by thousands of workers chanting "U-bal-di-ni, U-bal-di-ni." Although a month had passed since Ubaldini had lost control of the CGT, Menem's thirty minute speech was constantly interrupted by loud music and chants of "Oh, Ubaldini / it's a feeling that I can't stop / and everyday

85 "CGT: La Mayoria de los Gremios Respalda a la Mesa de Enlace," *Clarín*, August 29, 1989.
86 *Clarín*, October 16, 1989. 87 Author interview with Antonio Caló, December 26, 2019.
88 Author's calculation based on delegate counts available in "Como se Voto," *Clarín*, October 15, 1989.
89 "On the Labor Front: November 17: A Presidential Set-Back," *The Review of the River Plate*, November 30, 1989.

I love you more" and "Saúl, the people are with you."[90] In response, Menem hinted that if unions went on strike to oppose his reforms, he would use the power of the state to stop them; "to the groups that are already starting to show their claws, enough or we will have to cut them off."[91] The next morning, the front page of *Página/12* surveyed growing labor union opposition to Menem's economic reforms and announced that, "The Party is Over."[92]

This section tells the story of how such labor union opposition threatened to disrupt Menem's plans to open Argentina's economy, even after the CGT split in October 1989. Throughout 1990, the CGT–Azopardo led a series of successful strikes, rallied tens of thousands of workers against Menem's reforms, and proposed an alternative economic plan that was endorsed by politicians from opposition parties as well as the leader of Menem's own PJ. Yet this dramatic story of the CGT–Azopardo's struggle is routinely ignored by scholars of Argentine economic reforms, who tend to assume that these unions never posed a serious threat. For these scholars, the CGT–Azopardo's resistance was simply "out of step with the views of most unionized workers and the people at large regarding what Argentina must do to modernize its economy."[93] As Murillo argues, "the national labor confederation, the Peronist-dominated CGT, although surprised by the policy turnaround, accepted the market-oriented reforms."[94] Weyland argues that "most Peronists' willingness to follow the leader – a typical characteristic of populism – allowed Menem to marshal widespread acceptance of this drastic policy change inside the movement," and Levitsky and Way conclude that "the bulk of the labor movement remained loyal to the Menem government between 1989 and 1991."[95]

But the archives, labor union leaders, and Argentine government officials tell a very different story about Ubaldini, his stature in Argentine politics, and the threat that the CGT–Azopardo posed to Menem's reforms throughout the first year of his presidency. Although the CGT split undeniably weakened labor union opposition to Menem's reforms, support from several powerful union – especially the metalworkers – "helped to keep Ubaldini in a prominent position on the labour chess board."[96] With Argentina's hyperinflation and economic crisis worsening, "financial circles and city traders" worried that one of the "inevitable consequences" of the CGT split would be further strikes and protests that "could jeopardise the government's crash stabilisation programme." Menem's own allies among conservative leaders warned that Ubaldini's CGT–Azopardo posed a major political threat, that a series of strikes could leave Menem's government "in a shambles" and that Ubaldini would

90 "Oh Ubaldini / un sentimiento que no puedo parar / y cada día te quiero más" and "Saúl querido el pueblo está contigo."

91 "Long After Food Riots, Argentines Still Wary," *Washington Post*, November 26, 1989; "Un Llamado a la 'Batalla,'" *Página/12*, November 18, 1989.

92 "La Fiesta Se Acabo," *Página/12*, November 18, 1989. 93 Ranis 1992, 215.

94 Murillo 2001, 28. 95 Weyland 2002, 138; Levitsky and Way 1998, 174.

96 *The Review of the River Plate*, February 14, 1990, page 81.

then be well-positioned to challenge Menem in Argentina's next presidential election.[97] The hype and hysteria around Ubaldini reached a fever pitch; when Zulema Yoma, Menem's wife, met with Ubaldini for a five-hour dinner journalists speculated about whether she might be "working against her husband's re-election ambitions."[98]

Such concerns were rooted in a growing wave of strikes led by the CGT–Azopardo, soon after the CGT split. In early November 1989, a transport strike by bus, subway, and railroad workers paralyzed the city of Buenos Aires and the surrounding province. As one newspaper put it: "the expected test of wills between the Menem government and the unions has already begun to materialise."[99] In early December, Argentina was hit by a wave of railroad strikes against Menem's plans to privatize the country's railways. Ubaldini arranged a meeting for the government's "official surrender" in which he mediated directly between the CGT–Azopardo affiliated train drivers union and President Menem. According to *The Review of the River Plate*, "this was highly significant, because the railway unions now know their power and there is nothing to stop them repeating the experiment in pursuit of other demands. Nothing."[100] Rather than face crippling railroad strikes, the government chose to postpone its controversial privatization plan by two months. When discussing the government's broader economic reforms, journalists warned of the "alarming evidence that there is no real political will to press any decision home."[101]

Ubaldini was "heartened by his railway success" and sought to place himself and the CGT–Azopardo at the head of the growing opposition to Menem's economic reforms. Contemporary observers warned that politicians from both major parties – Menem's PJ and Alfonsín's Radical party – might join Ubaldini's coalition; "Menem will either have to back down yet again, or face something like a revolutionary general strike."[102] Pressure from labor unions continued to grow with a record number of strikes in January 1990 – a total of seventy-five – more than double the number of strikes in January 1988 when the CGT was fighting against Alfonsín's reforms.[103] Journalists noted that public confidence in the government's reforms "melted away as one surrender after another was made to … [anyone] willing and able to put pressure on the government."[104]

With Argentine newspapers warning of a "social upheaval," Menem traveled to the seaside resort town of Mar del Plata to meet with Ubaldini and

97 *Latin American Weekly Report*, October 26, 1989.
98 "Worries Over Prices & CGT Split," *Latin American Weekly Report*, November 2, 1989.
99 "Menem Faces Wave of Strike Actions," *Latin American Weekly Review*, November 23, 1989.
100 "Leading Events," *The Review of the River Plate*, December 14, 1989, 410.
101 "Why Bother with Plans and Pronouncements?" *The Review of the River Plate*, December 14, 1989, 407.
102 Ibid.
103 "Notes on News: The Last Opportunity," *The Review of the River Plate*, February 14, 1990, 72.
104 Ibid.

other labor union leaders to discuss a "social pact."[105] After the meeting, Menem announced that he and the union leaders shared "the desire for unity in the workers movement." While Menem hoped that a social pact would lead to unified CGT support for his economic reforms, Ubaldini cautioned that "we want a social pact, but to do that a change in the economic plan is necessary."[106]

Ubaldini and the CGT–Azopardo then released an alternative economic plan that called for a total rejection of Menem's reforms. The CGT–Azopardo's "Bases for a National Reactivation Plan" laid out the many differences between Menem's "liberal" economic proposals and the "justicialist" policies that Argentina had pursued since Juan Peron in the 1940s, with the strong backing of the CGT.[107] According to the union, "the liberal and the justicialist projects are supported by different social forces and differ, among other essential issues, in the functions assigned to the state, in the expansion of the internal market, in the development of certain economic sectors, in the distribution of income, in external relations and in the definition of what will be the engine of the economy."[108] The union called on Menem to continue the import–substitution industrialization policies that protected and fostered Argentina's domestic industries, and argued that due to Menem's narrow focus on modernizing some export sectors "the state is made useless, speculation is privileged over production, income is redistributed against wage-earners, and regional economies are destroyed, and national independence is renounced."[109]

Menem frequently claimed that his economic proposals were the only ones possible for Argentina's future, and that the CGT–Azopardo was clinging to a past to which it was impossible to return.[110] The CGT–Azopardo sought to turn this temporality on its head, arguing that Menem 'intended to return to the social injustice of the beginning of the century. That is why it is not true that the liberal plan is focused on the future; on the contrary, it aims to resuscitate the past. When in the name of international economic competitiveness, social

[105] Ibid, etc.

[106] "Union Leaders Support Menem's Social Agreement," *Clarín* [FBIS], January 25, 1990; "Government Call for Pact with Business, Labor," *Buenos Aires TELAM* [FBIS], 13 December 1989.

[107] This document is available in the CGT headquarters in Buenos Aires, Argentina or from the author upon request. Menem would later reject the "liberal" label and claim that his economic policy "is not in keeping with orthodox liberalism, but that it is a proposal, a humanized capitalism aimed at the development of the huge Argentine potential through a popular market economy." See "Menem Holds News Conference with Spanish Leader," *Buenos Aires TELAM* [FBIS], March 14, 1990.

[108] "Bases para un Plan Nacional de Reactivación," CGT, March 1990, author's translation.

[109] Ibid.

[110] In March 1990, Menem claimed that "there are currently two kinds of unions in the country, the nostalgic ones who live with the memory of the old Peronism, and the other, the workers movements who reject the Argentina of the past. This movement wants a dynamic and modern Argentina. I congratulate the union leaders who want a modern Argentina. I ask the others to adjust to a new reality. "Menem Interviewed on Goals of Reorganization," *O Estado De Sao Paulo* [FBIS], March 15, 1990.

justice is denied, the worst regression is being committed."[111] In other words, Menem's attempt to open the Argentine economy to international competition represented a return to the decades before Perón used trade protection and pro-labor legislation to increase workers' wages, build strong labor unions, and reduce income inequality.[112] The CGT–Azopardo argued that Menem "ignored that the root of the crisis is in the depression of the domestic market" and that by "dismantling the productive apparatus, [Menem] was setting up the retraction of the internal market and the deterioration of workers' purchasing power." In contrast, the CGT–Azopardo advocated continued trade protection, maintenance of state ownership, and a wage increase that would stimulate domestic demand and re-start the internal economy. While Menem planned to lower domestic prices by slashing Argentina's tariffs and increasing imports, the CGT–Azopardo argued that "emergency plans have little need of imported inputs."[113]

The CGT–Azopardo's alternative plan was publicly endorsed by Antonio Cafiero, the Governor of Buenos Aires and head of Menem's PJ party, eight PJ congressmen, and all five political parties that had formed an electoral alliance with the PJ just the year before.[114] Ubaldini even met with Alfonsín, the former president whose economic reforms were blocked by thirteen CGT general strikes, to discuss the possibility of unifying against Menem; Ubaldini told incredulous journalists that "historically, great political adversaries from one moment have later come together and united to overcome a country's difficulties."[115] As Héctor Recalde explained, "at that time, the opposition leader was Ubaldini. Not only of trade unionism, but of the opposition. He even nurtured leaders of other parties, not just the Justicialista."[116]

When the CGT–Azopardo called for a strike and protest outside Argentina's Congress in March of 1990, the head of Menem's own party announced that "if more than 60,000 people turn up, the Justicialista party is finished as a single unit."[117] Cafiero suggested that such high turnout for the protest would signal widespread opposition to Menem's economic reforms from within the labor movement, a key constituency of Menem's PJ. With the strike approaching, *Página/12* explained that "this week, the government faces its most difficult competition since Carlos Menem was inaugurated eighth months ago."[118] The sheer uncertainty of the moment – whether or not Menem and his economic reforms would survive labor opposition – was well captured by a newspaper

111 "Bases para un Plan Nacional de Reactivación," CGT, March 1990, author's translation.
112 Teubal 2001, 33.
113 "Bases para un Plan Nacional de Reactivación," CGT, March 1990, author's translation.
114 "CGT Muestra Las Uñas," *Página/12*, March 9, 1990; "D-day Approaches for Peronist Party," *Latin American Weekly Report*, March 29, 1990
115 "No Nos Une el Amore," *Página/12*, March 10, 1990.
116 Author interview with Héctor Recalde, December 16, 2019.
117 "D-day approaches for Peronist party," *Latin American Weekly Report*, March 29, 1990.
118 "Relaciones Peligrosas," *Página/12*, March [18–20], 1990. Exact date not included in archive of Fundacion Ubaldini.

article written right before the strike: "As this issue is being distributed, President Carlos Menem will be finding out if he can still be considered a Peronist President, or if a substantial part of his Justicialista party will break away and move into open opposition."[119] *Latin News* boasted that back in November 1989 it had reported that Ubaldini "might emerge as a challenger to Menem's leadership. In early March [1990], he clearly assumed that role, rejecting a 'social truce' requested by the President and openly rallying support for an alternative economic policy which would represent a complete reversal of course for the Menem administration."[120]

Beyond leading strikes and drawing attention from politicians and journalists, Ubaldini's popularity during this period can also be seen in public opinion polls. A poll conducted by the Demoskopia Institute in January 1990 found Ubaldini to be a serious candidate for Governor of the province of Buenos Aires, polling ahead of the incumbent Governor, Antonio Cafiero. Ubaldini's lead in the poll was especially impressive, given that Cafiero was the head of Menem's PJ and that the Argentine Constitution had recently been amended to allow Cafiero to run for re-election. Among voters who sympathized with the PJ, 23.91 percent favored Ubaldini while 22.46 percent preferred Cafiero.[121] Public opinion data from this period is especially important because scholars of Argentine reform often present Ubaldini's eventual electoral defeat in 1991 as evidence that the CGT–Azopardo did not pose a serious threat to Menem's economic reforms.[122] Levitsky and Way, for example, argue that Ubaldini's "candidacy was rejected by virtually the entire labor movement, and he received an embarrassing 2 percent of the vote."[123] It is therefore crucial to recognize that in 1990, when the CGT–Azopardo was widely seen as a major challenge to Menem's reforms, Ubaldini was actually more popular than the head of Menem's own political party.

The Defeat of the CGT–Azopardo

How did Menem's government overcome labor union opposition from the CGT–Azopardo? After the CGT–Azopardo won a series of strikes in the beginning of 1990, and Ubaldini reiterated that labor peace would require changing the government's economic plan, Menem launched an escalating campaign of labor repression. He declared specific strikes illegal, fired strikers, decertified striking unions, broke a strike with the military, and ultimately banned strikes on the eve of a general strike. This section tells the story of the government's escalating campaign of labor rights violations, which played a pivotal role in the collapse of the CGT–Azopardo in November 1990.

119 "D-day Approaches for Peronist Party," *Latin American Weekly Report*, March 29, 1990.

120 *Brazil and Southern Cone*, April 19, 1990.

121 "Ubaldini's Candidacy for Governship," *Buenos Aires SOMOS* [FBIS], February 21, 1990. Among all voters, 14.75 favored Ubaldini and 14 favored Cafiero. 53.25 percent, however, said that if the election came down to Ubaldini and Cafiero, they would vote for neither.

122 Hagopian and Mainwaring 2005, 77 123 Levitsky and Way 1998, 174.

Decreeing Strikes Illegal

In February 1990, the CGT–Azopardo-affiliated oil workers union (SUPE) announced a 48-hour strike in protest of the government's economic reforms. The union's secretary general, Diego Ibañez, was one of Ubaldini's earliest supporters, helping him survive the August 1989 vote on whether to remove him from the head of the CGT. When the CGT split in October 1989, Ibañez brought SUPE with Ubaldini to the CGT–Azopardo and continued vocal opposition to Menem's economic reforms. Menem's government announced that the February 1990 SUPE strike was illegal and the Minister of Labor threatened to deprive the union of its legal status if it went ahead with the strike.[124] The government went so far as to resurrect an old labor regulation from Argentina's military dictatorship – still on the books but long unused – that gave it the authority to physically force workers to return to their jobs during a strike. According to Carlos Tomada, the government only declared strikes illegal after threats to replace union leaders failed; "the declaration of illegality was the final point–before that, there were all kinds of threats."[125]

Menem then bragged to his cabinet members that his harsh crackdown on the SUPE strike demonstrated that "the government will act with firmness" to stop opposition to his economic reforms.[126] Contemporary journalists noted the change: "The government failed its first test of will, with the railways. It seems to be taking a firm line with SUPE."[127] The government's "firm line" – declaring the strike illegal, threatening to decertify the union and force strikers to return to work – was effective: SUPE backed down and called off the strike. The following week, the CGT–Azopardo-affiliated bank workers union launched a strike in opposition to the government's plan to close fourteen branches of the National Mortgage Bank. Menem's Interior Minister threatened to use "public forces" to break a sit-down strike by the union, and the Minister of Labor threatened to decertify the union if it followed through with the indefinite strike it had called for in all official banks. As one journalist explained, "the Ministry of Labor came up with the usual threat – and was again obeyed."[128]

Menem increasingly turned to such labor repression in February and March 1990, precisely when Ubaldini and the CGT–Azopardo were sharing their alternative economic plan and gaining momentum for a major strike and protest against Menem's economic reforms. It was during this period that the head of Menem's PJ party warned that a protest of more than 60,000 people could split the Peronist movement in half, cripple Menem's presidency, and

124 "Leading Events," *The Review of the River Plate*, February 28, 1990.

125 Author interview with Carlos Tomada, December 19, 2019.

126 "Official Denies Rumors of Cabinet Resignations," *Noticias Argentina* [FBIS], Feburary 16, 1990.

127 "Political Strikes Over Policy," *The Review of the River Plate*, February 28, 1990.

128 "On the Labour Front: Dollars, Pacts and Strikes – Mostly Dollars," *The Review of the River Plate*, February 28, 1990.

totally sideline Menem's economic agenda. When a three-day strike shut down the railroads in and around Buenos Aires in mid-March, Menem asked a court to suspend the legal registration of three railway unions, fired the striking workers, and requested that the Navy prepare naval engineers to break future strikes.[129] Triaca explained that "even if the union suspended its strike now, the proceedings aimed at removing the union's legal status will continue."[130] When Menem reflected on the railroad strike ending without mediation efforts, Menem glibly told the press that "we simply established conditions for the lifting of the strike."[131] As Manzetti explains, "the administration's tough stance softened labor opposition and dissuaded many unions from striking, as many workers were afraid of losing their jobs in the midst of the deep recession between 1989-90."[132]

Menem extended his threat to all unions that "insist on staging constant stoppages," warned that he would strip such unions of their legal status, and promised that if the unions go on with their struggles, "the government will also implement a battle plan [with] energetic measures."[133] Menem promised that in the future "the state will be inflexible [and] any strike that jeopardizes the peace and security of the Argentine people will not be tolerated."[134] Menem then threatened to declare a 'state of emergency' that would allow Labor Minister Triaca to suspend the registration of unions in most state-controlled services, including education and health.[135] As Juan Carlos Torre, an Argentine sociologist and member of Alfonsín's government, explained "Knowing Ubaldini, and knowing what he did, it is understandable that Triaca tried to create such an environment. Because the problem with Ubaldini was that he was crazy in the sense that he would do anything. It was a strategy to control Ubaldini."[136]

According to Carlos Tomada, Argentina's Minister of Labor for twelve years after Menem's presidency, the government knows that threatening to decertify unions is a powerful tool. Reflecting on Menem's tactics, Tomada explained that, "if I had begun to decree illegalities, at the fourth strike illegality, no one else is going to launch a strike. And here, this is what happened. It affected

129 "Rally Strengthens Menem's Hand," *Latin American Weekly Report*, April 19, 1990; "Argentina: Ferrocarriles. Historia de Traiciones y de Entregas," *ARGENPRESS*, September 23, 2008. Although four railway unions went on strike, Menem only decertified the three that were affiliated with the CGT–Azopardo, see Senén González 1999, 40.

130 "Government to Hire Train Operator Replacements," *DYN* [FBIS], April 11, 1990.

131 "Menem Discusses Railway Strike, Privatization," *Buenos Aires Domestic Service* [FBIS], April 12, 1990.

132 Manzetti, 97.

133 "Menem 'Warns' Unions of 'Government Battle Plan'," *Buenos Aires Herald* [FBIS], April 4, 1990.

134 "President Issues Warning against Future Strikes," *Buenos Aires TELAM* [FBIS], April 14, 1990.

135 "Rally Strengthens Menem's Hand," *Latin American Weekly Report*, April 19, 1990.

136 Author interview with Juan Carlos Torre, December 3, 2019.

the unions because it disciplined them."[137] Argentine union leaders agreed; according to Antonio Caló, the secretary general of the metalworkers union (UOM), "it's the same as if I threaten you: 'I'm going to put you in jail.' And well, if you don't want to go to jail, now you say 'well, let's not go on strike."'[138] Even the militant labor unions that have continued fighting against neoliberal economic policies up to the present day acknowledge that Menem's decision to declare these strikes illegal had an important impact on many unions. Argentine unions are often described as belonging to one of two different camps; a "combative" group that is ideologically committed to striking and protesting to protect workers and a "dialogue" group that is pragmatically committed to negotiating with the government. With this is mind, Héctor Recalde explained that such strike prohibitions "don't affect the combative unions. It gave excuses to the dialogist unions to break apart the CGT, which is what happened in the nineties."[139] Similarly, Víctor De Gennaro, secretary general of a state employees union (ATE) and founder of the militant CTA, claimed that such government threats stopped strikes in 1990, but only among unions that lacked ideological commitment; "It has an effect. Especially for leaders who want to have an excuse not to strike–for leaders who run their union like a business, it is a threat."[140]

The Ubaldini rally against Menem's economic policies went forward on March 21, 1990, albeit with mixed results. On the one hand, tens of thousands of protestors surrounded the Argentine Congress and called for the CGT–Azopardo to launch a general strike against Menem's economic reforms. Ubaldini told the crowd to "have no doubt that their union leaders will take the appropriate measures at the opportune moment," and that this rally was only "the first step in the fight plan."[141] The Argentine media reported that "Ubaldini's challenge is far from over. The "rebel" CGT has announced that it is gearing up for a nationwide general strike in the near future."[142] On the other hand, the rally also demonstrated that Menem's labor rights violations – his demonstrated willingness to break not only strikes, but the striking unions themselves – were beginning to reduce the ability of the CGT–Azopardo to mobilize workers. In the days leading up to the rally, Menem declared strikes by the oil and bank workers to be illegal and threatened to decertify the unions if they disobeyed; both unions then "turned their backs on the rally" and withheld support from Ubaldini's protest.[143]

137 Author interview with Carlos Tomada, December 19, 2019.
138 Author interview with Antonio Caló, December 26, 2019.
139 Author interview with Héctor Recalde, December 16, 2019.
140 Author interview with Víctor De Gennaro, December 9, 2019.
141 "Estatales Ubaldinistas Mostraron su Disconformidad," *Página/12*, March 22, 1990.
142 "Peronists Stick Together," *Latin American Weekly Report*, April 5, 1990.
143 "Estatales Ubaldinistas Mostraron su Disconformidad," *Página/12*, March 22, 1990.

The absence of these unions proved crucial, as journalists reported that the CGT–Azopardo mobilized precisely 60,000 workers, no more and no less than Cafiero's benchmark for a protest that could destabilize the Justicialista Party and threaten Menem's administration.[144] Rather than split the ranks of Menem's PJ party, the rally was followed by a public reconciliation between Menem and Cafiero.[145] According to *Página/12*, the rally's lower-than-feared turnout left Menem, his Cabinet, and PJ-leader Cafiero mutually satisfied that the government's economic plans "would continue their course tranquilly."[146] Ignoring the months of labor repression that deterred unions and workers from participating in the rally, Menem's Interior Minister announced that "we are winning the ideological battle."[147]

Menem then quickly turned toward rallying his own supporters in a pro-government rally held in the *Plaza de Mayo* on April 6, 1990. The rally was organized by what *Latin American Weekly Report* referred to as "conservative opinion groups," including a leading role from Bernardo Neustadt, a conservative Argentine radio host. The leaders of the CGT–San Martin joined the rally, but they did so alone and without the thousands of rank-and-file union members that would usually march in organized columns during such events.[148] While Ubaldini simply teased that "everyone at the rally was wearing a silk tie," *Página/12* argued that the rally may be "the founding point of a new political force that collects part of [the Peronist] tradition with conservative influences...a strange alliance of those that have nothing and those that are euphoric because 'the State will be small so that the motherland might be great.'" Scholars of Argentine politics echo these claims, concluding that during this period, "Menem's strategy aimed at forging a new conservative alliance with big domestic capital and conservative parties from Buenos Aires and other provinces of the country at the expense of unionism, the strongest and best organized group within the Peronist movement."[149]

Just as the Argentine press had used Cafiero's 60,000 threshold to judge Ubaldini's March rally, the turnout for that anti-Menem rally now became the baseline comparison for the pro-Menem rally. While some journalists estimated that "a similar number gathered" at both rallies, others reported that

144 *Latin American Weekly Report*, March 29, 1990. While the Buenos Aires police estimated the number of protestors at 15,000, the organizers claimed that roughly 80,000 participated in the rally outside the Argentine Congress. The *Buenos Aires Herald*, a conservative newspaper, estimated the turnout as between 50,000 and 100,000.

145 "Peronists Stick Together," *Latin American Weekly Report*, April 5, 1990.

146 "Optimismo en Gobierno," *Página/12*, March 22, 1990.

147 Ibid. 148 "Hombre Rico, Hombre Pobre," *Página/12*, April 7, 1990.

149 Manzetti et al. 1999, 77. Lupu argues that Menem's attempts to form "strange-bedfellow alliances with traditional rivals" was a common strategy among Latin American leaders at the turn of the twentieth century, see Lupu 2016, 3.

as many as 80,000 attended the April rally in favor of Menem's reforms.[150] Days later, Menem claimed that the rally was "spectacular and significant because it supported the government's decision, not to reverse, but to continue its policy."[151] The media had covered the March rally as Ubaldini's attempt "to test his strength against a defiant Menem," and Argentina's President now triumphantly asserted that his April rally was "a slap in the face of the doomsayers, the pessimists and losers who do not believe in the Argentine Republic."[152]

After the April rally, Menem was emboldened to further violate labor rights in order to weaken the CGT–Azopardo. According to the press, "President Carlos Menem seems to feel that the tide is turning in his favour, and that he can afford to get tough with organised labour."[153] Menem warned that "we have to give up certain things for the benefit of the country. This is what the union leaders should learn."[154] Apparently, one thing that Menem thought union leaders should give up was the right to strike; he reportedly toyed with the idea of issuing a presidential decree "sharply restricting the right to strike." When Menem's cabinet intervened and convinced him to seek congressional approval for the strike ban, he warned that if Congress did not approve a corresponding law within forty-five days, he would impose the strike ban by presidential decree nonetheless.[155]

While some legal experts rejected the constitutionality of such a prohibition, others noted that Menem had recently secured approval for his plan to increase the number of Supreme Court justices from five to nine, a packing of the court sufficient to uphold Menem's demands.[156] Rumors began to circulate that Menem would not convene the ordinary session of the Argentina Congress, and instead rule by decree. In response, Alfonsín gave a televised interview in which he warned that Argentina was "heading for authoritarianism."[157]

Breaking a Strike with the Military

At the same time that the government began declaring specific strikes to be illegal, Menem wrote an executive decree that permitted the Armed Forces to

150 "Comeback for Argentina's Left," *Latin American Weekly Report*, May 24, 1990; "Ya Nada es como Era Entonces," *Página/12*, April 7, 1990.

151 *Buenos Aires Domestic Service* [FBIS], April 12, 1990.

152 "D-day Approaches for Peronist Party," *Latin American Weekly Report*, March 29, 1990; "Hombre Rico, Hombre Pobre," *Página/12*, April 7, 1990.

153 "Rally Strengthens Menem's Hand," *Latin American Weekly Report*, April 19, 1990.

154 "Menem Discusses Railway Strike, Privatization," *Buenos Aires Domestic Service* [FBIS], April 12, 1990.

155 "Menem Gets Tough with State Workers," *Brazil and Southern Cone*, May 31, 1990.

156 Ibid.

157 "Alfonsín Warns of Threat to Congress," *Brazil and Southern Cone*, April 19, 1990. The existence of this scheme was confirmed by Peronist congressman Jorge Yoma, a family member of Menem's.

intervene in cases of "internal commotion" which endanger the "life, freedom, property or safety of the nation's inhabitants."[158] Deputies in Argentina's lower house of Congress demanded that the Minister of Defense testify regarding the government's motivation, and the leader of Argentina's Socialist Party (MAS) argued that "the government is seeking through repression what it is losing in popular support."[159] Days after the decree, a journalist interviewing Menem asked if the growing threat of a "social explosion" in opposition to his reforms was what "prompts you to think about the role that the Army might play in such cases?" When Menem denied the accusation, the journalist asked if he had ever heard of "Bordaberryism" (a reference to the dictator of Uruguay, who dissolved the general assembly and ruled by decree) and Menem simply said, "Please, that joke is in very bad taste."[160]

But it wasn't a joke; the military was called out just six months later to break a strike led by the CGT–Azopardo.[161] In September 1990, the Ubaldini-aligned telecommunications union in Buenos Aires (FOETRA-BA) launched a strike at ENTel, Argentina's national telecommunications company. The union demanded higher wages and voiced their opposition to the government's plans to privatize ENTel, which would be followed by large layoffs. The link with Ubaldini, as well as the larger political demands made by the union, quickly turned the strike into a precedent setting "showdown"; according to *Clarín*, "the strike has become an intense competition between the Ubaldanist FOETRA-BA and the Casa Rosada."[162] More specifically, the newspaper explained that "the idea is that this conflict is a test of the adjustment plan. . .and therefore its result will serve as a guide for future convulsions."[163]

Menem's government moved quickly not only to defeat the strike, but to send a clear signal that labor union opposition to its economic reforms would not be tolerated. Throughout the past year, Menem had declared various strikes illegal, occasionally fired striking worker, and decertified unions. Although Menem had decreed that the Armed Forces could be used to quell "internal commotion," he insisted that such measures would only be used during violent riots or coup attempts. In September 1990, Menem systematically combined all of these repressive tactics and focused their force on the FOETRA-BA union members occupying the ENTel offices in Buenos Aires. The Labor Ministry demanded that the union enter mandatory conciliation. When the union refused, the government declared the strike illegal. When ENTel started firing strikers, the union declared that their strike would continue for an indeterminate length. Two days later, the government agreed to the union's original wage demands but refused to rehire the 147 strikers that had already been fired. When the union continued the strike, ENTel fired an addition 110 strikers and met with

158 "Decree Gives Military Role in Domestic Conflicts," *Buenos Aires Herald*, March 4, 1990.
159 Ibid. 160 Ibid. 161 McGuire 1996.
162 "La Marche del Adjuste," *Clarín*, September 10, 1990.
163 "Quien es Quien en el Pleito," *Clarín*, September 11, 1990.

Argentina's Joint Staff of the Armed Forces to discuss the possibility of using military personnel to "ensure telephone services."

An Argentine bishop, Rodolfo Bufano, then proposed a temporary suspension of the strike and offered to help mediate the conflict. However, Menem's government "did not want the conflict mediation in the hands of Monsignor Bufano, a bishop that maintains excellent relations with Saúl Ubaldini" and refused to negotiate until the strike was permanently ended.[164] As ENTel's manager explained, "President Carlos Menem has been very clear on this point. The fact that the labour ministry has declared the strike by the Buenos Aires branch illegal forbids any kind of talks with those outside the law."[165] On September 6, the seventh day of the strike, a lieutenant colonel and twenty troops from the Armed Forces entered three ENTel offices, evicted the FOETRA strikers, and resumed telephone services. The same day, ENTel announced the firing of an additional ninety-three strikers, bringing the total to 350. According to *La Nación*, the FOETRA strikers were non-violent and the military was able to "peacefully evict" the workers.[166]

The government's use of the Armed Forces to repress a peaceful strike marked a fundamental change in Argentine labor relations and further clarified the extremes to which Menem was willing to go to defend his reforms from labor union opposition. Six months earlier, when Menem decreed that the Armed Forces could be used for "internal commotion," he forcefully denied that the military would be used to break strikes. Menem claimed that the Armed Forces would only be used for disturbances such as the infamous La Tablada attack, in which a left-wing guerrilla group attacked an Argentine Army barracks and killed thirty-nine people. He promised that "only when the security forces [police] cannot cope with cases of that nature is the President authorized to order the Armed Forces to intervene."[167] Contemporary observers were shocked: Menem's own Vice President, Eduardo Duhalde, announced that ENTel's actions were "irresponsible" and "were out of step with the country's delicate situation."[168] The head of Argentina's Socialist Party declared that "the government sending military troops to intimidate the just striker of the telephone workers' union is an unprecedented action not seen since the time of the military dictatorship."[169]

The manager of ENTel, Maria Julia Alsogaray, not only defended her actions but clarified just how high-up the decision had been made; in an interview with the *Buenos Aires Herald* Alsogaray insisted that "the use of the military personnel to replace striking workers at the ENTel phone company

164 "Hubo Cambio de Actores," *Clarín*, September 11, 1990.

165 "Alsogaray Defends Actions," *Buenos Aires Herald*, September 9, 1990.

166 "Entel: Continuaran este Fin de Semana las Negociaciones para Solucionar el Conflicto," *La Nación*, September 8, 1990.

167 "Menem Interviewed on Goals of Reorganization," *O Estado De Sao Paulo* [FBIS], March 15, 1990.

168 "Ratificaron la Continuidad del Paro Telefónico," *La Nación*, September 8, 1990. 169 Ibid.

was authorized by President Carlos Menem."[170] She also suggested that the government's forceful response was influenced by the fact that the FOETRA-BA leader "is closely aligned with Saúl Ubaldini, secretary general of the rebel Azopardo branch of the CGT" and that "the Buenos Aires union has brought politics into the conflict because it is opposed to the privatization of the company." Alsogaray dismissed criticism of her decision to break the strike with the Armed Forces and lamented that "the trouble is that some people still feel the Armed Forces almost should not exist. This is not the President's feeling and he's the commander of the Armed Forces."[171] The FOETRA strike, broken by a democratic government with the use of the military, was a turning point for Ubaldini and labor union opposition to Menem's economic reforms. As McGuire explains, "Menem's supporters have compared it with British Prime Minister Margaret Thatcher's defeat of the coal miners and U.S. President Ronald Reagan's defeat of the air traffic controllers, which launched a decade of low strike activity."[172]

Menem and the CGT–Azopardo General Strike

Despite a year of labor repression – the bomb in Ubaldini's car, the replacement of dissident union leaders, the manipulation of union finances, the declaration that certain strikes were illegal, the decertification of unions and firing of strikers, the decree permitting the Armed Forces to intervene into domestic affairs and the subsequent use of the military to break a strike – the CGT – Azopardo continued to oppose Menem's economic reforms. On October 17, 1990 the CGT–Azopardo met and unanimously voted to launch a general strike to demonstrate their "resistance to the liberal economic adjustment plan...and the demand for a recovery plan based on national employment and production."[173] In response, Menem immediately signed Decree 2148/90, which banned strikes by public sector unions – a key part of the CGT–Azopardo's coalition. The specific date of Menem's decree was also important for symbolic reasons; October 17 is Loyalty Day in Argentina, a day when Peronists celebrate the labor protests that led to Juan Perón's release from a military prison in 1945. The decree was therefore immediately seen as a "symbolic event destined to be recorded in history" – a Peronist president revoking a basic labor right guaranteed in Argentina's constitution on the day that celebrates Peronist ties with the labor movement.[174]

The strike ban is often mentioned in passing when scholars discuss how "Menem refused to give in to labor demands; indeed, he was often openly defiant of them."[175] Similarly, Levitsky and Way mention the strike ban in a long list of other "adjustment programs" that Menem implemented.[176] They

170 "Alsogaray Defends Actions," *Buenos Aires Herald*, September 9, 1990.
171 Ibid. 172 McGuire 1996, 145.
173 *Periodico Mensual de la Confederacion General del Trabajo*, November 1990.
174 Senén González 1999, 45. 175 Lupu 2016, 73. 176 Levitsky and Way 1998.

note that Menem slashed public spending, opened the country to international trade, and privatized the country's state enterprises, before writing that "the government also assaulted union privileges, banning strikes in a wide range of public services."[177] McGuire recognizes the potential importance of the ban but concludes that it had limited effect because strikes subsequently decreased in the private sector sector just as much as the public sector.[178] The strike ban is thereby acknowledged by scholars, but readers are left without any sense of how the ban fits in with other instances of labor rights violations or how it was related to the government's broader strategy.

In reality, the strike ban was the culmination of a year of labor repression aimed at weakening and isolating the CGT–Azopardo, with the ultimate goal of stopping a general strike. When the CGT–Azopardo met on October 17th and voted to launch a general strike, the Argentine Congress was still refusing to pass the anti-strike legislation that Menem proposed months earlier. With the threat of a CGT–Azopardo general strike coming to a head, Menem signed a presidential decree that effectively declared the general strike to be illegal.[179] As Senén Gonzáez explained, "the government will try to hinder him [Ubaldini]. One method will be a warning...of the consequences of taking part in the strike." Careful not to leave any doubts, Menem's Minister of Labor, Jorge Triaca, spent the weeks between the October 17 decree and the general strike planned for November 15 explicitly warning that workers joining the strike would be fired and that participating unions would be decertified. Triaca openly stated that Menem's intention was that "the right to strike was not used by those who express their opposition to the policy changes that President Menem embodies today."[180] Triaca then told journalists that he had "hung up his boots" as a labor leader; "I have dedicated myself to the government. I am Menem's man."[181] Andreoni, head of the pro-government CGT–San Martin mocked, "holding a strike or a march in these circumstances is like trying to get a kite off the ground when there is no wind."[182]

The strike ban ultimately led Lorenzo Miguel, the leader of 300,000 unionized metalworkers (UOM), to abandon Ubaldini and the CGT–Azopardo just before the general strike. Although Miguel had voted for the general strike on October 17th, when Menem banned strikes by decree and Triaca warned that the new decree would apply to the upcoming general strike, Miguel began to warn the CGT–Azopardo to reconsider. Perhaps they could launch a march or a rally, he suggested, but a general strike in defiance of the new decree appeared

177 Levitsky and Way 1998, 172. 178 McGuire 1996.

179 "Leading Events: CGT Calls for Strike," *The Review of the River Plate*, October 31, 1990.

180 Senén González 1999, 40.

181 "On the Labour Front" The Rights to Strike: the Decree and the Possible Bargains," *The Review of the River Plate*, November 14, 1990.

182 Ibid.

too costly.[183] With Miguel and other Ubaldini allies on the fence, and turnout for the general strike uncertain, the government approached Miguel with a compensation offer. To be clear, Miguel had rejected earlier government efforts to purchase his support. In April, Miguel rejected a government plan that would have incorporated the CGT–San Martin unions into a union coalition led by Miguel all while leaving Ubaldini and the CGT–Azopardo in the cold.[184] In June, Miguel rejected Menem's offer to formally represent Argentina at the ILO in exchange for removing his support for Ubaldini as the head of the CGT. Now with the November general strike approaching, Luis Barrionuevo, the head of ANSSAL and controller of union healthcare funds, "almost indulged in blackmail when he claimed that Miguel would not join the strike because he was 'loyal to the President.'"[185]

By decreeing public sector strikes illegal, promising to fire strikers, and threatening to decertify striking unions, Menem further decreased the probability that the CGT–Azopardo would be able to mobilize workers for a successful general strike. With the writing on the wall, Miguel finally cut a deal. Although there is no formal record, newspapers reported that ANSSAL transferred ten million dollars to the UOM's healthcare fund (*Obras Sociales*).[186] Miguel, now ready to acquiesce to Menem's economic reforms, told the press that the strike should be called off because Menem had already agreed to 70 percent of what union leaders had requested.[187] Miguel dramatically withdrew from the CGT–Azopardo on November 14, 1990, just one day before the planned general strike. In the following weeks, Menem overflowed with compliments, telling journalists that "we must not forget that there are leaders like Lorenzo Miguel . . . at the head of the UOM, and they think more than just of their union, they think of their own country. At times like this the Argentine Republic needs gestures of this type."[188]

The CGT–Azopardo – now shorn of many of its most powerful original members – went through with an anemic general strike on November 15, 1990. According to *La Prensa*, "the unsuccessful and almost inconsequential rally in the plaza reaffirmed this time more than ever that Saúl Ubaldini is on the decline."[189] The pathetic turnout for the strike and rally immediately led to further defections. Rubén Pereyra, the secretary general of the Waterworkers'

183 *The Review of the River Plate*, November 14, 1990

184 "Alfonsín's Decline, CGT Problems Analyzed," *La Prensa* [FBIS], April, 12, 1990.

185 "On the Labour Front: The Rights to Strike: the Decree and the Possible Bargains," *The Review of the River Plate*, November 14, 1990, 293.

186 "Miguel's Strategy," *La Prensa* [FBIS], November 15, 1990.

187 Recalde was at that meeting and told a great story about Miguel lying and Menem putting his arm on his shoulder and promising that everything would be OK.

188 "Menem on Jurisdiation for Rebels; Union Attitudes," *Buenos Aires TELAM* [FBIS], December 12, 1990.

189 "Ubaldini's Decline," *La Prensa* [FBIS], November 21, 1990.

Union (FENTOS), withdrew his union from the CGT–Azopardo despite being one of Ubaldini's original and most loyal supporters; at the March 1990 rally, Pereyra and Ubaldini had been the only two speakers.[190] As one Argentine journalist explained, labor union opposition to Menem's reforms had now "begun what could be described as the last stage of its decline."[191]

When the dust settled from the failed general strike, the CGT–Azopardo's most powerful original allies were almost all gone; unions representing workers in industries from metal, oil, water, light and power, and banking had now all migrated into an "independent" group of unions that soon joined the CGT–San Martin. After months of speculation that an Ubaldini-led general strike could sideline Menem's reforms, newspapers now ran headlines that pronounced, "The Decline of Ubaldini."[192] Less than two weeks later, with labor opposition silenced, Menem signed a decree enabling 120,000 public sector workers to be fired over the next three years.[193] The waves of privatization and trade liberalization that followed led to hundreds of thousands of job losses. Membership in the once powerful metalworkers union imploded, dropping from 300,000 members before the reforms to just 60,000 after the reforms were implemented. According to Antonio Caló, the secretary general of the UOM, "Menem opened the economy, he tossed away everything that was manufactured in Argentina, privatized everything ... He was a disaster, in my opinion, the worst president there was in Argentina."[194]

CONCLUSION

This chapter told the story of how President Carlos Menem used the violation of labor rights – labor repression – to facilitate the opening of Argentina's economy in the 1990s. The first part of this chapter focused on the opening four months of Menem's presidency (July–October 1989), when a united CGT posed a serious threat to Menem's efforts to implement trade liberalization and other neoliberal economic reforms. When Argentina's previous President, Raúl Alfonsín, proposed similar reforms in the 1980s, the CGT launched thirteen general strikes that destabilized the government and helped to maintain high tariffs. When Menem called on unions to support his reforms and pledge not to strike, CGT secretary general Saúl Ubaldini flatly rejected both requests and threatened to continue launching general strikes.[195] After the majority of Argentine unions voted to keep the militant Ubaldini at the head of the CGT,

190 "Waterworkers Union Pulls Out of Confederation," *Buenos Aires Herald*, November 20, 1990; "State Workers Hold Anti-govt Protest," *Buenos Aires Herald*, March 22, 1990.

191 "Ubaldini's Decline," *La Prensa* [FBIS], November 21, 1990.

192 *La Prensa* [FBIS], November 21, 1990.

193 "Leading Events," *The Review of the River Plate*, November 30, 1990.

194 Author interview with Antonio Caló, December 26, 2019.

195 "No Soy Obsecuente de Nadie, Aseguró Saúl Ubaldini," *Clarín*, July 27, 1989; Senén González 1999, 29.

Menem launched a campaign of labor rights violation that ultimately split the CGT into two weakened factions. Menem replaced dissident union leaders and used government control over union finances to coerce union leaders to abandon Ubaldini. It was during this period of Menem's open intervention into CGT affairs that a bomb exploded in Ubaldini's car, sending a clear message concerning "what opponents of the Menem's new economic proposals might expect."[196]

The second part of this chapter focused on the year after the CGT split (November 1989–November 1990), when Ubaldini's CGT–Azopardo continued to launch strikes that journalists and politicians saw as major obstacles to Menem's economic reforms.[197] In March 1990, the head of Menem's own party endorsed the CGT–Azopardo's alternative economic proposals and called for the government to maintain high tariffs and other policies associated with Argentina's history of import-substitution industrialization.[198] When the CGT–Azopardo led a series of successful strikes against Menem's reforms, the Argentine media concluded that Menem would either continue to give in to union demands or else face a "revolutionary general strike" that could leave his government in shambles.[199]

In order to weaken the CGT–Azopardo, Menem further increased his campaign of labor repression. As the CGT–Azopardo began to gather momentum in early 1990, the government responded by declaring strikes by CGT–Azopardo unions to be illegal, fired strikers, and decertified unions that disobeyed government orders. These labor rights violations contributed to labor unions abandoning the CGT–Azopardo right before a crucial March 1990 protest, which contemporary politicians and journalists saw as having the potential to permanently undermine Menem's leadership and ability to implement his reforms. When the CGT–Azopardo then launched a strike seen as "the acid test" for Menem's ability to overcome labor union opposition to his reforms, Menem ordered the military to break the strike.[200]

When the CGT–Azopardo finally announced plans for a long-anticipated general strike, Menem declared the strike illegal and threatened to decertify participating unions and to fire striking workers. These labor rights violations contributed to the powerful metalworkers union (UOM) abandoning the CGT–Azopardo the day before the general strike.[201] With the loss of the UOM's 300,000 union members, turnout for the general strike was embarrassingly

196 Author interview with Héctor Palomino, December 23, 2019.

197 "Alfonsín Warns of Threat to Congress," *Brazil and Southern Cone*, 19 April 1990.

198 "CGT Muestra Las Uñas," *Página/12*, March 9, 1990.

199 "Why Bother with Plans and Pronouncements?" *The Review of the River Plate*, December 14, 1989, 407.

200 "On the Labour Front: The Right to Strike, Employment Flexibility and Bond Payments," *The Review of the River Plate*, September 14, 1990, pg. 150.

201 "The Right to Strike: the Decree and the Possible Bargains," *The Review of the River Plate*, November 14, 1990, 293.

low and the CGT–Azopardo quickly lost so many affiliated unions that the Argentine press finally announced the "the decline of Ubaldini."[202]

Of course, labor repression was only a part of Menem's broader strategy to split the Argentine labor movement in half and then to isolate, weaken, and ultimately defeat the unions that continued to oppose his economic reforms. Strong partisan ties between the Argentine labor movement and the PJ party helped Menem maintain a base of support amongst many Argentine union leaders. Menem also provided compensation in the form of government positions and financial resources to union leaders that agreed to support his reforms. Yet, as shown above, partisan loyalty between unions and the PJ only led a minority of unions to support Menem's reforms; Menem only garnered enough union support to remove Ubaldini from the CGT after a car bomb, the replacement of dissident union leaders, and the manipulation of union finances helped to tilt the balance. Similarly, although compensation played an important role in unions abandoning the CGT–Azopardo, Menem's escalating campaign of labor repression clearly helps to explain the timing and logic of those defections.

By overlooking the threat posed by the CGT–Azopardo, scholars regularly commit what John Dewey called the "historical fallacy." According to Dewey, this fallacy occurs when "a state of things characterizing an outcome is regarded as a true description of the events which led up to this outcome; when, as a matter of fact, if this outcome had already been in existence, there would have been no necessity for the process."[203] Scholars incorrectly draw conclusions about the CGT–Azopardo's original power based on the final outcome of the union's efforts to resist Menem's reforms. It is true that Ubaldini and the CGT–Azopardo failed to launch a general strike in the opening years of Menem's presidency, but that does not mean that the CGT–Azopardo did not pose a serious threat to Menem's reforms during that period. In fact, Argentine journalists and politicians believed that Ubaldini's growing coalition in 1990 represented a major obstacle to Menem's leadership of the Peronist movement and his ability to implement trade liberalization and other economic reforms.

Critical junctures are easy to observe when things change, when a trajectory is suddenly altered. They are more difficult to identify when things stay the same, that is, when efforts to alter the trajectory of events fail. Once defeated, such challenges are often written-out of our conventional histories and become paths not taken and soon forgotten. Looking back, it is easy to see Menem consciously twisting the Argentine narrative in this way. In April 1990, Menem addressed a pro-reform rally from the balcony of the *Casa Rosada*. When he came back inside to his office, journalists were waiting to interview him and the first question was, "What would you say to Ubaldini, and those that didn't come?"[204] Menem responded, "if they decide to join from now on it's up to

[202] "Ubaldini's Decline," *La Prensa* [FBIS], November 21, 1990. [203] Dewey 1896, 367.
[204] "Hombre Rico, Hombre Pobre," *Página/12*, April 7, 1990.

them. Because nobody here closes the door to anyone. The doors are open, I am not the one that closes them or opens them, so now they will do what they decide."[205]

Of course, Menem knew that labor unions were not left free to decide whether or not to oppose his economic reforms. Menem's systematic violation of labor rights – the manipulation of union finances, intervention into union elections, the banning of strikes – were all doors that he opened and closed in order to decrease the ability of unions to launch strikes and protests. If we accept Menem's rhetoric, we are one step closer to falling for the historical fallacy that Dewey warned about. For scholars that believe that Menem passively waited for unions to make up their minds, the collapse of the CGT–Azopardo implies that labor union opposition dissolved on its own. In fact, the eventual weakness of the CGT–Azopardo – the lack of a general strike against Menem's reforms – is even held up as an illustration of how unnecessary labor repression would have been. In contrast, this chapter showed the numerous ways in which Menem used labor repression to help avoid general strikes. The goal of such revisionist history was well captured by Víctor De Gennaro, an Argentine labor union leader who played an active role in the story told above: "There is an Argentine song that says, 'if history is written by those who win, then that means that there is another history.' Recovering all these little pieces of that history is therefore a triumph."[206]

205 Ibid. 206 Author interview with Víctor De Gennaro, December 9, 2019.

6

Conclusion

Before the sun rose on September 19, 1985, Juan Lechín Oquendo and hundreds of other Bolivian labor union leaders were taken to internment camps in the Amazon jungle.[1] Hours earlier, they had been lying on cots in a union office off of La Paz's colonial *Plaza San Francisco*, two weeks into a general strike and three days into a national hunger strike. The union's protests were an effort to block trade liberalization and other neoliberal economic reforms announced by their country's newly elected President, Victor Paz Estenssoro.[2] Bolivia's democratic government sent the police to crack down on such union opposition, banish union leaders to the outskirts of the country, and forcefully break the general strike.[3] The next morning, the government confirmed the circulating rumors that they had declared a 'state of siege' but refused to release the names of the union members being detained.[4]

Shocking as it may sound, this is a central part of the story of how Bolivia and many other democratic developing countries opened their economies in the late twentieth century. Half-way around the world, Turkey's newly-elected democratic government was lowering tariffs while the country's union leaders sat in prison awaiting trial. A few years later, Argentina's democratic government manipulated union elections and banned strikes in order to avoid the general strikes that had helped to block trade liberalization throughout the 1980s. In the early 1990s, the democratic government of India – a country with a reputation for strong pro-labor legislation – preventively arrested tens

1 "CBO Goes Underground," *Paris AFP* [FBIS], September 20, 1985.

2 "COB Message Calls for National Hunger Strike," *La Paz Cadena Panamericana* [FBIS], September 17, 1985; Nazmi 1995.

3 "Mass Arrests, Curfew Follow," *Madrid EFE* [FBIS], September 19, 1985. Polity, Varieties of Democracy, and the Unified Democracy Score all consider Bolivia to have been a democracy in 1985.

4 "Union Leaders Banished," *Paris AFP* [FBIS], September 19, 1985.

of thousands of union members in an effort to decrease turnout for a general strike launched against the government's plan to open the economy. In these ways, *Opening Up By Cracking Down* has told the story of how democratic developing countries used labor repression to overcome union opposition and thereby facilitate the process of trade liberalization.

During the late twentieth century many democratic developing countries followed one of two different paths toward free trade. The first path started with labor repression and then added democracy. This occurred when developing countries transitioned from autocracy to democracy but maintained the high levels of labor repression practiced by the previous regime. Democracy empowered demands for trade liberalization from the general public and export-oriented capital while labor repression weakened union pleas for continued trade protection. For countries on this path, democratization triggered trade liberalization and tariffs fell fast.

The second path started with democracy, and then added labor repression. This trajectory started when developing countries not only transitioned to democracy but also established high levels of respect for labor rights. Labor unions, more often than not, led the democratization struggles that gave birth to such pro-labor democracies. The mix of democracy and labor rights politically empowered labor unions, which joined protectionist industrialists and fought to maintain the tariffs that promised high wages alongside high profits. The more these democracies continued to respect labor rights, the more likely they were to continue to protect their economies with high tariffs. Trade liberalization became more likely – whether it took four years or forty years – when these democratic governments increased labor repression to weaken union opposition.

My argument places labor repression at the heart of the history of international trade in developing countries and suggests that scholars must think differently to understand the tensions and trade-offs between democracy, labor rights, and free trade. First, it challenges a common argument in international political economy, which holds that democracy, on its own, was a sufficient condition for trade liberalization.[5] This work often starts with the Heckscher–Ohlin model of international trade to predict that workers in developing countries, who constitute the majority of the population, overwhelmingly support trade liberalization.[6] It then uses the median voter theorem to predict that democratic governments lower tariffs in response to the pro-trade demands of the average worker. This approach precludes labor union opposition to trade liberalization, cannot explain why many developing countries maintained high tariffs after transitioning to democracy, and fails to recognize that democracies that repressed labor unions were the most likely to embrace free trade.

5 Milner and Kubota 2005; O'Rourke and Taylor 2006; Eichengreen and Leblang 2008; Chaudoin et al. 2015.

6 Rogowski 1989; Hiscox 2002.

Second, it poses a fundamental challenge to the widespread assumption that democracies do not use labor repression to reduce labor unions' policy influence. This assumption can be traced back to the 1980s, when scholars used a false dichotomy to theorize about why many authoritarian regimes were opening their economies more rapidly than democracies. According to this perspective, dictatorships like Pinochet's Chile could use labor repression to overcome labor union opposition while democratic governments like Alfonsín's Argentina were precluded from violating basic labor rights. When democratic governments later began to lower their tariffs, many scholars implicitly used this framework to search for the non-repressive tactics that democracies used to overcome union opposition. Many argued that democracies used welfare compensation – unemployment insurance, job retraining programs – to overcome opposition from groups harmed by free trade.[7] Others argued that economic crises weakened the ability of unions to mobilize workers, or that partisan ties between unions and political parties led unions to acquiesce to reforms.[8] While these non-repressive tactics often played important roles, a generation of scholarship has remained unjustifiably silent on the many ways in which democratic developing countries routinely used labor repression to overcome labor union opposition to trade liberalization.

This book tested my theory with a multi-method approach that combined rigorous quantitative and qualitative evidence. Together, these different types of research built a constellation of evidence that demonstrated how labor repression facilitated the process of trade liberalization in many democratic developing countries at the turn of the twentieth century. Chapter 2 used regression analysis and quantitative data from 126 developing countries from 1985 to 2010 to show that tariff levels vary with democracy and labor rights in the general ways predicted by my theory. As my theory's first path toward free trade predicts, increases in democracy were more likely to be associated with trade liberalization if respect for labor rights was low. At higher levels of respect for labor rights, increases in democracy were associated with continued trade protection. As my theory's second path toward free trade predicts, in countries with an established democratic government, an increase in labor repression was associated with a decrease in tariff levels. These findings not only established the generalizability of my argument across the developing world, but also showed that these dynamics cannot be explained by many of the alternative explanations developed by previous studies.

While this regression analysis was ideal for establishing the general relationships between trade policy, democracy, and labor rights, it was unable to explore the causal mechanisms that link labor repression to trade liberalization in democratic developing countries. How does labor repression increase the probability of trade liberalization in democratic developing countries? Is my

7 Ruggie 1982; Garrett and Lange 1995; Etchemendy 2004; Walter 2010; Menendez 2016.
8 Nelson and Waterbury 1989; Geddes 1995; Murillo 2001; Levitsky 2003; Teitelbaum 2011.

theory correct that labor repression weakens the ability of labor unions to launch protests and strikes against government efforts to lower tariffs? In order to begin answering these questions, Chapter 3 presented a series of case studies of trade politics in Argentina, Mexico, Bolivia, Turkey, and India during the late twentieth century. Using a mix of cross-case and within-case comparisons, this chapter illustrated three key causal mechanisms of my theory – (1) how democracy increased demands for trade liberalization, (2) how democratic developing countries frequently used labor repression to weaken union opposition, and (3) how variation in the scope of union mobilization influenced trade policy outcomes.

Chapter 3 began with a cross-case comparison of Argentina (1983–1989) and Mexico (1982–1994), most-similar cases that both started the period with authoritarian governments facing economic crises, subsequently democratized, witnessed governments propose trade liberalization, and had protectionist labor union confederations that opposed the reforms. These cases show how the degree to which an increase in democracy led to trade liberalization depended on the degree to which governments respected labor rights or repressed labor unions. In Mexico, democratization was accompanied by labor repression that weakened union opposition and facilitated the government's ability to lower tariffs. In Argentina, democratization was combined with respect for labor rights, which permitted unions to launch general strikes that contributed to the government's decision to maintain high tariffs.

A within-case comparison of trade politics in Bolivia (1982–1989) illustrated how a similar dynamic played out over the course of the country's first two democratically-elected presidents. These cases illustrated how Bolivia's democratization in 1982 led to a new democracy that respected labor rights and maintained high tariffs. Bolivia's democratic government faced new domestic demands for trade liberalization, but union protests and general strikes made such reforms unlikely. Bolivia did not lower its tariffs until 1985, when a newly-elected president increased labor repression – the mass arrest of labor union leaders discussed above – in order to silence labor union opposition to trade liberalization and other economic reforms. The cases clearly illustrate how an increase in democracy led to the maintenance of high tariffs when the government respected labor right (1982–1985), as well as how an increase in labor repression in an established democracy facilitated the country's move toward free trade (1985–1989).

The case studies then moved beyond Latin America to demonstrate how the same dynamics shaped trade policy outcomes in developing countries in other regions of the world. A within-case comparison of Turkey in the 1960s through the 1980s explored the trade policy consequences of two very different democratic transitions. In 1961, Turkey transitioned to democracy, elected a government that respected labor rights, and went on to maintain high tariffs. In 1980, a military coup ushered in an authoritarian regime that brutally repressed labor unions. In 1983, Turkey transitioned back to democracy, elected a government that maintained the high levels of labor repression practiced by the previous military regime, and quickly implemented trade liberalization. The Turkish cases illustrate how an increase in democracy led to the maintenance of high tariffs when labor rights were protected (1960s and 1970s), as well as how an increase in democracy led to trade liberalization when labor unions were repressed.

Finally, Chapter 3 presented a case study of trade politics in the long-established democracy of India, a case that is "most different" from the relatively new democracies analyzed in the rest of the chapter. The Indian case study illustrates how Prime Minister Rajiv Gandhi's attempts to lower tariffs between 1985 and 1987 triggered union-led general strikes that helped to reverse the reforms. Despite the numerous differences between India (1985–1987), Argentina (1983–1989), Bolivia (1982–1985), and Turkey (1961–1980), all of these countries maintained high tariffs after facing union-led general strikes that were enabled by high levels of respect for labor rights. Across all five country cases analyzed in this chapter, labor unions demanded continued trade protection, and democratic governments were more likely to implement trade liberalization if they repressed such labor union opposition.

While Chapter 3 explored Argentina and India in the 1980s, the next two chapters continued these stories into the 1990s. In both cases, labor rights and high tariffs in the 1980s gave way to labor repression and trade liberalization in the 1990s. Chapter 4 explained how Narasimha Rao was elected Prime Minister of India in 1991 and quickly set out to avoid the labor-led general strikes that had blocked trade liberalization in the 1980s. When India's labor unions announced a general strike against Rao's New Economic Policy, the government offered the unions compensation programs and policy consultation in exchange for canceling the strike. The unions refused and paralyzed the country with a general strike joined by ten million workers. When the unions called for another general strike six months later, Rao's government fought back by arresting tens of thousands of union members and holding them in prison until after the strike was over. Such "preventive arrests" reduced the unions' ability to picket and spread the general strike, thus reducing turnout and political influence. Rao's use of labor repression thus facilitated India's move toward free trade, even while continued labor union opposition compelled the country to lower its tariffs more slowly than most other developing countries.

Chapter 5 explained how Carlos Menem was elected President of Argentina in 1989 and quickly took aim at the CGT, the labor union confederation that led thirteen general strikes against neoliberal economic reforms during the 1980s. Drawing on archival research in Washington, D.C. and Buenos Aires, as well as fieldwork interviews with Argentine labor union leaders and government officials, this chapter described how Menem interfered in union elections, manipulated union finances, decertified unions and fired workers that launched strikes against his reforms, broke a strike with the military, and ultimately banned strikes on the eve of a CGT general strike. This campaign of labor repression helped to split the CGT in half and slowly defeated the labor unions that continued to oppose his reforms. Argentine labor union leaders repeatedly rejected compensation offers from the government and continued to oppose Menem's reforms until labor repression ultimately made continued resistance a lost cause. A within-case comparison of Argentina in the 1980s and 1990s, respectively, illustrated why democracies that respected labor rights were more likely to maintain high tariffs as well as how established democracies used labor repression to facilitate trade liberalization.

DEMOCRACY, FREE TRADE, AND INTERNATIONAL POLITICAL ECONOMY

Scholars of international political economy have long recognized that democracy, on its own, may not lead to trade liberalization in *developed* countries. Traditionally, the field has seen this as a normative problem that ought to be fixed for the benefit of consumers around the world, and especially workers in developing countries. As Krugman argues, "while fat-cat capitalists might benefit from globalization, the biggest beneficiaries are, yes, Third World workers."[9] Drawing on work by neoclassical economists, IPE scholars generally hold that some groups may be harmed by trade liberalization but that governments can tax the winners, redistribute income to the losers, and ultimately leave everyone better off.[10] Despite these broad benefits, democracy permits narrow interest groups to capture the policymaking process and secure trade protection.[11] In this vein, the field tends to see demands for trade protection, whether they come from labor unions in declining industries, environmentalists concerned about climate change, or human rights activists concerned about labor conditions abroad, as rent-seeking behavior that harms consumers in the United States and workers in developing countries.[12]

A common IPE solution to the tension between democracy and free trade has been that countries should create international institutions. By working through multilateral institutions such as the World Trade Organization, countries could negotiate binding commitments to trade liberalization that would "tie the hands" of governments and thereby help them to overcome domestic demands for trade protection.[13] This approach embraced un-democratic strategies – international delegation and the "insulation" of policymakers – to achieve outcomes that were believed to benefit the majority.[14] As Farrell and Knight argue, IPE scholars thereby "defend the dominant features of the international political economy – international institutions and economic openness – as democratically justified forms of delegation that serve demonstrable public needs."[15] Trade liberalization was a democratic outcome achieved by less-than democratic means.

9 Krugman 1997. 10 Feenstra and Lewis 1994. 11 Grossman and Helpman 1994.
12 e.g. Krueger 1974; Goldstein and Martin 2000. 13 Milner 1998. 14 Moravcsik 2004.
15 Farrell and Knight 2017.

After years of advocating trade liberalization and delegation to international institutions, the Great Recession and the rise of populism have left the field of international political economy in a "crisis of legitimacy." As Keohane explains,

> Those of us who have celebrated as well as analyzed globalization share some responsibility for the rise of populism. We demonstrated that an institutional infrastructure was needed to facilitate globalization, but this infrastructure was constructed by and for economic elites. . .Global finance and global business had a privileged status, and there was little regard for the interests of ordinary workers.[16]

In short, the field's solution to the tension between free trade and democracy contributed to the pursuit of trade policies that harmed workers in developed countries and bred distrust in multilateral institutions. In the United States, trade shocks wreaked havoc on local communities, triggered a backlash against globalization and elite policymakers, and fueled support for authoritarianism.[17] The IPE solution to square democracy with free trade in developed countries may have ultimately undermined both.[18]

This book suggests that a similar reckoning is needed with regards to the relationship between democracy and free trade in developing countries. If international institutions made democracy compatible with trade liberalization in developed countries, it was often labor repression that permitted democratic developing countries to pursue trade liberalization. If viewed over the *longue durée*, there are signs that IPE scholars are slowly recognizing the unpopular roots of trade liberalization in developing countries. For example, the neoclassical trade models used by IPE scholars have gradually decreased the size of the group of workers purported to gain from trade liberalization in developing countries. Rogowski's groundbreaking work in the 1980s introduced the Heckscher–Ohlin model, along with its prediction that trade liberalization would increase wages for all workers in developing countries.[19] Frieden's use of the Ricardo–Viner model predicted that the benefits of trade would be more narrow, but still extend to all workers in export-oriented industries.[20] More recent work in IPE uses what is called "New New Trade Theory" to predict that trade liberalization only benefits a small number of "superstar firms," which account for the vast majority of exports.[21]

Over the course of forty years, the expected beneficiaries of trade liberalization in developing countries progressively shrank from all workers, to all workers in export-oriented industries, to the small number of relatively high-skilled workers employed by a handful of firms. In this vein, Menendez, Owen, and Walter recently called on scholars to consider how the narrow benefits of trade liberalization in developing countries may change our "expectations about the politics of trade in emerging and developing countries."[22] That is,

[16] Keohane 2016.
[17] Autor et al. 2016; MacWilliams 2016; Dean 2018; Broz et al. 2019; Dean and Kimmel 2019.
[18] Colgan and Keohane 2017. [19] Rogowski 1989. [20] Frieden 1991.
[21] Madeira 2016; Osgood et al. 2017; Kim and Osgood 2019. [22] Menendez et al. 2018.

why did democracies in developing countries end up opening their economies, if trade predominately benefitted a small minority of its citizens? And how could the pro-trade demands of a few exporting firms outweigh the protectionist demands of labor unions hurt by globalization? This book has argued that democratic governments in developing countries were more likely to implement trade liberalization if they used labor repression to weaken union opposition. That such labor-repressive democracies pursue trade policies that may only benefit a small segment of the population is, perhaps, less puzzling.

Are democracies justified in using labor repression to liberalize trade policy if only a minority of the country benefits from free trade? Answering this question requires that we also consider the broader negative consequences of labor repression. Independent of international trade, labor repression weakens labor unions and therefore lowers workers' wages, increases income inequality, and weakens demands for welfare spending.[23] Some scholars even point to the decline of labor unions as a proximate cause of the erosion and decline of democracy around the globe.[24] A virtuous circle of democracy, free trade, and the empowerment of workers in developing countries makes for a great story. It's just not what actually happened.

In this book, I have tried to tell a different story, one more focused on the labor unions that opposed trade liberalization and the ways in which democratic governments frequently used labor repression to weaken protests and break strikes. Many of these tales, such as the preventive arrest of tens of thousands of union members in India or the bomb that blew up CGT Secretary General Ubaldini's car in Argentina, are conspicuously absent from conventional histories of economic reform at the turn of the twenty-first century. I hope that the revisionist histories presented throughout this book improve our understanding of trade liberalization by conveying more of what really happened in democratic developing countries. Building a global economy of democracies that respect labor rights will require, at the very least, an honest reckoning with the labor repression that facilitated the last wave of globalization.

23 Rudra 2002; Kerrissey 2015; Yang and Kwon 2019.
24 Schmitter 1993; Budd et al. 2018; Baccaro et al. 2019.

Appendix

This appendix presents additional information concerning the cross-national statistical analysis presented in Chapter 2 as well as the industry-level analysis of Indian tariffs and union membership presented in Chapter 4.

The regression analyses presented in Chapter 2 included all countries for which data was available in Latin America, Africa, the Middle East (excluding Israel), Asia (excluding Japan), and Eastern Europe. Table A.1 presents a list of the 126 developing countries included in the analyses. Table A.2 presents the descriptive statistics for the variables included in the regression analysis in Chapter 2.

INDIA'S TARIFFS AND UNION MEMBERSHIP

This section provides additional information on the analysis of Indian tariffs presented in Chapter 4. The analysis focused on industry-year level tariff levels, using data from the World Bank's World Integrated Trade Solution.[1] Data on unweighted average tariffs is available for 16 different industries, including agriculture, mining, and manufacturing from 1990 to 2016.[2] According to this data, India's highest tariffs – 144 percent – were in the food products industry in 1990. India's lowest tariffs – 9 percent – were in the hides and skin industry in 1997. India's tariffs were gradually reduced during the 1990s, from a starting mean of 78 percent in 1990 to a mean of 32 by 1999. The mean industry-year tariff during the 1990s was 47.2 percent.

1 https://wits.worldbank.org

2 Data on the following sectors are available, based on the Harmonized Commodity Description and Coding System: Animal, Vegetable, Food Products, Minerals, Fuels, Chemicals, Plastic or Rubber, Hides and Skins, Wood, Textiles and Clothing, Footwear, Stone and Glass, Metals, Machinery and Electrical, Transportation, and Miscellaneous.

TABLE A.1. *The 126 developing countries analyzed in Chapter 2*

Albania, Algeria, Angola, Argentina, Armenia, Azerbaijan, Bahrain, Bangladesh, Belarus, Benin, Bhutan, Bolivia, Botswana, Brazil, Bulgaria, Burkina Faso, Burundi, Cambodia, Cameroon, Central African Republic, Chad, Chile, China, Colombia, Comoros, Costa Rica, Cote d'Ivoire, Croatia, Cuba, Czech Republic, Democratic Republic of the Congo, Djibouti, Dominican Republic, Ecuador, Egypt, El Salvador, Equatorial Guinea, Eritrea, Estonia, Ethiopia, Gabon, Gambia, Georgia, Ghana, Guatemala, Guinea, Guinea-Bissau, Guyana, Haiti, Honduras, Hungary, India, Indonesia, Iran, Jordan, Kazakhstan, Kenya, Kuwait, Kyrgyz Republic, Laos, Latvia, Lesotho, Liberia, Libya, Lithuania, Macedonia, Madagascar, Malawi, Malaysia, Mali, Mauritania, Mauritius, Mexico, Moldova, Mongolia, Morocco, Mozambique, Namibia, Nepal, Nicaragua, Niger, Nigeria, Oman, Pakistan, Panama, Papua New Guinea, Paraguay, Peru, Philippines, Poland, Qatar, Romania, Rwanda, Saudi Arabia, Senegal, Sierra Leone, Singapore, Slovak Republic, Slovenia, Solomon Islands, South Africa, South Korea, Sri Lanka, Sudan, Suriname, Swaziland, Syria, Tajikistan, Tanzania, Thailand, Togo, Trinidad and Tobago, Tunisia, Turkey, Turkmenistan, Uganda, Ukraine, United Arab Emirates, Uruguay, Uzbekistan, Venezuela, Vietnam, Yemen, Zambia, Zimbabwe

TABLE A.2. *Descriptive statistics*

	N	Mean	SD	Min	Max
Tariff	1422	16.9	12.5	0	106.5
Polity	1422	11.5	6.71	0	20
LaborRights	1422	23.6	7.54	2.50	37
Population (log)	1422	16.3	1.55	12.8	21.0
GDPpc (log)	1422	7.45	1.30	3.97	11.0
WTO	1422	0.57	0.50	0	1
Left Exec	1422	0.29	0.45	0	1
Manufacturing (% GDP)	1243	16.5	7.57	1.42	41.7
IMF-Trade	1422	2.89	4.80	0	49.0
IMF-Labor	1422	0.86	2.37	0	22.0
Debt Crisis	1384	0.01	0.09	0	1
Bank Crisis	1384	0.04	0.18	0	1
Currency Crisis	1384	0.04	0.20	0	1
Welfare (% GDP)	709	3.999	4.61	0	21.07

Testing my argument at a subnational level required gathering data on industry-level labor union power in India. The analysis below utilizes data on union membership available from the Indian Labour Year Book produced annually by India's Ministry of Labour and Employment. Since only 10 to 25 percent of registered Indian labor unions provide membership information in any given year, this data represents a low estimate of union membership.

In order to address considerable variation from year-to-year within each industry, the analysis uses a three-year running average of union membership. Union members in India, in absolute numbers, are most likely to be found in the agricultural sectors; in 1999, 1.1 million union members were employed in the production of plant-based foods, while 260,000 union members manufactured food products. Of the 1.5 million union members in India's mining and manufacturing industries in 1990, roughly 75 percent were employed in the textile, metal, machinery, and transportation equipment industries. The total number of union members increased from 1990 (2.1 million) to 1999 (3.1 million), with the largest increase coming from the production of plant-based foods and the largest decrease coming from textiles.

The analysis below uses the number of labor union members as a measure of industry-year level labor power, rather than a measure of union density (percentage of workers that are unionized). This properly captures the basic logic of my argument, which is that the Indian government formulated trade policy in a way that would minimize labor opposition. All else being equal, lowering tariffs on an industry with a large number of protectionist union members would therefore be more politically difficult than lowering tariffs on an industry with a smaller number of union members. Although union density is a good proxy for labor power vis-a-vis employers, the number of union members is a better proxy for labor power vis-a-vis the government.

India's original commitment to high tariffs and import–substitution industrialization was based on the goal of increasing production, employment, and profitability in industrial manufacturing. The lowering of tariffs in the 1990s opened the Indian economy to global competition and threatened to harm these previously prized sectors. To address the possibility that industry characteristics besides union membership influenced tariff levels, the analysis controls for industry-level employment, fixed capital, and profitability using data from the Economic and Political Weekly Research Foundation India Time Series.[3] To address the possibility that tariff levels were influenced by changes in overall employment levels, the analyses controls for annual employment in both manufacturing and agriculture using data from the Centre for Monitoring Indian Economy.[4]

The analysis presented in Table A.3 explores the relationship between industry-year level tariffs and labor union membership using ordinary least squares regression. In order to address the decline of tariff levels over time, the model includes a year time trend. I address concerns about serial correlation in tariff levels with an AR(1) correction and estimate panel-corrected standard errors in order to control for the panel heteroskedasticity and contemporaneously correlated errors associated with panel data.[5] To focus the analysis on variation within industries over time, the analysis also introduces industry-level fixed effects. Tariff levels and union membership are both logarithmically

3 http://epwrfits.in 4 https://economicoutlook.cmie.com 5 Beck and Katz 1995.

TABLE A.3. *OLS regression results. DV = log(Tariff)*

	Model 1	Model 2	Model 3	Model 4
Union Membership	0.098***	0.073*	0.083**	0.104**
	(0.021)	(0.029)	(0.027)	(0.037)
Year	−0.087***	−0.091***	−0.098***	−0.093***
	(0.016)	(0.016)	(0.015)	(0.011)
Number of Workers		0.071	0.063	
		(0.063)	(0.057)	
Fixed Capital		−0.035	−0.023	
		(0.052)	(0.048)	
Profits		0.008	0.007	
		(0.022)	(0.021)	
Manufacturing			−0.184	−0.239
			(0.151)	(0.131)
Agriculture			0.346	0.125
			(0.632)	(0.603)
Industry Fixed-Effects	no	no	no	yes
Observations	288	192	192	288
R^2	0.861	0.910	0.913	0.896

AR(1) correction and panel-corrected standard errors in parentheses.
* $p < 0.05$, ** $p < 0.01$, *** $p < 0.001$.

transformed to address their non-normal distribution, and the coefficients reported below therefore represent elasticities.

The regression results reported in Table A.3 suggest a positive relationship between industry-year tariff levels and union membership. Model 1 regresses tariff levels on to union membership and a time trend. Model 2 introduces industry-level controls for the number of workers, fixed capital, and profitability. Model 3 includes additional controls for total employment in manufacturing and agriculture. Since the industry-level variables are relatively stable over time, the model cannot include these controls at the same time as industry-level fixed effects. Model 4 therefore drops these controls and introduces industry-level fixed effects.

Across all four models, the coefficient on *Union Membership* is positive and statistically significant. This elasticity means that a 10 percent increase in industry-level union membership is associated with a roughly 1 percent increase in industry-level tariff protection. In other words, throughout the reform period, the Indian government maintained higher levels of tariff protection for industries that employed larger numbers of union members. This relationship cannot be explained by industry-level employment, profitability, or fixed capital, stable differences across India's industries, changes in manufacturing or agricultural employment, or temporal trends in trade policy. Although the relationship between union membership and tariff levels may also run in the opposite direction (e.g., tariff cuts cause layoffs), the model's controls focus the analysis on union membership while holding industry-level employment constant. Since non-unionized workers are likely to be laid-off before unionized workers, there is less reason to worry about reverse causality; tariff cuts are unlikely to lead to more layoffs for union members than non-union members.[6] While the small number of controls raise concerns about omitted variables that may explain the correlation between tariffs and union membership, these regression results provide additional support for my argument that labor union power in India was associated with higher levels of tariff protection.

6 Abraham and Medoff 1984.

Bibliography

Abraham, Katharine G., and Medoff, James L. 1984. Length of service and layoffs in union and nonunion work groups. *ILR Review*, 38(1), 87–97.

Acemoglu, Daron. 2003. Patterns of skill premia. *The Review of Economic Studies*, 70(2), 199–230.

Acemoglu, Daron, and Robinson, James A. 2006. *Economic Origins of Dictatorship and Democracy*. Cambridge University Press.

2008. Persistence of power, elites, and institutions. *American Economic Review*, 98(1), 267–293.

Adsera, Alicia, and Boix, Carles. 2002. Trade, democracy, and the size of the public sector: The political underpinnings of openness. *International Organization*, 56(2), 229–262.

Ahlquist, John S., and Levi, Margaret. 2014. *In the Interest of Others: Organizations and Social Activism*. Princeton University Press.

Ahlquist, John S., Clayton, Amanda B., and Levi, Margaret. 2013. Unionization and workers' attitudes toward international trade: The ILWU puzzle. *International Organization*, 68(1), 33–75.

Ahluwalia, Montek S. 2002. Economic reforms in India since 1991: Has gradualism worked? *Journal of Economic Perspectives*, 16(3), 67–88.

Ahmad, Feroz. 1993. *The Making of Modern Turkey*. Vol. 264. Routledge London.

1998. The economy of Turkey since liberalization. *Studies in Comparative International Development*, 33(2), 126–129.

Albertus, Michael, and Menaldo, Victor. 2014. Gaming democracy: Elite dominance during transition and the prospects for redistribution. *British Journal of Political Science*, 44(3), 575–603.

2018. *Authoritarianism and the Elite Origins of Democracy*. Cambridge University Press.

Anderson, Leslie E. 2016. *Democratization by Institutions: Argentina's Transition Years in Comparative Perspective*. University of Michigan Press.

Arrighi, Giovanni, Silver, Beverly J., and Brewer, Benjamin D. 2003. Industrial convergence, globalization, and the persistence of the North-South divide. *Studies in Comparative International Development*, 38(1), 3–31.

Aswathappa, Kemal. 2005. *Human Resource and Personnel Management*. Tata McGraw-Hill Education.

Autor, David, Dorn, David, Hanson, Gordon, and Majlesi, Kaveh. 2016. Importing political polarization? *NBER Working Paper*.

Babb, Sarah. 2013. The Washington Consensus as transnational policy paradigm: Its origins, trajectory and likely successor. *Review of International Political Economy*, 20(2), 268–297.

Baccaro, Lucio, Benassi, Chiara, and Meardi, Guglielmo. 2019. Theoretical and empirical links between trade unions and democracy. *Economic and Industrial Democracy*, **40**(1), 3–19.

Bailey, Michael, Goldstein, Judith, and Weingast, Barry. 1997. The institutional roots of American trade policies. *World Politics*, **49**(3), 309–338.

Baker, Andy. 2005. Who wants to globalize? Consumer tastes and labor markets in a theory of trade policy beliefs. *American Journal of Political Science*, **49**(4), 924–938.

2009. *The Market and the Masses in Latin America: Policy Reform and Consumption in Liberalizing Economies*. Cambridge University Press.

Banga, Rashmi, and Das, Abhijit. 2010. Role of Trade Policies in Growth of Indian Manufacturing Sector. *Munich Personal RePEc Archive* Paper No. 35236 https://mpra.ub.uni-muenchen.de/35236/

Bates, Robert H. 2014. *Markets and States in Tropical Africa: The Political Basis of Agricultural Policies*. University of California Press.

Bates, Robert H., and Krueger, Anne. 1993. *Political and Economic Interactions in Economic Policy Reform*. Oxford: Blackwell.

Bearce, David H., and Velasco-Guachalla, V. Ximena. 2020. How can we explain regime type differences if citizens don't vote based on foreign economic policy? *Foreign Policy Analysis*, **16**(3), 492–503.

Beck, Nathaniel. 2011. Of fixed-effects and time-invariant variables. *Political Analysis*, **19**(2), 119–122.

Beck, Nathaniel, and Katz, Jonathan N. 1995. What to do (and not to do) with time-series cross-section data. *American Political Science Review*, **89**(3), 634–647.

1996. Nuisance vs. substance: Specifying and estimating time-series-cross-section models. *Political Analysis*, **6**(1), 1–36.

Beck, Thorsten, Clarke, George, Groff, Alberto, Keefer, Philip, and Walsh, Patrick. 2001. New tools in comparative political economy: The database of political institutions. *The World bank Economic Review*, 15(1), 165–176.

Betz, Timm, and Pond, Amy. 2019. The absence of consumer interests in trade policy. *The Journal of Politics*, 81(2), 585–600.

Bhagwati, Jagdish. 2007. *In Defense of Globalization*. Oxford University Press.

Blanchflower, David G., Oswald, Andrew J., and Sanfey, Peter. 1996. Wages, profits, and rent-sharing. *The Quarterly Journal of Economics*, 111(1), 227–251.

Blyth, Mark, 2002. *Great Transformations: Economic Ideas and Institutional Change in the Twentieth Century*. Cambridge University Press.

Boix, Carles. 1997. Privatizing the public business sector in the eighties: Economic performance, partisan responses and divided governments. *British Journal of Political Science*, **27**(04), 473–496.

Brambor, T., Clark, W.R., and Golder, M. 2006. Understanding interaction models: Improving empirical analyses. *Political Analysis*, **14**(1), 63–82.

Broz, J. Lawrence, Jeffry Frieden, and Stephen Weymouth. 2021. "Populism in place: The economic geography of the globalization backlash." *International Organization* 75(2), 464–494.

Budd, John W., Lamare, J. Ryan, and Timming, Andrew R. 2018. Learning about democracy at work: Cross-national evidence on individual employee voice influencing political participation in civil society. *ILR Review*, 71(4), 956–985.

Burstein, Paul, and Linton, April. 2002. The impact of political parties, interest groups, and social movement organizations on public policy: Some recent evidence and theoretical concerns. *Social Forces*, **81**(2), 380–408.

Buyukuslu, Ali Riza. 1998. The changing nature of Turkish trade unions since 1980. *Irish Journal of Management*, **19**(1), 65.

Cameron, David R. 1978. The expansion of the public economy: A Comparative analysis. *American Political Science Review*, **72**(04), 1243–1261.

Candland, Christopher. 2007. *Labor, Democratization and Development in India and Pakistan*. Routledge.

Centeno, Miguel Angel. 1993. The new Leviathan: The dynamics and limits of technocracy. *Theory and Society*, **22**(3), 307–335.

Chaudoin, Stephen, Milner, Helen V., and Pang, Xun. 2015. International systems and domestic politics: Linking complex interactions with empirical models in international relations. *International Organization*, **69**(02), 275–309.

Chorev, Nitsan. 2005. The institutional project of neo-liberal globalism: The case of the WTO. *Theory and Society*, **34**(3), 317–355.

Chwieroth, Jeffrey M. 2009. *Capital Ideas: The IMF and the Rise of Financial Liberalization*. Princeton University Press.

Colgan, Jeff D., and Keohane, Robert O. 2017. The liberal order is rigged: Fix it now or watch it wither. *Foreign Affairs*, **96**, 36.

Collier, David, and Cardoso, Fernando Henrique. 1979. *The New Authoritarianism in Latin America*. Princeton University Press.

Collier, Ruth Berins. 1999. *Paths Toward Democracy: The Working Class and Elites in Western Europe and South America*. Cambridge University Press.

Conaghan, Catherine M. 1995. The private sector and the public transcript: The political mobilization of business in Bolivia. In Bartell, Ernest, and Payne, Leigh A. (eds.), *Business and Democracy in Latin America*. University of Pittsburgh Press.

Conaghan, Catherine M., and Malloy, James. 1995. *Unsettling Statecraft: Democracy and Neoliberalism in the Central Andes*. University of Pittsburgh Pre.

Conaghan, Catherine M., Malloy, James M., and Abugattas, Luis A. 1990. Business and the "boys": The politics of neoliberalism in the Central Andes. *Latin American Research Review*, **25**(2), 3–30.

Confederacion General del Trabajo. 1989a. *Memoria y Balance 1986 and 1990*. Confederacion General del Trabajo.

1989b. *Propuesta para una Plataforma de Liberacion Nacional*. Movimiento Obrero Peronista.

Cook, M.L. (1995). 'Regional integration and transnational labor strategies under NAFTA'. In Cook, M.L. and H. C. Katz, Regional Integration and Industrial Relations in North America, Proceedings. Ithaca, NY: Cornell University Press, pp. 142–66.

Coppedge, Michael, Gerring, John, Lindberg, Staffan I., Skaaning, Svend-Erik, and Teorell, Jan. 2017. V-Dem comparisons and contrasts with other measurement projects. *V-Dem Working Paper*, **45**.

Cyr, Jennifer. 2015. Making or breaking politics: Social conflicts and party-system change in democratic Bolivia. *Studies in Comparative International Development*, 50(3), 283–303.

Davenport, Christian. 2007. *State Repression and the Domestic Democratic Peace.* Cambridge University Press.

2017. Performing Order: An examination of the seemingly impossible task of subjugating large numbers of people, everywhere, all the time. In Morgan, Kimberly J, and Orloff, Ann Shola (eds.), *The Many Hands of the State: Theorizing Political Authority and Social Control.* Cambridge University Press.

Davis, Diane E. 1992. Mexico's new politics: Changing perspectives on free trade. *World Policy Journal*, 9, 655–671.

de la Garza Toledo, Enrique. 1994. *Mexican Labor Unions Facing the Free Trade Agreement (NAFTA).* Presented at Conference on International Trade Unionism at the Current Stage of Economic Globalization and Regionalization, Saitama University, Japan.

Dean, Adam. 2015a. Power over profits: The political economy of workers and wages. *Politics & Society*, 43(3), 333–360.

2015b. The gilded wage: Profit sharing institutions and the political economy of Trade. *International Studies Quarterly*, 59(2), 316–329.

2016. *From conflict to coalition: Profit-sharing institutions and the political economy of trade.* Cambridge University Press.

2018. NAFTA's Army: Free trade and US military enlistment. *International Studies Quarterly*, 62(4), 845–856.

Dean, Adam, and Kimmel, Simeon. 2019. Free trade and opioid overdose death in the United States. *SSM-Population Health*, 8, 100409.

Dewey, John. 1896. The reflex a concept in psychology. *Psychological Review*, 3(4), 357–370.

Deyo, Frederic C. 1989. *Beneath the Miracle: Labor Subordination in the New Asian Industrialism.* University of California Press.

Dinler, Demet Şahende, and Büro, Friedrich-Ebert-Stiftung. 2012. *Trade Unions in Turkey.* Friedrich-Ebert-Stiftung, Department for Central and Eastern Europe.

Dogan, Mustafa G. 2010. When neoliberalism confronts the moral economy of workers: The final spring of Turkish labor unions. *European Journal of Turkish Studies. Social Sciences on Contemporary Turkey*, 11, 1–20.

Doğangün, Gökten. 2005. *State tradition and business in Turkey: The Case of TUSIAD.* M.Phil. thesis.

Dunkerley, James. 1990. Political transition and economic stabilisation: Bolivia, 1982–1989. *ISA Research Papers.*

Dutta, Puja Vasudeva. 2007. Trade protection and industry wages in India. *ILR Review*, 60(2), 268–286.

Edwards, Sebastian. 1996. Crisis and reform in Latin America: From despair to hope. *American Economist*, 40(2), 98.

Eichengreen, B., and Leblang, D. 2008. Democracy and globalization. *Economics & Politics*, 20(3), 289–334.

Etchemendy, Sebastián. 2004. Repression, exclusion, and inclusion: Government-union relations and patterns of labor reform in liberalizing economies. *Comparative Politics*, 36(3), 273–290.

2011. *Models of Economic Liberalization: Business, Workers, and Compensation in Latin America, Spain, and Portugal.* Cambridge University Press.

Fairbrother, Malcolm. 2014. Economists, capitalists, and the making of globalization: North American free trade in comparative–historical perspective1. *American Journal of Sociology*, **119**(5), 1324–1379.

Farrell, Henry, and Knight, Jack. 2017. *Dewey's Democratic Account of International Politics.*

Feenstra, Robert C., and Lewis, Tracy R. 1994. Trade adjustment assistance and Pareto gains from trade. *Journal of International Economics*, **36**(3–4), 201–222.

Fischer, Karin. 2009. The influence of neoliberals in Chile before, during, and after Pinochet. In Mirowski, Philip and Plehwe, Dieter (eds.), *The Road from Mont Pelerin: The Making of the Neoliberal Thought Collective*, Harvard University Press.

Fourcade-Gourinchas, Marion, and Babb, Sarah L. 2002. The rebirth of the liberal creed: Paths to neoliberalism in four countries. *American Journal of Sociology*, **108**(3), 533–579.

Franzese, Robert J., and Kam, Cindy. 2007. *Modeling and Interpreting Interactive Hypotheses in Regression Analysis*. University of Michigan Press.

Freeman, R., and Pelletier, J. 1990. The impact of industrial relations legislation on British Union Density. *British Journal of Industrial Relations*, **28**(2), 141–164.

Freeman, Richard B., and Medoff, James L. 1984. What do unions do? *Industrial & Labor Relations Review*, **38**, 244.

Frieden, Jeffry A. 1991. Invested interests: The politics of national economic policies in a world of global finance. *International Organization*, **45**(4), 425–451.

1999. Actors and preferences in international relations. In Lake, David, and Powell, Robert (eds.), *Strategic Choice and International Relations*. Princeton University Press.

Gallagher, Kevin P. 2007. Understanding developing country resistance to the Doha Round. *Review of International Political Economy*, **15**(1), 62–85.

Gamarra, Eduardo. 1991. *The System of Justice in Bolivia: An Institutional Analysis*. Vol. 4. Centro para la Administración de Justicia, Florida International University.

Garrett, Geoffrey. 2000. The causes of globalization. *Comparative Political Studies*, **33**(6–7), 941–991.

Garrett, Geoffrey, and Lange, Peter. 1995. Internationalization, institutions, and political change. *International Organization*, **49**, 627–655.

Gaventa, John. 1982. *Power and Powerlessness: Quiescence and Rebellion in an Appalachian Valley*. University of Illinois Press.

Geddes, Barbara. 1995. The politics of economic liberalization. *Latin American Research Review*, **30**(2), 195.

George, Alexander L., and Bennett, Andrew. 2005. *Case Studies and Theory Development in the Social Sciences*. MIT Press.

Gerchunoff, Pablo, and Torre, Juan Carlos. 1996. La política de liberalización económica en la administración de Menem. *Desarrollo económico*, **36**(143), 733–768.

Gereffi, Gary, and Wyman, Donald L. 1990. *Manufacturing Miracles: Paths of Industrialization in Latin America and East Asia*. Princeton University Press.

Ghosh, Arunabha. 2006. Pathways through financial crisis: India. *Global Governance*, **12**, 413.

Giugni, Marco. 2008. Political, biographical, and cultural consequences of social movements. *Sociology Compass*, **2**(5), 1582–1600.

Godard, John. 2003. Do labor laws matter? The density decline and convergence thesis revisited. *Industrial Relations: A Journal of Economy and Society*, 42(3), 458–492.

Goertz, Gary. 2017. *Multimethod Research, Causal Mechanisms, and Case Studies: An Integrated Approach*. Princeton University Press.

Goldberg, Pinelopi Koujianou, and Pavcnik, Nina. 2007. Distributional effects of globalization in developing countries. *Journal of Economic Literature*, 45(1), 39–82.

Goldstein, Judith, and Martin, Lisa L. 2000. Legalization, trade liberalization, and domestic politics: A cautionary note. *International organization*, 54(3), 603–632.

Gourevitch, Alex. 2018. The right to strike: A radical view. *The American Political Science Review*, 112(4), 905–917.

Green, Donald P., Kim, Soo Yeon H., and Yoon, David. 2001. Dirty pool. *International Organization*, 55(02), 441–468.

Greenhill, Brian, Mosley, Layna, and Prakash, Aseem. 2009. Trade-based diffusion of labor rights: A panel study, 1986–2002. *American Political Science Review*, 103(04), 669–690.

Grinspun, Ricardo, and Kreklewich, Robert. 1994. Consolidating neoliberal reforms: "Free Trade" as a conditioning framework. *Studies in Political Economy*, 43(1), 33–61.

Grossman, Gene M., and Helpman, Elhanan. 1994. Protection for sale. *The American Economic Review*, 84(4), 833.

Guisinger, Alexandra. 2017. *American Opinion on Trade: Preferences without Politics*. Oxford University Press.

Haggard, Stephan. 1990. *Pathways from the Periphery: The Politics of Growth in the Newly Industrializing Countries*. Cornell University Press.

Haggard, Stephan, and Kaufman, Robert R. 1995. *The Political Economy of Democratic Transitions*. Princeton University Press.

2008. *Development, Democracy, and Welfare states: Latin America, East Asia, and Eastern Europe*. Princeton University Press.

Hagopian, Frances, and Mainwaring, Scott P. 2005. *The Third Wave of Democratization in Latin America: Advances and Setbacks*. Cambridge University Press.

Hainmueller, Jens, Mummolo, Jonathan, and Xu, Yiqing. 2019. How much should we trust estimates from multiplicative interaction models? Simple tools to improve empirical practice. *Political Analysis*, 27, 163–192.

Hamann, Kerstin, Johnston, Alison, and Kelly, John. 2013. Unions against governments: Explaining general strikes in Western Europe, 1980–2006. *Comparative Political Studies*, 46(9), 1030–1057.

Hanson, Gordon H. 2003. *What has happened to wages in Mexico since NAFTA?* Tech. rept. National Bureau of Economic Research.

Harvey, David. 2005. *A Brief History of Neoliberalism*. Oxford University Press Oxford.

Hathaway, Dale A. 1997. *Mexico's Frente Auténtico del Trabajo: Organizing Beyond the PRI and Across Borders*. Presented at the 1997 meeting of the Latin American Studies Association.

2002. Mexico's Frente Autentico del Trabajo and the problem of unionizing Maquiladoras. *Labor History*, 43(4), 427–438.

Held, David, McGrew, Anthony, Goldblatt, David, and Perraton, Jonathan. 1999. *Global Transformations: Politics, Economics and Culture*. Stanford University Press.

Hicks, Raymond, Milner, Helen V., and Tingley, Dustin. 2013. Trade policy, economic interests, and party politics in a developing country: The political economy of CAFTA-DR. *International Studies Quarterly*.

Hiscox, Michael J. 2002. *International Trade and Political Conflict: Commerce, Coalitions and Mobility*. Princeton University Press.

Huntington, Samuel P. 1993. *The Third Wave: Democratization in the Late Twentieth Century*. Vol. 4. University of Oklahoma Press.

Ianchovichina, Elena, and Martin, Will. 2001. Trade liberalization in China's accession to WTO. *Journal of Economic Integration*, 16(4), 421–445.

India. 1985. *Budget Speech of Minister of Finance 1985–1986*. Government of India.

1986. *Budget Speech of Minister of Finance 1986–1987*. Government of India.

1987. *Budget Speech of Minister of Finance 1987–1988*. Government of India.

1991. *Budget Speech of Minister of Finance 1991–1992*. Government of India.

1992. *Budget Speech of Minister of Finance 1992–1993*. Government of India.

Indian National Trade Union Congress. 1990. *206th Meeting of the Working Committee of INTUC*.

International Confederation of Free Trade Unions. 1990. *Annual Survey of Violations of Trade Union Rights*.

1993. *Annual Survey of Violations of Trade Union Rights*.

Jameson, Kenneth P. 2019. Austerity programs under conditions of political instability and economic depression: The case of Bolivia. Pages 81–103 In *Paying the Costs of Austerity in Latin America*. Routledge.

Jenkins, Rhys. 1997. Trade liberalisation in Latin America: The Bolivian case. *Bulletin of Latin American Research*, 16(3), 307–325.

Jenkins, Rob. 1999. *Democratic Politics and Economic Reform in India*. Vol. 5. Cambridge University Press.

Jinks, Derek P. 2000. The anatomy of an institutionalized emergency: Preventive detention and personal liberty in India. *Michigan Journal of International Law*, 22(2), 311.

Karacan, Elifcan. 2015. *Remembering the 1980 Turkish Military Coup d 'État: Memory, Violence, and Trauma*. Springer.

Katzenstein, Peter J. 1985. *Small States in World Markets: Industrial Policy in Europe*. Cornell University Press.

Kay, Tamara. 2011. *NAFTA and the Politics of Labor Transnationalism*. Cambridge University Press.

Kaya, Muzaffer. 2018. "We Too Have a Word to Say": Enactment of the 1963 Collective Bargaining, Strike, and Lockout Law in Turkey. *The Journal of Interrupted Studies*, 1(1), 48–68.

Kentikelenis, Alexander E., Stubbs, Thomas H., and King, Lawrence P. 2016. IMF conditionality and development policy space, 1985–2014. *Review of International Political Economy*, 23(4), 543–582.

Keohane, Robert O. "International Institutions in an Era of Populism, Nationalism, and Diffusion of Power." The Warren and Anita Manshel Lecture in American Foreign Policy, Harvard University. Available at https://wcfia.harvard.edu/lectureships/manshel/2016/transcript (2016).

Kerrissey, Jasmine. 2015. Collective labor rights and income inequality. *American Sociological Review*, 80(3), 626–653.

Kim, In Song, and Osgood, Iain. 2019. Firms in trade and trade politics. *Annual Review of Political Science*, **22**, 399–417.

Kim, Sung Eun, and Margalit, Yotam. 2017. Informed preferences? The impact of unions on workers' policy views. *American Journal of Political Science*, **61**(3), 728–743.

Kleinfeld, Rachel, and Barham, Elena. 2018. Complicit states and the governing strategy of privilege violence: When weakness is not the problem. *Annual Review of Political Science*, 21(1), 215–238.

Kofas, Jon V. 1995. The politics of austerity: The IMF and US foreign policy in Bolivia, 1956–1964. *The Journal of Developing Areas*, **29**(2), 213–236.

Kohli, Atul. 1987. *The State and Poverty in India: The Politics of Reform*. Cambridge University Press.

1989. Politics of economic liberalization in India. *World Development*, 17(3), 305–328.

2004. *State-Directed Development: Political Power and Industrialization in the Global Periphery*. Cambridge University Press.

2006. Politics of economic growth in India, 1980–2005: Part I: The 1980s. *Economic and Political Weekly*, **41**(13), 1251–1259.

2012. *Poverty Amid Plenty in the New India*. Cambridge University Press.

Kolben, Kevin. 2009. Labor rights as human rights. *Virginia Journal of International Law*, **50**, 449.

Korpi, Walter. 2006. Power resources and employer-centered approaches in explanations of welfare states and varieties of capitalism: Protagonists, consenters, and antagonists. *World Politics*, **58**(02), 167–206.

Krueger, Anne O. 1974. The political economy of the rent-seeking society. *The American Economic Review*, **64**(3), 291–303.

Krugman, Paul. 1997. In praise of cheap labor. *Slate*, March, **21**, 1997.

Kuruvilla, Sarosh C. 1995. Industrialization strategy and industrial relations policy in Malaysia. In Frenkel, Stephen J., and Harrod, Jeffrey (eds.), *Industrialization and Labor Relations: Contemporary Research in Seven Countries*. Cornell University Press.

1996. Linkages Between industrialization strategies and industrial relations/human resource policies: Singapore, Malaysia, the Philippines, and India. *Industrial and Labor Relations Review*, **49**(4), 635–657.

Lake, David A. 2009. Open economy politics: A critical review. *The Review of International Organizations*, **4**(3), 219–244.

Lerena, Roberto García. 2007. *Saúl Ubaldini: crónicas de un militante obrero peronista*. Runa Comunicaciones.

Levitsky, Steven. 2003. *Transforming Labor-Based Parties in Latin America: Argentine Peronism in Comparative Perspective*. Cambridge University Press.

Levitsky, Steven, and Way, Lucan A. 1998. Between a shock and a hard place: The dynamics of labor-backed adjustment in Poland and Argentina. *Comparative Politics*, **30**(2), 171–192.

Levy, Frank, and Temin, Peter. 2009. Institutions and wages in post–World War II America. In Brown, Clair, Eichengreen, Barry J., and Reich, Michael (eds), *Labor in the Era of Globalization*, Cambridge University Press.

Lindvall, Johannes. 2013. Union density and political strikes. *World Politics*, **65**, 539.

Lockwood, Erin. 2020. The international political economy of global inequality. *Review of International Political Economy*, **28**(2), 1–25.

Lukes, Steven. 2004. *Power: A radical view*. Macmillan International Higher Education.

Lupu, Noam. 2016. *Party Brands in Crisis: Partisanship, Brand Dilution, and the Breakdown a of Political Parties in Latin America*. Cambridge University Press.

MacWilliams, Matthew C. 2016. Who decides when the party doesn't? Authoritarian voters and the rise of Donald Trump. *PS: Political Science & Politics*, **49**(4), 716–721.

Madeira, Mary Anne. 2016. New trade, new politics: Intra-industry trade and domestic political coalitions. *Review of International Political Economy*, **23**(4), 677–711.

Madrid, Raúl L. 2003. Labouring against neoliberalism: Unions and patterns of reform in Latin America. *Journal of Latin American Studies*, **35**(1), 53–88.

Malloy, James M. 1991. Democracy, economic crisis and the problem of governance: The case of Bolivia. *Studies in Comparative International Development*, **26**(2), 37–57.

Manger, Mark S., and Shadlen, Kenneth C. 2014. Political trade dependence and North–South trade agreements. *International Studies quarterly*, **58**(1), 79–91.

Manzetti, Luigi, et al. 1999. *Privatization South American Style*. Oxford University Press on Demand.

Margheritis, Ana, and Pereira, Anthony W. 2007. The neoliberal turn in Latin America: The cycle of ideas and the search for an alternative. *Latin American Perspectives*, **34**(3), 25–48.

Marshall, Monty G., Jaggers, Keith, and Gurr, Ted Robert. 2002. Polity IV project: Dataset users' manual. *College Park: University of Maryland*.

Marx, Axel, Soares, Jadir, and Aker, Wouter Van. 2015. *Global Governance of Labour Rights: Assessing the Effectiveness of Transnational Public and Private Policy Initiatives*. Edward Elgar Publishing.

Masilamani, Samuel. 1995. *Economic Reforms and Trade Unions in India*. Friedrich Ebert Stiftung.

Mathur, Ajeet N. 1993. The experience of consultation during structural adjustment in India (1990–92). *International Labour Review*, **132**, 331.

McGuire, James W. 1992. Union political tactics and democratic consolidation in Alfonsin's Argentina, 1983–1989. *Latin American Research Review*, **27**, 37–74.

1996. Strikes in Argentina: Data sources and recent trends. *Latin American Research Review*, **31**(3), 127–150.

1999. *Peronism Without Perón: Unions, Parties, and Democracy in Argentina*. Stanford University Press.

Medrano, Juan Díez, and Braun, Michael. 2012. Uninformed citizens and support for free trade. *Review of International Political Economy*, **19**(3), 448–476.

Menendez, Irene. 2016. Globalization and welfare spending: How geography and electoral institutions condition compensation. *International Studies Quarterly*.

Menendez, Irene, Owen, Erica, and Walter, Stefanie. 2018. *Low skill products by high skill workers: The distributive effects of trade in developing countries*. American Political Science Association. Annual Meeting, Boston, 30 August 2018–2 September 2018.

Meschi, Elena, and Vivarelli, Marco. 2009. Trade and income inequality in developing countries. *World Development*, **37**(2), 287–302.

Middlebrook, Kevin J., and Middlebrook, Kevin J. 1995. *The Paradox of Revolution: Labor, the State, and Authoritarianism in Mexico*. JHU Press.

Milner, Helen V. 1998. Rationalizing politics: The emerging synthesis of international, American, and comparative politics. *International Organization*, **52**(4), 759–786.

Milner, Helen V., and Kubota, Keiko. 2005. Why the move to free trade? Democracy and trade policy in the developing countries. *International Organization*, **59**(01), 107–143.

Milner, Helen V., and Mukherjee, B. 2009. Democratization and economic globalization. *Annual Review of Political Science*, **12**, 163–181.

Morales, Juan Antonio. 1995. Bolivia and the slowdown of the reform process. *PSD Occasional Paper*.

1996. Economic policy in Bolivia after the transition to democracy. Pages 30–48 In *Economic Policy and the Transition to Democracy*. Springer.

Moravcsik, Andrew. 2004. Is there a "democratic deficit" in world politics? A framework for analysis. *Government and Opposition*, **39**(2), 336–363.

Mosley, Layna. 2010. *Labor Rights and Multinational Production*. Cambridge University Press.

2011. *Replication Data for: Collective Labor Rights Dataset*. Tech. rept. http://hdl.handle.net/1902.1/15590 Layna Mosley [Distributor] V1 [Version].

Mukherjee, Bumba. 2016. *Democracy and Trade Policy in Developing Countries*. University of Chicago Press.

Mukherji, Rahul. 2013. Ideas, interests, and the tipping point: Economic change in India. *Review of International Political Economy*, **20**(2), 363–389.

Munck, Ronaldo. 1989. *Latin America: The Transition to Democracy*. Zed Books.

Murillo, Maria Victoria. 2001. *Labor Unions, Partisan Coalitions, and Market Reforms in Latin America*. Cambridge University Press.

Nazmi, Nader. 1995. *Economic Policy and Stabilization in Latin America*. ME Sharpe.

Nelson, Joan M., and Waterbury, John. 1989. *Fragile Coalitions: The Politics of Economic Adjustment*. Vol. 12. Transaction Publishers.

Nichols, Theo, Sugur, Nadir, and Demir, Erol. 2002. Beyond cheap labour: Trade unions and development in the Turkish metal industry. *The Sociological Review*, **50**(1), 23–47.

Noronha, Ernesto, Beale, David, and Hurd, Richard. 2011. India, Neo-liberalism and union responses–unfinished business and protracted struggles. In Gall, Gregor, and Wilkinson, Adrian (eds.), *The International Handbook of Labour Unions: Responses to Neo-liberalism*. Edward Elgar Pub.

Oatley, Thomas. 2011. The reductionist gamble: Open economy politics in the global economy. *International Organization*, **65**(02), 311–341.

Olson, Mancur. 1965. *The Logic of Collective Action: Public Goods and the Theory of Groups*. Harvard University Press.

Önder, Nilgün. 1998. Integrating with the global market: The state and the crisis of political representation: Turkey in the 1980s and 1990s. *International Journal of Political Economy*, **28**(2), 44–84.

Öniş, Ziya, and Türem, Umut. 2002. Entrepreneurs, democracy, and citizenship in Turkey. *Comparative Politics*, **34**(4), 439–456.

Öniş, Ziya, Webb, Steven Benjamin, and Mundial, Banco. 1992. *Political Economy of Policy Reform in Turkey in the 1980s*. WPS 1059. World Bank.

O'Rourke, K.H., and Taylor, A.M. 2006. Democracy and protectionism. *Working Paper, Department of Economic, University of California David*.

Osgood, Iain, Tingley, Dustin, Bernauer, Thomas, Kim, In Song, Milner, Helen V., and Spilker, Gabriele. 2017. The charmed life of superstar exporters: Survey evidence on firms and trade policy. *The Journal of Politics*, **79**(1), 133–152.

Oyejide, T. Ademola. 1973. Tariff protection and industrialization via import substitution: An empirical analysis of the Nigerian experience. *The Bangladesh Economic Review*, 1(4), 331–340.

Özkiziltan, Didem. 2013. *A Political Economy of Insecurity?: State and Socio-economic Actors in the Making of Industrial Relations in Modern Turkey*. Ph.D. thesis, University of Bath.

2020. Protection of capitalism as a regime of rationality: A historical institutionalist rereading of modern Turkey's industrial relations. *The Journal of Development Studies*, 56(4), 732–747.

Palomino, Héctor. 2000. *Unions and Civil Society in Contemporary Argentina*.

Pavcnik, Nina. 2017. *The impact of trade on inequality in developing countries*. Tech. rept. National Bureau of Economic Research.

Pemstein, Daniel, Meserve, Stephen A., and Melton, James. 2010. Democratic compromise: A latent variable analysis of ten measures of regime type. *Political Analysis*, 18(4), 426–449.

Pepinsky, Thomas B. 2018. Visual heuristics for marginal effects plots. *Research & Politics*, 5(1), 2053168018756668.

Polanyi, Karl. 1944. *The Great Transformation: The Political and Economic Origins of our Time*. Beacon Press.

Pop-Eleches, Grigore. 2008. *From economic crisis to reform: IMF programs in Latin America and Eastern Europe*. Princeton University Press.

Pozzi, Pablo Alejandro, and Schneider, Alejandro M. 1994. *Combatiendo al capital: crisis y recomposición de la clase obrera argentina (1983–1993)*. El Bloque Ed.

Przeworski, Adam. 1991. *Democracy and the Market: Political and Economic Reforms in Eastern Europe and Latin America*. Cambridge University Press.

Raj, Krishna. 1987. Public sector – lenient view. *Economic and Political Weekly*, **Vol. 22**(Issue No. 4).

Ranis, Peter. 1992. *Argentine Workers: Peronism and Contemporary Class Consciousness*. University of Pittsburgh Press.

Razmi, Arslan, and Blecker, Robert A. 2008. Developing country exports of manufactures: Moving up the ladder to escape the fallacy of composition? *The Journal of Development Studies*, 44(1), 21–48.

Reuveny, Rafael, and Li, Quan. 2003. Economic openness, democracy, and income inequality: An empirical analysis. *Comparative Political Studies*, 36(5), 575–601.

Robben, Antonius CGM. 2005. *Political Violence and Trauma in Argentina*. University of Pennsylvania Press.

Rodrik, Dani. 1992. *The rush to free trade in the developing world: Why so late? Why now? Will it last?* Tech. rept. National Bureau of Economic Research.

2018. Populism and the economics of globalization. *Journal of International Business Policy*, 1(1-2), 12–33.

Rogowski, Ronald. 1987. Trade and the variety of democratic institutions. *International Organization*, 41(2), 203–223.

1989. *Commerce and Coalitions: How Trade Affects Domestic Political Alignments*. Princeton University Press.

Rosenfeld, Jake. 2010. Economic determinants of voting in an era of union decline. *Social Science Quarterly*, 91(2), 379–395.

Rudra, Nita. 2002. Globalization and the decline of the welfare state in less-developed countries. *International Organization*, 56(2), 411–445.

2005. Globalization and the strengthening of democracy in the developing world. *American Journal of Political Science*, **49**(4), 704–730.

Rueschemeyer, Dietrich, Stephens, Evelyne Huber, Stephens, John D., et al. 1992. *Capitalist Development and Democracy*. Vol. 22. Cambridge Polity.

Ruggie, John Gerard. 1982. International regimes, transactions, and change: Embedded liberalism in the postwar economic order. *International Organization*, **36**(2), 379–415.

Sachs, Jeffrey D., and Collins, Susan M. 2019. *Developing Country Debt and Economic Performance, Volume 3: Country Studies–Indonesia, Korea, Philippines, Turkey*. University of Chicago Press.

Schamis, Hector E. 1999. Distributional coalitions and the politics of economic reform in Latin America. *World Politics*, 236–268.

Schmitter, Philippe C. 1993. Some propositions about civil society and the consolidation of democracy. *Working Paper No. 10, Institut für Höhere Studien*.

Schumpeter, Joseph. 1928. The instability of capitalism. *The Economic Journal*, **38**(151), 361–386.

Senén González, Santiago. 1999. *El sindicalismo en tiempo de Menem. Los ministros deTrabajo en la primera presidencia de Menem: sindicalismo y Estado (1989–95)*. Corregidor.

Şener, Meltem Yılmaz. 2004. The Relationship Between Neoliberalism and Authoritarian States: The Case of Turkey.

Shadlen, Kenneth C. 2002. Orphaned by democracy: Small industry in contemporary Mexico. *Comparative Politics*, **35**(1), 43–62.

Shastri, Vanita. 1997. The politics of economic liberalization in India. *Contemporary South Asia*, **6**(1), 27–56.

Shenoy, P.D. 2006. *Globalization: Its Impact on Industrial Relations in India*. New Dawn Press (IL).

Sheppard, Eric. 2005. Constructing free trade: From Manchester boosterism to global management. *Transactions of the Institute of British Geographers*, **30**(2), 151–172.

Shirk, David A. 2005. *Mexico's New Politics: The PAN and Democratic Change*. Lynne Rienner Publishers.

Silver, Beverly J. 2003. *Forces of Labor: Workers' Movements and Globalization Since 1870*. Cambridge University Press.

Simmons, Erica S. 2016. *Meaningful Resistance: Market Reforms and the Roots of Social Protest in Latin America*. Cambridge University Press.

Sinha, Aseema. 2016. *Globalizing India*. Cambridge University Press.

Smith, William C. 1990. Democracy, distributional conflicts and macroeconomic policymaking in Argentina, 1983–89. *Journal of Interamerican Studies and World Affairs*, **32**(2), 1–42.

Spalding, Rose J. 2014. *Contesting Trade in Central America: Market Reform and Resistance*. University of Texas Press.

Stokes, S.C. 2001. *Mandates and Democracy: Neoliberalism by Surprise in Latin America*. Cambridge University Press.

Stone, Randall W. 2008. The scope of IMF conditionality. *International Organization*, **62**(4), 589–620.

Sturzenegger, Federico. 1995. Bolivia: From stabilization to what? Pages 239–288 of: *Reform, Recovery, and Growth: Latin America and the Middle East*. University of Chicago Press.

Swamy, Dalip S., and Singh, Kavaljit. 1994. *Against Consensus: Three Years of Public Resistance to Structural Adjustment Programme*. Public Interest Research Group.

Tarrow, Sidney G. 1994. *Power in Movement: Social Movements and Contentious Politics*. Cambridge University Press.

Teitelbaum, Emmanuel. 2011. *Mobilizing Restraint: Democracy and Industrial Conflict in Post-Reform South Asia*. Ilr Press.

2017. India's weakened unions face a push for reform. *Current History*, **116**(789), 142–147.

Teorell, Jan, Coppedge, Michael, Lindberg, Staffan, and Skaaning, Svend-Erik. 2019. Measuring polyarchy across the globe, 1900–2017. *Studies in Comparative International Development*, **54**(1), 71–95.

Teubal, Miguel. 2001. From import substitution industrialization to the "open" economy in Argentina: The role of Peronism. *Miraculous metamorphoses: The neoliberalization of Latin American populism. London: Zed Books*, 22–59.

Thacker, Strom C. 2000. *Big Business, the State, and Free Trade: Constructing Coalitions in Mexico*. Cambridge University Press.

Tilly, Charles. 1995. Globalization threatens Labor's rights. *International Labor and Working-Class History*, **47**, 1–23.

Uba, Katrin. 2005. Political protest and policy change: The direct impacts of Indiananti-privatization mobilizations, 1990–2003. *Mobilization: An International Quarterly*, 10(3), 383–396.

Valenzuela, J. Samuel. 1989. Labor movements in transitions to democracy: A framework for analysis. *Comparative Politics*, **21**(4), 445–472.

Varshney, Ashutosh. 1998. Mass politics or elite politics? India's economic reforms in comparative perspective. *The Journal of Policy Reform*, **2**(4), 301–335.

Verma, Arvind. 1997. Maintaining law and order in India: An exercise in police discretion. *International Criminal Justice Review*, **7**(1), 65–80.

von Mettenheim, Kurt, and Malloy, James M. 1998. *Deepening Democracy in Latin America*. University of Pittsburgh Press.

Wade, Robert. 2010. After the crisis: Industrial policy and the developmental state in low-income countries. *Global Policy*, **1**(2), 150–161.

Wallerstein, Michael. 1987. Unemployment, collective bargaining, and the demand for protection. *American Journal of Political Science*, **31**(4), 729–752.

Walter, Stephanie. 2010. Globalization and the welfare state: Testing the microfoundations of the compensation hypothesis. *International Studies Quarterly*, **54**(2), 403–426.

Western, Bruce. 1997. *Between Class and Market: Postwar Unionization in the Capitalist Democracies*. Cambridge University Press.

Weyland, K. 2002. *The Politics of Market Reform in Fragile Democracies: Argentina, Brazil, Peru, and Venezuela*. Princeton University Press.

Wilhite, Al. 1988. Union PAC contributions and legislative voting. *Journal of Labor Research*, **9**(1), 79–90.

Wisniewski, Tomasz Piotr, Lambe, Brendan John, and Dias, Alexandra. 2020. The influence of general strikes against government on stock market behavior. *Scottish Journal of Political Economy*, **67**(1), 72–99.

Yadirgi, Veli. 2017. *The Political Economy of the Kurds of Turkey: From the Ottoman Empire to the Turkish Republic*. Cambridge University Press.

Yang, Jae-jin, and Kwon, Hyeok Yong. 2019. Union structure, bounded solidarity and support for redistribution: Implications for building a welfare state. *International Political Science Review*, 0192512119887535.

Zagha, Roberto. 2000. Labour and India's economic reforms. In Sachs, Jeffrey, Varshney, Ashutosh, and Bajpai, Nirupam (eds.), *India in the Era of Economic Reforms*. Oxford University Press.

Ziblatt, Daniel. 2006. How did Europe democratize. *World Politics*, 58, 311–338.

Zucker, Noah. 2020. Free trade and forms of democratization. *The Journal of Politics*, 83(4), 1867–1871.

Index

Other books in the series **(*continued from page ii*)**

Kelly H. Chang,
Appointing Central Bankers: The Politics of Monetary Policy in the United States and the European Monetary Union
Tom S. Clark,
The Supreme Court: An Analytical History of Constitutional Decision Making
Peter Cowhey and Mathew McCubbins, eds.,
Structure and Policy in Japan and the United States: An Institutionalist Approach
Gary W. Cox,
The Efficient Secret: The Cabinet and the Development of Political Parties in Victorian England
Gary W. Cox,
Making Votes Count: Strategic Coordination in the World's Electoral System
Gary W. Cox,
Marketing Sovereign Promises: Monopoly Brokerage and the Growth of the English State
Gary W. Cox and Jonathan N. Katz,
Elbridge Gerry's Salamander: The Electoral Consequences of the Reapportionment Revolution
Tine De Moore,
The Dilemma of the Commoners: Understanding the Use of Common-Pool Resources in Long-Term Perspective
Adam Dean,
From Conflict to Coalition: Profit-Sharing Institutions and the Political Economy of Trade
Mark Dincecco,
Political Transformations and Public Finances: Europe, 1650–1913
Mark Dincecco and Massimiliano Gaetano Onorato,
From Warfare to Weath: The Military Origins of Urban Prosperity in Europe
Raymond M. Duch and Randolph T. Stevenson,
The Economic Vote: How Political and Economic Institutions Condition Election Results
Jean Ensminger,
Making a Market: The Institutional Transformation of an African Society
David Epstein and Sharyn O'Halloran,
Delegating Powers: A Transaction Cost Politics Approach to Policy Making under Separate Powers
Kathryn Firmin-Sellers,
The Transformation of Property Rights in the Gold Coast: An Empirical Study Applying Rational Choice Theory
Clark C. Gibson,
Politicians and Poachers: The Political Economy of Wildlife Policy in Africa

Daniel W. Gingerich,
Political Institutions and Party-Directed Corruption in South America
Avner Greif,
Institutions and the Path to the Modern Economy: Lessons from Medieval Trade
Jeffrey D. Grynaviski,
Partisan Bonds: Political Reputations and Legislative Accountability
Stephen Haber, Armando Razo, and Noel Maurer,
The Politics of Property Rights: Political Instability, Credible Commitments, and Economic Growth in Mexico, 1876–1929
Ron Harris,
Industrializing English Law: Entrepreneurship and Business Organization, 1720–1844
Anna L. Harvey,
Votes Without Leverage: Women in American Electoral Politics, 1920–1970
Shigeo Hirano and James M. Snyder, Jr.
Primary Elections in the United States
Murray Horn,
The Political Economy of Public Administration: Institutional Choice in the Public Sector
John D. Huber,
Rationalizing Parliament: Legislative Institutions and Party Politics in France Jack Knight, Institutions and Social Conflict
Sean Ingham,
Rule of Multiple Majorities: A New Theory of Popular Control
John E. Jackson, Jacek Klich, Krystyna Poznanska,
The Political Economy of Poland's Transition: New Firms and Reform Governments
Jack Knight,
Institutions and Social Conflict
Michael Laver and Kenneth Shepsle, eds.,
Cabinet Ministers and Parliamentary Government
Michael Laver and Kenneth Shepsle, eds.,
Making and Breaking Governments: Cabinets and Legislatures in Parliamentary Democracies
Michael Laver and Kenneth Shepsle, eds.,
Cabinet Ministers and Parliamentary Government
Margaret Levi,
Consent, Dissent, and Patriotism
Brian Levy and Pablo T. Spiller, eds.,
Regulations, Institutions, and Commitment: Comparative Studies of Telecommunications
Leif Lewin,
Ideology and Strategy: A Century of Swedish Politics (English Edition)
Gary Libecap,
Contracting for Property Rights
John Londregan,
Legislative Institutions and Ideology in Chile

Arthur Lupia and Mathew D. McCubbins,
The Democratic Dilemma: Can Citizens Learn What They Need to Know?
C. Mantzavinos,
Individuals, Institutions, and Markets
Mathew D. McCubbins and Terry Sullivan, eds.,
Congress: Structure and Policy
Gary J. Miller,
Above Politics: Bureaucratic Discretion and Credible Commitment
Gary J. Miller,
Managerial Dilemmas: The Political Economy of Hierarchy
Ilia Murtazashvili,
The Political Economy of the American Frontier
Douglass C. North,
Institutions, Institutional Change, and Economic Performance
Elinor Ostrom,
Governing the Commons: The Evolution of Institutions for Collective Action
Sonal S. Pandya,
Trading Spaces: Foreign Direct Investment Regulation, 1970–2000
John W. Patty and Elizabeth Maggie Penn,
Social Choice and Legitimacy
Daniel N. Posner,
Institutions and Ethnic Politics in Africa
J. Mark Ramseyer,
Odd Markets in Japanese History: Law and Economic Growth
J. Mark Ramseyer and Frances Rosenbluth,
The Politics of Oligarchy: Institutional Choice in Imperial Japan
Stephanie J. Rickard, Spending to Win: Political Institutions,
Economic Geography, and Government Subsidies
Jean-Laurent Rosenthal,
The Fruits of Revolution: Property Rights, Litigation,
and French Agriculture, 1700–1860
Michael L. Ross,
Timber Booms and Institutional Breakdown in Southeast Asia
Meredith Rolfe,
Voter Turnout: A Social Theory of Political Participation
Shanker Satyanath,
Globalization, Politics, and Financial Turmoil: Asia's Banking Crisis
Alberto Simpser,
Why Governments and Parties Manipulate Elections: Theory, Practice,
and Implications
Norman Schofield,
Architects of Political Change: Constitutional Quandaries
and Social Choice Theory
Norman Schofield and Itai Sened,
Multiparty Democracy: Elections and Legislative Politics
Alastair Smith,
Election Timing

Pablo T. Spiller and Mariano Tommasi,
The Instituional Foundations of Public Policy in Argentina: A Transactions Cost Approach
David Stasavage,
Public Debt and the Birth of the Democratic State: France and Great Britain, 1688–1789
Charles Stewart III,
Budget Reform Politics: The Design of the Appropriations Process in the House of Representatives, 1865–1921
George Tsebelis and Jeannette Money,
Bicameralism
Georg Vanberg,
The Politics of Constitutional Review in Germany
Nicolas van de Walle,
African Economies and the Politics of Permanent Crisis, 1979–1999
Stefanie Walter,
Financial Crises and the Politics of Macroeconomic Adjustments
John Waterbury,
Exposed to Innumerable Delusions: Public Enterprise and State Power in Egypt, India, Mexico, and Turkey
David L. Weimer, ed.,
The Political Economy of Property Rights Institutional Change and Credibility in the Reform of Centrally Planned Economies
Adam Dean,
Opening Up By Cracking Down: Labor Repression and Trade Liberalization in Democratic Developing Countries

For EU product safety concerns, contact us at Calle de José Abascal, 56–1°, 28003 Madrid, Spain or eugpsr@cambridge.org.

www.ingramcontent.com/pod-product-compliance
Ingram Content Group UK Ltd.
Pitfield, Milton Keynes, MK11 3LW, UK
UKHW022148080726
473066UK00010B/841

* 9 7 8 1 1 0 8 7 4 5 8 9 5 *